# Studies in the History of Law and Justice

Volume 33

The purpose of this book series is to publish high quality volumes on the history of law and justice. Legal history can be a deeply provocative and influential field, as illustrated by the growth of the European universities and the *Ius Commune*, the French Revolution, the American Revolution, and indeed all the great movements for national liberation through law. The study of history gives scholars and reformers the models and courage to question entrenched injustices, by demonstrating the contingency of law and other social arrangements. Yet legal history today finds itself diminished in the universities and legal academy. Too often scholarship betrays no knowledge of what went before, or why legal institutions took the shape that they did.This series seeks to remedy that deficiency.

Studies in the History of Law and Justice will be theoretical and reflective. Volumes will address the history of law and justice from a critical and comparative viewpoint. The studies in this series will be strong bold narratives of the development of law and justice. Some will be suitable for a very broad readership.

Contributions to this series will come from scholars on every continent and in every legal system. Volumes will promote international comparisons and dialogue. The purpose will be to provide the next generation of lawyers with the models and narratives needed to understand and improve the law and justice of their own era. The series includes monographs focusing on a specific topic, as well as collections of articles covering a theme or collections of article by one author.

Zuzanna Augustyniak

# Marriage in the Ethiopian Empire

## Between Custom and Code

Springer

Zuzanna Augustyniak
Faculty of Asian and African Cultures
University of Warsaw
Warsaw, Poland



ISSN 2198-9842 ISSN 2198-9850 (electronic)
Studies in the History of Law and Justice
ISBN 978-3-032-26064-2 ISBN 978-3-032-26065-9 (eBook)
https://doi.org/10.1007/978-3-032-26065-9

Translation from the Polish language edition: "Ewolucja instytucji małżeństwa w świetle etiopskich kodeksów prawnych" by Zuzanna Augustyniak, © Zuzanna Augustyniak 2018. Published by Elipsa Publishing House. All Rights Reserved.

This work was supported by University of Warsaw.



This Springer imprint is published by the registered company Springer Nature Switzerland AG
The registered company address is: Gewerbestrasse 11, 6330 Cham, Switzerland

# Contents

# Chapter 1
# Introduction

The Federal Democratic Republic of Ethiopia, like the Ethiopian Empire earlier, is a multicultural and multi-ethnic country, in which not only numerous languages but also various traditions and customs co-exist. These cultures do not function in isolation, but quite the opposite—they interact with each other to a greater or lesser extent. Over the centuries, the dominant ethnic group were the Amhara, who played the main role in the cultural, social, economic and political formation of Ethiopia. Most of the rulers of the Ethiopian Empire came from this ethnic group, while the Amharic culture and language influenced both the development of the institution of marriage and that of Ethiopian legislation. As a result, the majority of the issues discussed in this book refer to the Amhara.

In Amharic, the official language on the federal level in Ethiopia, there are two fundamental words that refer to marriage. The first of these is *tədar*, derived from the verb *darä*. Noteworthy, the verb signifies not only "to marry off" but also "to sell an object at a good price" (Kane 1990, pp. 1732–1733), which brings to one's mind the theories of eighteenth-century anthropologists who maintained that initially marriage was a business transaction involving purchase of a bride. Among related words, *dərä gäb* (Kane 1990, p. 1732) denotes a woman who has recently divorced her first husband; the term *fät dar* (Kane 1990, p. 1732) refers to a divorced woman who has remarried, while *loga dar* (Kane 1990, p. 1732) signifies a woman who was married off at a young age. An analysis of the Amharic corpus has not revealed any set phrases, in which the word *tədar* would be used in the legal context, while the only phrase referring to this aspect of the term is *ḥəgg wäṭ tədar* (Kane 1990, p. 33), i.e., a legally unsanctioned relationship between a man and a woman.

The verb *ᵓagäbba*—"to marry" (Kane 1990, 1967)—is much richer in meaning, as it is a verb from which the nouns *gabəčča*—"marriage, matrimony" (Kane 1990, 1970, 1981) and *gəbbi*—"the institution of marriage" (Kane 1990, 1969) originate. It is from this verb, and not from the verb *darä*, that more words are derived showing links to the institution of marriage, for example *magbiya*—"means for, time or place of taking a wife" (Kane 1990, 1971) and *ᵓaggäbab/ ᵓagbäb*—"marriage customs or ceremony" (Kane 1990, 1971). It is also worth noting that the word



Z. Augustyniak, *Marriage in the Ethiopian Empire*, Studies in the History of Law and Justice 33, https://doi.org/10.1007/978-3-032-26065-9_1

*əgban*—“appeal (judicial)” (Kane 1990, 1971) and the phrase *ᵓagbäb ᵓaläw*—“to have jurisdiction over (of a public authority)” (Kane 1990, 1971) come from the verb *gäbba*.

The Amharic language exhibits comparable richness in the terminology linked to jurisprudence. The term “law” itself has three equivalents in Amharic. The most important of these is the aforementioned *ḥəgg*, which comes from the Semitic root HGG, referring to codified law or a normative act (Leslau 1991, p. 227). According to Claude Sumner, who studied Ethiopian philosophical treaties, the term *ḥəgg* refers to natural law, i.e., God-given law. For example, because such is God’s will, it is natural law that one man marries one woman (Sumner 1978, pp. 159, 252). As a result, the law linked to the institution of marriage is referred to as *ḥəgg ᵓawsəbo* (literally, “marriage laws” [Kane 1990, p. 33]). Kane’s *Amharic-English Dictionary*, in turn, indicates that the word *ḥəgg* itself can be used to refer to a religious marriage, while *ḥəgg gäbba* means also “to get married in a church ceremony which admits of no divorce” (Kane 1990, p. 33). The last term also means “to be engaged to a virgin” as—according to the sixteenth-century Ethiopian codex *Fəṭḥa Nägäśt*—only a virgin had the right to be married in a church. A virgin married off during a church ceremony is then called the legitimate wife (*yäḥəgg mist* [Kane 1990, p. 33]), while the man is referred to as the *balä ḥəgg* (“husband” [Kane 1990, p. 33]). Another important phrase is *ḥəgg ᵓafärräsä*, i.e., “one who violates the law” (Kane 1990, p. 33), however when used to refer to a member of the clergy, it signified one who had committed the sin of adultery or wanted to enter into another marriage, which is forbidden by Ethiopian canon law.

Another legal term (in Ge’ez) is the word *fəth̩* (*fätäḥ*) (Kane 1990, p. 2308), from which expressions are formed that refer to various types of law, for example *fəṭḥ mänfäsawi* (“canonical law”) (Kane 1990, p. 2308), *fəṭḥ səgawi* (“secular law”) (Kane 1990, p. 2308) or *Fəṭḥa Nägäśt* (“Law of the Kings” [Kane 1990, p. 2308]—the title of the first official legal code in the Ethiopian Empire). Noteworthy, the noun *fəṭḥ* comes from the verb *fätḥa*, which means “set free, solve, do justice” (Leslau 1991, p. 170). This suggests that the superordinate purpose of law is solving contentious issues. In connection with the above word, *fəṭḥ* is always used in a broader context, because it encompasses the widest semantic field.

The last word designating law—*sərat* (Kane 1990, p. 481) refers directly to the issuing of imperial edicts and is associated with *wäg* (Kane 1990, p. 1576), i.e., “right sanctioned by custom”. The former word is also linked to the expressions *sərat betä mängəst* (“court rules or etiquette” [Kane 1990, p. 481]) and *sərat betä krəstiyan* (“church laws or canons” [Kane 1990, p. 481]). The word *särr*—customary law, custom (Kane 1990, p. 480)—has the same etymology. It can be assumed that the term *sərat* appeared earlier than *ḥəgg* and *fəṭḥ*, because in all of its meanings it refers to usage, unwritten law or legal precedence.

The present study focuses on the period from the beginning of the state until the fall of the Ethiopian Empire in 1974. Although the search for the sources of Ethiopian law started in the cradle of the Empire, the ancient city-state of Axum, it became apparent very soon that more than eight centuries of Ethiopian statehood had not brought about significant changes in terms of the legislation related to the institution of marriage. Thus, the theory proposed by Lewis Morgan (1871) has been confirmed, i.e., that marriage is a sphere of social life that changes very slowly and that the terminology used in the kinship system reflects previous systems and types of marriage that no longer exist.

The development of Ethiopian legislation does not end with the dethronement of the last emperor. The post-1974 family law codes (1995 and 2000) reflected not only social but also political changes. After 1974, Ethiopia transformed from an absolute monarchy to a communist regime state. However, none of the legal codes produced during the Därg government period introduced as many changes in the legal understanding of the institution of marriage as the 1960 code. As a result, the present study discusses Ethiopian legislation only until the times of the Great Codification[1] and the period following it. However, this does not mean that the topic of Ethiopian legislation on marriage has been exhausted. The opening up to the Western world following the fall of the communist regime in 1991 and the emergence of new concepts in the social sphere began a new chapter in the history of Ethiopian legal development. The changes that occurred in the legislation regarding marriage in the Federal Democratic Republic of Ethiopia deserve a separate study.

The aim of this book is not to provide a legal analysis of Ethiopian family law, nor to offer guidance for navigating contemporary legislation. Rather, its purpose is to present an ethno-historical study of the institution of marriage in Ethiopia, tracing the development of the relevant concepts, practices and legal notions within their broader cultural and social context. By examining linguistic evidence, customary norms and the evolution of formal legislation, the book seeks to show how deeply embedded the institution of marriage is in Ethiopia's historical experience and how slowly it has changed over the centuries. In doing so, it hopes to offer readers—especially those unfamiliar with Ethiopia—a clearer understanding of the cultural foundations upon which Ethiopian marriage law has been built.

## 1.1 The Sources

The study presented here is an attempt to describe the processes that led to changes in the legal perception of the institution of marriage. I have consulted Ethiopian sources and confronted them with material from European and American sources. The Ethiopian sources include—above all—the sixteenth-century *Fətḥa Nägäśt* and the 1960 Civil Code. Imperial chronicles, documents, and memoirs were of no lesser importance. To the Western scholar, the subject of marriage in Ethiopia is very interesting, especially when one considers the multitude of types of marriages and associated rituals. However, for imperial chroniclers, writers, and diarists,

[1] I use the term "Great Codification" to refer to the period of intensive development of Ethiopian legislation that took place in the 1950s and 1960s, characterised by the issuance of a series of legal codes, including the Penal Code and the Civil Code.

marriage ceremonies were a part of daily life so common as to be unworthy of wasting any ink or devoting any time. As an example of this approach, the memoirs of *Blatten Geta* Mahtämä Śəllase Wäldä Mäsqäl's can be quoted, who in the chapter on the marriages of aristocrats wrote: "[...] I think it is much more important to remember the church wedding ceremonies than those entered into by the emperor's subjects" (Mahtämä Śəllase Wäldä Mäsqäl 1982, p. 581). In Ethiopian sources, usually only titbits of information can be found—that one person or another married a woman named this or that. Only minor marginal comments, mentioning that before the wedding ceremony the bride received the sacrament of baptism, may indicate that some of the imperial wives were not Christians. Apart from the scant information available on the development of the institution of marriage and the customs associated with it, an additional complication is the fact that although all the ethnic groups inhabiting the Ethiopian Empire followed their own customary laws, these were rarely written down, but rather passed down orally from generation to generation. Thus, it is possible that as certain forms of marriage disappeared, the laws that pertained to them were forgotten. Yet another problem is that until the nineteenth century there were no records of any legal trials, and no information survives about the precedence that later became binding law. Some of the Amharic or Ge'ez sources used in this work have been translated into European languages. These editions, which include valuable comments, were obviously useful; however, wherever possible the original Amharic texts were used.

The external sources primarily include accounts of European travellers and missionaries, for whom the Ethiopian Empire was either a destination or a stop on their journey across the African continent; their descriptions, although often exaggerated, preserved an image of the everyday lives of the Ethiopians. Another group of external sources consists of studies on Ethiopian culture by Western scholars who, however, addressed the topic of marriage only in two contexts: the ethnographic one (e.g., Andrea Nicolas, Rita Pankhurst) or the historical and political one (e.g., Häran Säräkä-Bərhan, Bairu Tafla, Richard Pankhurst). These studies provide a great deal of cultural information, but little data on the place the institution of marriage holds in legislation. More light is shed on the subject in the works of European scholars on the development of law in the Ethiopian Empire. The writings of Heinrich Scholler or French jurists invited by Emperor Ḫaylä Śəllase I to co-write Ethiopian legal codes (Jacques Vanderlinden, Nathan Marein, George Krzeczunowicz) focused on such issues. Their work is particularly relevant when considering the evolution of Ethiopian legislation during the Great Codification period. Finally, the doctoral dissertation of the Ethiopian scholar Abera Jembere should be mentioned, which, despite its shortcomings, is a valuable attempt at providing a compendium covering the history of the development of law in Ethiopia.

## 1.2 Language, Transcription, Quotations and Dates

Until the thirteenth century, Ethiopian documents were written in Ge'ez, the literary language of Ethiopia used by the imperial court and clergy. From the fourteenth century onwards, Amharic gradually took over, and by the nineteenth century it had become the most widely used language in Ethiopian literature. Both languages belong to the Afro-Asiatic family of languages, the South Semitic group. This subgroup also includes other languages spoken in Ethiopia, such as Tigre, Tigrinya, Harari, Argobba, and the Guragie group of languages. Both the Ge'ez and Amharic languages are written using a syllabic alphabet. Several transcription systems exist for the Amharic language; however, none of them has been recognised as binding. Here, unless in quotations, the transcription follows that of the *Encyclopaedia Aethiopica*.

Foreign terms have been italicised in the text. All quotations have been translated into English.

The Ethiopian calendar is based on the Coptic calendar, which in turn derives from the ancient Egyptian calendar (von Beckerath 1980). According to the Ethiopian calendar, a year consists of twelve thirty-day months plus one month amounting to five days (six on leap years). The Ethiopian calendar era is also distinct from the Christian one, as the years are counted from the birth of Christ, calculated by Annonios of Alexandria to have been in 9 CE. This means that the Ethiopian calendar is seven or eight years behind the Gregorian calendar. The Ethiopian dates are marked with the abbreviation A. M. from the expression *ʾamätä məḥret*—"year of grace" in Ge'ez.

For convenience, all dates are given according to the Gregorian calendar. Where relevant to the argument, the Ethiopian date is provided in parentheses with the appropriate notation. Unless otherwise noted, dates given next to the names of rulers and patriarchs indicate the years of their reign.

## References

Kane TL (1990) Amharic-English dictionary, vol 1-2. Harrassowitz, Wiesbaden
Leslau W (1991) Comparative dictionary of Geᶜez. Otto Harrassowitz, Wiesbaden
Morgan L (1871) Systems of consanguinity and affinity of the human family. Smithsonian Institution, Washington DC
Sumner C (1978) Ethiopian philosophy, vol III. Addis Ababa University, Addis Ababa
von Beckerath J (1980) Kalender. In: Helck W, Westendorf W (eds) Lexikon der Ägyptologie, vol 3. Harrassowitz, Wiesbaden. col 297-299
Wäldä Mäsqäl MŚ (1982) Zəkrä Nägär. Artistik, Addis Abäba

legal institutions function within these societies as attributes of power, law was still considered as subject only to the will of the ruler or that of a small ruling class or a few privileged individuals. It was argued that the rules of conduct in the clan, family or community lacked any external pressure, while the societies having no ruling authorities at all were treated as if the rules of conduct were not compulsory.

Ignoring clear evidence of the concept of law among 'primitive' societies, ethnologists created or—as Malinowski wrote—"framed" (Malinowski 1934, p. xxi) a theory of primitive law. According to it, none of the components of 'primitive' culture suggest the existence of any legal devices. The rules acknowledged in 'primitive' societies were considered to form a whole, obeyed only as a result of inane deference to existing norms, customs and practices. The anthropologists at the time assumed that any elements of what is considered law in western culture only appeared in cases of evident violation of social code, while the only crystallised form of law was criminal law. This view was shared by the most renowned theorists of ethno-sociology, including Alfred Radcliffe-Brown, who—taking as a basis the definition of law created by Roscoe Pound (Malinowski 2000, p. xxiii)—considered all 'primitive' societies to have customs supported by sanctions and only some of them had laws. Radcliffe-Brown proposed that in reference to 'primitive' societies one should use the terms "private and public delicts" instead of the terms "civil and criminal law" (Malinowski 2000, p. xxiii), with the former applied to acts (delicts) which provoke:

> ...an organised and regular procedure by the whole community or by the constituted representatives of social authority which results in the fixing of responsibility upon some person within the community and the infliction by the community or by its representatives of some hurt or punishment upon the responsible person. (Malinowski 1934, p. xxiii)

According to him, such a reaction to a crime aims to maintain a sense of moral righteousness among the members of the society. In his article on the subject, Radcliffe-Brown (1952, pp. 205–211) also provides a list of acts that are subject to criminal sanctions organised in this manner. These include incest, sorcery and sacrilege as well as crimes against tribal custom.

The definition of law formulated by Roscoe Pound (1914) and Radcliffe-Brown's theory on private and public delicts (1952: 212–231) was rejected by Adamson E. Hoebel (1954) and Bronisław Malinowski (1934). Hoebel defined the legal form as one for transgression of which a socially established sanction was impending and this ascribed all societies with having legal systems, regardless of whether they had even a rudimentary centralised political organisation. Malinowski, in turn, criticised Radcliffe-Brown's division of law. He claimed that the fundamental reason to obey a law is not fear of sanctions but rather the rule of reciprocity, which in turn is the fundament of social ties. This means that members of a society fulfil their responsibilities towards one's neighbour, ruler and community not because of a sense of obligation but rather due to various long-term benefits. Following the law leads to rewards in the form of exchanged services, while non-compliance with the rules results not in direct violence, but in natural retaliation, which amounts to the withdrawal of exchanged services, criticism, and social discontent. Denial of services results in the complete disorganisation of any cooperating group, which in turn affects its survival.

According to Malinowski, there is another element of the dynamic mechanism of legal compulsion, and namely the systematic interdependence of legal obligations. This means that a duty of one party towards another creates a further duty for the latter towards the former. For example, a husband's obligation to provide for his wife results in her obligation to prepare meals for him from the resources he has earned, and the obligation of community members to pay tribute to a chief will result in the chief's obligation to organise and finance tribal ceremonies.

Since reciprocity works in all societies, and refusal to comply to it leads to sanctions, it can be assumed that every society, even with rudimentary formal structures, has laws. Legislative systems around the world are developed to an extent dependent on the societies' development, but in all of them two branches can be seen, derived directly from the principle of reciprocity, i.e., criminal law and civil law.

## 2.2 Law in Societies with Non-complex Social Structures

In politically organised societies, the term "law" can be understood in two ways: either with reference to actions performed by an authority to enforce a citizen's obligation (legislation), or as what is referred to as subjective rights, i.e., those accrued to individuals or entire social groups. Among them is the right to work and rest, the right to remuneration for work done, or human rights. In politically organised societies, the two concepts are often complementary. For example, subjective rights are superimposed on the laws that govern those rights.

For the discussion on the formation of law, the term "subjective law" seems more relevant, as it is a broader concept that can be applied even to societies that do not have political authorities. In the case of such societies, the classical definition of law as "[...] norms derived from the will of those in power or at least norms supported by state enforcement" (Kurczewski 1973, p. 9) does not find practical application. Pre-state societies, however, are not entirely devoid of law. In many such cultures, examples can be found of non-institutionalised forms of public law, which are expressed as norms for the violation of which there is a sanction and a negative reaction from the community. In such cases, subjective law is constructed on the basis of the interdependencies—both negative and positive—that exist in these societies. These interdependencies, in turn, derive from the aforementioned principle of reciprocity.

The notion of law, understood both as a subjective right and as positive law, is inseparably linked to the sociological notion of social control, understood as pressures that aim at shaping the attitudes and behaviour of individuals in accordance with certain patterns. The concept of social control is most often used to describe behaviour within a given group when an individual is controlled by the environs to which he belongs and with which he has a personal relationship. This aspect distinguishes social control from state control, the objectives of which are the same, but—unlike the former—state control (and thus the law) does not presuppose subjective ties and is exercised over all persons residing within a certain territory.

In a narrower sense, social control is "[...] the process of one's environs comparing an individual's actual behaviour with environmentally recognised patterns that define normal behaviour or behaviour symptomatic of normal mental states" (Kurczewski 1973, p. 74). On the other hand, in a broader sense, social control means the process of transmitting models of behaviour, for example in the form of general norms or comparing behaviour with the models, and reacting to situations in which behaviour is inconsistent with the model. The purpose of the social control process is to maintain a certain social order. The process can be illustrated by the following diagram:

establishing a model → transmitting the model → comparing behaviour with the model → corrective reactions[2]

This process can slightly differ between cultures. It is not always the group that sets the model (in which case, it comes from the outside), and the person whose behaviour is being controlled has not always been informed of the model. Most often, however, behavioural models are passed on in the process of upbringing, which in more developed societies takes the form of initiation. An extreme case occurs when the same person sets the model, controls the behaviour, and rules over the controlled. Such a situation occurs most often in micro-communities, for example, in a clan, in which its leader is the person who establishes a given pattern of behaviour.

In European societies, there are various organisations in charge of controlling the behaviour of individuals and groups. The activities of these organisations are regulated by the applicable law, which sometimes prescribes certain corrective reactions (e.g., detecting crimes and punishing their perpetrators), sometimes allows for these reactions (e.g., voluntary visits to the doctor), and sometimes prohibits the control of individual behaviour (e.g., the possibility of practicing any religion).

The issue of social control looks completely different in communities without any state authority, even a basic one, like a ruler or tribal court. Repeating after Kurczewski, these are the simplest communities that fulfil two conditions at the same time: they base their material existence on the acquisition (through hunting and/or gathering) of products of nature, and they are organisationally simple, "[they exist] primarily in the form of local communities consisting of individual family groups and lacking institutionalised authority" (Kurczewski 1973, p. 76). The question arises as to how, in the absence of forms of authority to control behaviour and maintain behavioural models, those patterns are nevertheless maintained. Is the order observed in this type of community conscious or mechanical, that is, an order resulting from the sameness of the experiences of individual members of the community? Legal anthropologists do not have a clear answer to this question, because there is no single way of organising life in such communities. For some, the guardian of the models is the family, while for others it is a local group or individuals, such as the elders:

[2] The scheme after Kurczewski (1973), p. 74.

> There is no organised government in an Andaman village. The affairs of the community are governed entirely by the older men and women. [...] In addition to respect for seniority, there is another important factor regulating community life – respect for certain personal qualities. [...] The man who possesses these qualities is undoubtedly likely to gain an influential position in the community, and in all matters his opinion may carry more weight than that of other, even older men. (Kurczewski 1973, p. 80)

In such a case, the elders constitute the social group that establishes the model, watches over its observance, and decides the punishment for one whose behaviour is found to be contrary to the existing standard. Thus, it can be assumed that in such social groups, it is the elders who make the law, and the punishments they set for particular crimes can be treated as criminal law regulations.

There are also societies in which only one person is in charge of policing social norms, e.g., the chief, chosen by the community from among its members. The basis of power is the possession of personal prestige or what some anthropologists refer to as charisma. Another important quality expected from a ruler is the ability to win over allies. A chief elected by the community does not have coercive means and leadership is maintained through the generous distribution of goods and privileges rather than violence. Claude Lévi-Strauss added that "[...] power is founded, psychologically speaking, in consent" (Lévi-Strauss 1961, p. 308), which in everyday life is expressed through a continuous exchange of mutual benefits, privileges, services, and obligations between the chief and the rest of the community.[3] In this case, the chief does not make the law himself. Rather, he is the guardian of patterns of behaviour observed by the entire community, who, in his authority (bestowed on him by the community), has the right to watch over the observance of these patterns and has the right to punish those who behave contrary to the imposed pattern on behalf of the entire community.

A third form of political and sacral authority that establishes a pattern of behaviour—and thus law—is the institution of the witch doctor (in African cultures) or the shaman (in Asian cultures). The witch doctors or shamans are not elected by the members of the community as leaders, but rather owe their position to their supposed association with supernatural forces. An influential witch doctor/shaman may demand the dissolution of a marriage to obtain a woman for himself or impose a certain taboo on a community member. Disobedience may result in the rebel's banishment. The witch doctor/shaman watches over the observance of behavioural patterns, although he does not establish them. However, he has the power to punish the person who does not follow the model. It is worth noting here that witch doctors/shamans most often live on the margins of social life. Moreover, this function is sometimes performed by people with psychological features that differ from the norm recognised in the given society. Paradoxically, this means that the person whose own behaviour differs from the norm is in charge of guarding the observance of patterns.

---

[3] According to J. Kurczewski, this pattern is the highest possible level of institutionalisation of individual power that occurs in a hunter-gatherer group. Cf. Kurczewski (1973), p. 83.

However, there are societies so non-complex that none of the three aforementioned forms of government is present to establish or enforce a pattern. In such a society, the response to the misdeeds of one member of the community is the collective reaction of the rest of the community, without a specific social factor. Collin M. Turnbull gives an example of such a reaction when describing the actions of the Bambuti people towards a member of the group:

> Nobody really minded Pepei's stealing, because he was a born comic and a great storyteller. But he had gone too far in stealing from old Sau, who had lost her husband and was supported by her son Amabosu and his wife. So the men ran out of their huts angrily and caught hold of Pepei, while the youths broke off thorny branches and whipped him until he managed to break away. He went running, as fast as he could into the forest; he cried bitterly and wrapped his arms around himself for comfort. He stayed in the forest for nearly twenty-four hours, and when he came back the next night he went straight to his hut, unseen, and lay down to sleep. His hut was between mine and Sau's, and I heard him come in; and I heard him crying softly because even his brother wouldn't speak to him. (Turnbull 1968, pp. 120–121)

This example shows that the reaction of the community is immediate and there is no person or persons who would first make the decision regarding punishing the offender and then lead the repressive action.

In other societies, it happens that the punishment is administered not by the whole community, but by one person who had first received the support of the whole community. This is the case, for example, with the Inuit. In this community, a single murder leads to bloody revenge from the family of the slain. However, in the case of repeated or multiple murders, the entire community must react, because the murderer is a threat to the community. In such a case, a community member can take the initiative to remove the recidivist. He can ask all the adult males in turn whether they think the murderer should be killed. If there is unanimous agreement, then the killing takes place at the earliest opportunity, and the relatives of the murdered man have no right to avenge the death. The execution is usually carried out by the current leader of the group, although this is not the rule.

The examples presented above show two mechanisms for punishing offenders. In the first case, the reaction is immediate and the punishment is administered by members of the society. In the second case, one person undertakes administering punishment, but only with the approval of the other members of the group. Based on these observations, one can conclude that in societies having no complex political structure, it is the whole community that watches over the observance of behavioural patterns and punishes those who do not follow them. This means that members of these societies possess both legislative (establishing the pattern of behaviour), judicial (deciding the punishment for the crime), and executive (carrying out the sentence) powers. The more politically complex a society becomes, the more separable these functions can be, as seen in the second example.

According to the legal anthropologists of the Victorian period, such as Maine, "in olden times [...] every man, living during the greater part under patriarchal despotism, was practically controlled in all his actions by a regime not of law but of caprice" (Maine 1861, after Kuper 1997, p. 29). Gradually, the place of capricious patriarchal despots was taken by rulers who when making their judgements began to invoke divine inspiration. They in turn were supplanted by aristocracy, which in the Western world took the form of a political oligarchy. Its power over the law consisted in the fact that it had exclusive knowledge of common law. The power of the oligarchs did not last long.

The next step in the development of legislation was the codification of law, which according to Henry Maine consisted simply in the process of writing down common law. Maine believed that there was a point in the history of legislation when common law was ripe for codification. Moreover, some societies, while codifying their laws, introduced some advantageous legal reforms into the common law. As confirmation of his own thesis, he quoted the example of the Roman code, which was written at a time when common law was still in force, but the further lack of codification could have had disastrous consequences. According to Maine, three mechanisms were behind the changes in Roman common law: the law of equity, legislation, and legal fiction.

The law of equity was intended to resolve disputes between parties, but on the basis of principles of conscience, fairness, and justice rather than of legal rules. The law of equity was thus tied to social norms, and judgments were to be made according to one's conscience and common sense. Legislation, in turn, was to be the final mechanism, which, along with codification, represented the pinnacle of the evolution of law, not its starting point, as Henry Maine's chief opponents, Jeremy Bentham and John Austin, would have it.

According to Bentham, legal fiction is "[...] a wilful falsehood, having for its object the stealing of legislative power, by and for the hands which could not, or durst not, openly claim it, and but for the delusion thus produced could not exercise it" (Kuper 1997, p. 30). In turn, Maine claimed the opposite—that it serves the mechanisms of progressive reform. According to him, under the guise of legal fictions, the elite were to introduce reforms, keeping the conservative part of society convinced that nothing was changing. In Roman society, seen by Maine as the model, reforms were first carried out on the basis of legal fictions, then the law of equity was adopted, and finally, as laws became more complex, they were codified (Kuper 1997, p. 30).

Along with social, political and geographical development came the evolution of legislation. Individual states evolved, and with them their laws developed. Over time, state laws that were similar to each other were combined into legal families. Currently, in the legislation of the Western world, two legal families can be distinguished—the Anglo-Saxon family of precedent law (*common law*) and the family of continental law (*civil law*).[4] They were distinguished on the basis of two criteria. The first is ideological—one legal family includes countries that are similar in religious or philosophical terms, or have similar political, economic and social

[4] A third group orbits around these two families, generally referred to as "other systems," which include Talmudic law, Hindu law, Muslim law, and the youngest group of African and Malagasy laws.

structures. The second criterion are the principles of legislative technique, i.e., common or similar rules for the construction of normative acts by legislators.

## 2.3 The Continental Legal System and Common Law

Continental law is a continuation of the tradition of Roman law. The source of Roman law was customary law, which was nothing more than (mostly) unwritten patterns of behaviour. In Rome, custom was elevated to the status of a legal norm when it was recognised by the society as necessary and had been applied unchanged for a sufficiently long time. Customary law primarily referred to matters of everyday life, so Roman law placed the individual at the centre of legislation. Many laws reflect the way of life of the Romans: marriage was considered the union of a man and a woman, and bigamy was forbidden. Concubinage was permitted, although children born of this union had no right to inherit and belonged to the mother's family, and not to that of the father. Divorce was also permitted (Nicholas 1962, pp. 82–92).

As the Empire grew, Roman law spread to the northern (Germany) and western (the British Isles) frontiers of the state. However, it was the law of the invaders, and most conquered societies did not welcome it with enthusiasm. When the Romans were forced to withdraw from previously conquered territories, the inhabitants returned to their customary laws. Roman law spread through Europe once again between the eleventh and thirteenth centuries. Confronted by the uniform legislation in the Arab world, which had begun to dominate the Mediterranean, Europe faced the challenge of normalizing its legislation. It was therefore necessary to regulate (and often to write down) the customary laws of individual European countries, with Roman law serving as the model.[5] The changes that occurred in European legislation at the time provided the basis for the creation of the system of continental law.

Modern continental law is based on laws created by parliaments or legislatures. Codes are considered the highest form of legislation, and it is primarily criminal and civil laws that are codified. In countries that apply continental law, courts play a much lesser social role than in countries that apply Anglo-Saxon law. Courts are called upon to apply the law, but unlike in the system of case law, they cannot create it. Consequently, legal judgments are not treated as sources of law. Moreover, there is a strict hierarchy of legal acts in continental law. The most important of these is the constitution, while acts of field law are lowest in level.[6]

[5] A huge role in the process of the codification of law was played by the Church, which functioned as a unifying factor.

[6] However, it should be remembered that in the continental legal system, the Supreme Court's decisions are important in later interpretations of positive law and can initiate a line of case law, even though the decisions of these courts are much less significant than the court decisions in the *common law* system.

Raoul C. van Caenegem argued that the Norman conquest of the British Isles was the reason behind the formation of precedence law (Glenn 2010, p. 238). The Normans, upon settling in England, decided to create a new legal system. It was to be based on modern (for those times) legal concepts originating from Europe, adapted to the legal, social and political circumstances found in the territories conquered by the Normans.

The Norman kings created the bases of precedence law within a century and a half of William the Conqueror's invasion in 1066. The royal court was the institution responsible for formulating law. This was the legal order known in the Norman kingdom and according to the rulers this was the only reasonable option in these circumstances, as they were surrounded by a hostile population whose legal mechanisms (and even language) they did not understand. Uncertain of the loyalty of local noblemen and without any local legal doctrine to refer to, the new rulers decided to create an independent court institution. In contrast to the tradition of Roman legislation, where sentences could only be passed by Roman citizens, those who were appointed as judges were not French aristocrats, but priests, who could not only read and write, but were also well acquainted with canon law and Roman civil law. As a result, each sentence was accompanied by a written legal justification. Then, these notes became the basis for the passing of similar sentences in comparable cases. Unlike the Romans, the Normans did not impose their laws on the English and the judgements passed by the judges were not only based on the laws created on the European continent, but also on local customary law.[7]

Precedence law developed smoothly throughout the entire Middle Ages. Its basis, as mentioned above, was the constantly growing number of royal sentences and orders, which had legal force. These orders frequently had the form of letters to the royal officials, in which the king expressed his opinion on this or that category of crime (rather in a general form than referring to any specific case) along with an instruction on what each administrator could do to accelerate the course of the criminal proceedings. For example, the defendant's property could have been withheld until his innocence was proven or a Council of Judges was convened who would decide in a particular case.

Contemporary Anglo-Saxon law has only marginally departed from the premises held by the Norman rulers who created it. The courts still participate in formulating law, and not only in using it. This means that when a court passes the sentence in a specific new case, it creates a precedence which subsequent courts refer to when passing decisions in similar cases. As a result, the court's task is to decide in specific cases, rather than to create a generally applied norm. This law can only be changed by the court which previously passed the law or by a superior court.

[7] Glenn (2010) is of the opinion that initially the legal institutions in England were under the strong influence of Islamic traditions. It should be remembered that at that time Europe was aspiring to standardise its legislation, while Islamic law was a profound source of inspiration for these actions.

## 2.4 Law in Sub-Saharan African Countries

Considering the multiplicity and diversity of African cultures, it is difficult to speak of a single African law. If African societies were to be researched the same way the first anthropologists of law did, i.e., by studying the structures related to marriage and family, private property, the state, it would turn out that also in terms of its laws Africa is very diverse. There are societies with both monarchic and democratic structures, but also those with rudimentary social structures. The family as the basic social unit can be both patrilineal and matrilineal, while between these two types there are also many variants. The system of land division is also different in particular societies. As a result, it is hard to state there is one African law. It is rather a cluster of laws, independent of each other, which have in common that all of them derive from custom (see David and Brierley 1978, p. 505; Supatajew 1984).

The diversity of social structures implies, obviously, a diversity of customs and customary laws. However, an attempt can be made to find a common denominator for these laws. Primarily, this would be the constancy of the law, in terms of both legal acts and institutions. This means, for example, that African customary laws generally lack regulations concerning the sale of land, as in African cultures land belongs to the ancestors, and it is inherited, and not bought.[8] Such terms as "limitation periods" and "acquisitive prescriptions" are unknown, as deeds are remembered forever and hospitality is never refused (David and Brierley 1978, p. 507).

Yet another common feature is that African laws are not focused on the interest of an individual, but rather that of the entire community, regardless of whether this was a rural, caste or ethnic community. The community is the fundamental legal unit (David and Brierley 1978, p. 507). Due to such a perception of the group, a fair sentence does not necessarily signify punishing the guilty person, but rather proposing such a solution that would ensure reconciliation between the conflicted parties and would not cause harm to the whole community.[9] Also the institution of marriage, being rather a legal agreement entered into by two families than a relationship between two people, shows the priority given to the group over an individual.

In African customary laws, much more emphasis is placed on the responsibilities of an individual. These were imposed depending on one's social position; however, it is difficult to distinguish between the legal responsibilities and those imposed by the adopted moral approach. European researchers of African laws have to a various extent attempted to create such a distinction, but for the Africans themselves this did not hold much significance when there were no lawyers (understood as a professional group) within their societies and law was not pursued as an academic

[8] This example should exclude Muslim cultures, observing religious law that includes legal regulations on land trade.

[9] Once again, Muslim cultures should be excluded, within which the well-being of the community is favoured over the well-being of an individual, but punishment of the guilty party is frequently a form of a just sentence.

discipline (David and Brierley 1978, p. 507). There was no distinction between criminal and civil law, property rights, tort law, contract law, etc.

The arrival of the Europeans in Africa was a turning point in the history of African legislation. Western legal concepts appeared on the continent along with the settlers from Europe. If the settlements were founded in already inhabited territories, the existing law remained in force, even though attempts were made to merge them into one legal system with the law of the newly arrived (Glenn 2010, p. 274). Various methods were used to achieve this aim. English colonisers used a strategy H. Patrick Glenn refers to as the "*hands-off approach*" (Glenn 2010, p. 274), i.e., the existing law was applied to the autochthones, while the English law—to the new arrivals, although there were some exceptions. Nonetheless, this does not mean that the British were not interested in the customary laws applied in their colonies. Quite the opposite, in fact. Colonial authorities/administration made use of the work of scholars such as S. Nadel, who helped in creating regional courts in Nupe in Nigeria, or G. Brown, who provided information about marriages, divorces and the extent of the practice of polygamy in what was at the time referred to as Tanganyika, to improve the management of the colonies. Field studies conducted by anthropologists were also used during the re-organisation of the administrative territories of the Gold Coast.

French colonisers, on the other hand, considered their law to be universal, to be followed by all the inhabitants of the colonies. Despite this approach, during the colonial period, the French colonial administrators collected about 150 sets of laws. Unfortunately, some manuscripts are poorly written and preserved, resulting in only half of them being published (David and Brierley 1978, p. 509).

In both cases, after some time had passed, the law of the colonisers began to dominate over local customary law, even though the latter was never forgotten, and this for two reasons. The first was the resistance shown by the autochthonous societies, who ignored some of the colonisers' laws, replacing them with their own. The second reason for customary law surviving was—paradoxically—the activities of the colonial judges. To a large extent, they are responsible for the unwritten law of the autochthonous population having survived. As they could not interpret the regulations of European law in such a way that would fit the social and economic situation of a particular colony, the judges frequently applied existing elements of customary law to find the optimal solution to a conflict, and this most often happened in cases linked to marriage and inheritance (Glenn 2005, p. 67).

Another turning point in the history of African legislation came in the twentieth century along with the decolonisation of Africa. A need to systematise and codify law appeared along with independence. Due to the specific historical development of the region, the national legal systems of African states created at that time contained both elements of colonial law, as well as those of religious (Christian, Islamic, Hindu) law and customary law, which continued to function in many aspects of social life, exerting political and legal, but also economic and social impact on the development of African states.

The newly formed African countries faced the challenge of creating new legislative systems. In almost all cases, it was decided to modify the existing legal system that had been in place during the colonial period. The reforms mainly involved the removal of regulations that were discriminatory towards the African population. The majority of countries rapidly developed and announced constitutional drafts, which to a greater or lesser extent were based on European models and were written with the aid of lawyers originating from Europe. Some African lawyers opted also for introducing a regulation into the constitution, which would include respecting the customary law of each ethnic group inhabiting the given country (Glenn 2010, p. 90). This concept was in a sense similar to the English principle of the "*hands-off approach*" and seems appropriate for multi-ethnic societies, which are predominant on the African continent.

Contemporary African legal systems attempt to reverse the colonial order, in which homogeneous legislation was supposed to pertain to all autochthonous inhabitants. This is a natural process, characteristic for societies that for many years lived in systems imposed upon them. However, not all the European legal regulations were rejected by the Africans. Some were retained, especially those pertaining to aspects of the legal system which had previously been unknown to the autochthonous population. The mentioned regulations referred to such aspects as maritime, international, property and labour law. Looking at the development of African legislation, one can observe a distinctive change in the colonial order, in which the colonial legal system took precedence. Currently, in African countries, it is the codified autochthonous legislation that is superior, with some elements of European law included.

## References

David R, Brierley JEC (1978) Major legal systems in the world today: an introduction to the comparative study of law. The Free Press, New York

Glenn HP (2005) On common laws. Oxford University Press, Oxford

Glenn HP (2010) Legal traditions of the world. Sustainable diversity in law. Oxford University Press, Oxford

Hoebel EA (1954) The Law of a Primitive Man. A Study in Comparative Legal Dynamics. Cambridge, Massachusetts, Harvard University Press

Kuper A (1997) The invention of primitive society. Transformations of an illusion. Routledge, London and New York

Kurczewski J (1973) Prawo prymitywne. Wiedza Powszechna, Warszawa

Lévi-Strauss C (1961) Tristes tropiques (trans: Russell J). Criterion Books, New York

Maine H (1861) Ancient law. Henry Holt and Company, New York

Malinowski B (1934) Introduction. In: Hogbin HI (ed) Law and order in Polynesia: a study of primitive legal institutions. Harcourt, Brace and Co., New York, pp xvii–lxxii

Malinowski B (2000) Prawo, zwyczaj, zbrodnia w społeczności dzikich. DeAgostini, Altaya, Warszawa

Nicholas B (1962) An Introduction to Roman Law. Oxford, Clarendon Press

Radcliffe-Brown AR (1952) Structure and Function in Primitive Society. London, Cohen and West
Supatajew MA (1984) Obycznoje prawo w stranach Wostocznoj Afriki. Izdatielstwo "Nauka,", Moskva
Turnbull CM (1968) The forest people. Touchstone, New York

# Chapter 3
# The Institution of Marriage in Ethiopia

*"[...] the study of such an issue as exogamy 'belongs properly to that interesting, but difficult and almost unworked subject, the Comparative jurisprudence of the lower races, and no one not versed in Civil Law could do it justice'."*

*(Tylor 1865, p. 277, after Kuper 1997, p. 3)*

## 3.1 Stages in the Development of the Institution of Marriage

According to Max Gluckman (1965, p. 10), the second field of interest for early anthropologists—after religious life—was marriage and the development of the family as an institution. The first to study this topic was the American lawyer, Lewis Morgan. In 1851, he conducted a study of the kinship system among the Iroquois living in North America. Morgan noted that the Iroquois used the same word for mother and mother's sister. Further research proved that similar terminology is used not only among other indigenous peoples of the Americas but also (with variations) among other societies around the world. The findings led Morgan to believe that the kinship system is closely related to the institution of marriage. Moreover, he found that the terminology associated with the kinship system changes very slowly; thus, the nomenclature used for family ties reflects earlier rather than functioning types of marriage (Gluckman 1965, p. 10).

Morgan's theory as related by Gluckman states that in 'primitive' societies initially there was a stage of "promiscuity" (Gluckman 1965, p. 10) and no rule defining incest. This stage ended rather quickly, and no traces of it can be found in any community. The second stage of development was the "consanguine family" (Gluckman 1965, p. 10), in which marriages between siblings occurred, but parent-child marriages were prohibited.[1] Similarly, according to Morgan, no trace remains of this stage. The fact that marriages of this type were possible is evidenced by the

[1] In many cultures, a particular ruler was considered the founder of the institution of marriage, usually one who was remembered by posterity as charismatic and 'enlightened'. See Ringrose (1911), p. 7.



Z. Augustyniak, *Marriage in the Ethiopian Empire*, Studies in the History of Law and Justice 33, https://doi.org/10.1007/978-3-032-26065-9_3

system of designating kinship among the Hawaiians, where all mothers' brothers are called fathers, as they were once able to marry their sisters.

In his book, *Systems of Consanguinity and Affinity of the Human Family* (Morgan 1871), Lewis Morgan lists seventeen stages in the development of the institution of marriage, ending with monogamous marriages in western societies. His work later became the basis for the research of subsequent anthropologists, who treated the particular customs of various ethnic groups as source material on previous forms of social organisation.

Basing on Lewis Morgan's theory, later researchers sought to prove that originally inheritance was matrilineal. Since sexual freedom prevailed in the first stage of family development, only the mother of a child was known. Consequently, a child could only inherit matrilineally, or—more precisely—from the mother's brother or brothers. This rule changed only in the later stages of family development, when men sought wives outside their group, kidnapping them from neighbouring settlements. When a kidnapped woman gave birth to a child, it no longer belonged to her family but to the man's family and inherited from him.[2]

Although the above reasoning applied by anthropologists was based on an unverifiable assumption about the first stages of family development, it functioned for many years as a valid model precisely because it could not be definitively refuted or fully accepted. It was only twentieth-century anthropologists who began questioning Lewis Morgan's theory, wondering why particular forms of marriage were found in primitive societies and disappeared in institutionalised societies.

One of them was Max Gluckman,[3] who studied law and social relations (and therefore also marriage) among ethnic groups living in southern Africa. Gluckman argued that in 'primitive' societies, even the richest men could not afford to accumulate wealth. Goods could not be accumulated; food quickly spoiled or eaten by insects, clothing could rapidly become damaged, and houses built of clay and organic fibres would not last long. Under such subsistence conditions, a well-to-do man used his wealth not to improve the quality of his life, but rather to attract the less wealthy members of the community, to gain their favour and ultimately power over them (Gluckman 1965, p. 13). Using his wealth, a man would gain vassals, but in order to attract people equal in social status and wealth he had to enter into kinship relations. The most common way was to invoke a common ancestor, and if such was lacking, the solution was a marriage between representatives of the two families. Bound together through blood brotherhood, the two families were obliged to help and support each other in need. Arranged marriages were also a way to resolve conflicts between families.

[2] The wedding custom, present in many cultures, involving the symbolic kidnapping of a woman by the groom-to-be and his friends, is supposedly a remnant of this stage. Max Gluckman (1965, p. 12) also claimed that the custom of carrying the bride over the threshold known within Western societies has the same origins.

[3] Aside from Gluckman, kinship systems (and the related issue of the institution of marriage) were the research focus of such researchers as E. Leach, A.A. Radcliffe-Brown, E.E. Evans-Pritchard and Claude Lévi-Strauss.

## 3.2 Marriage as a Legal Contract

Max Gluckman's theory was a development of Bronislaw Malinowski's concept; the latter argued that it is in the field of kinship that the principle of mutual obligations, mentioned in the previous chapter, is most clearly evident. Malinowski considered the institution of the family, with such aspects as marriage, parenthood, extended kinship and clanship, to be the focal point of the kinship system (Malinowski 1934, p. xlvi).

Among the above-mentioned aspects of the family, the most symmetrical institution is marriage as it has symmetry of structure, mutuality of obligations and mutuality of benefits. According to Malinowski, if the act of entering into marriage is to be analysed as the legal establishment of a permanent social relationship between two contracting parties in accordance with the principle of reciprocity, we find that the previously presented image of marriage in 'primitive' societies was distorted. The relationship was usually considered from the male point of view, so with regard to such concepts as purchasing or kidnapping, it was automatically assumed that the woman was the object of the transaction.[4] Moreover, as Malinowski argued, marriage was described solely through its rituals and symbolism, in isolation from its context.

> To put it bluntly, I should say that the symbolic, representative or ceremonial contents of marriage are of secondary importance to the anthropologist. To insist that enshrined in a ceremonial act there remain large chunks of history, condensed and pickled souvenirs of past ages, is simply a case of antiquarian obsession. [...] The range of symbolic interpretation covers absolutely every aspect of marriage; sex undoubtedly and permanently; procreation, with fertility, potency and mutual satisfaction, preference for male or female offspring as the case may be; cooking, joint eating, sartorial details and so on and so forth. (Ethnography has not yet discovered any marriage ritual symbolising the darning of socks.) (Malinowski 1934, p. xlviii)

According to Malinowski, the essence of marriage is not symbolism being a reflection of the whole past history of marriage, but rather the fact that through the execution of a very simple or sometimes—quite the opposite—a very complex ritual, two

[4] Claude Lévi-Strauss, mentioned in the previous chapter, argued against B. Malinowski's statement, claiming that an important role in considering the essence of marriage was occupied by what is referred to as marital exchange. Lévi-Strauss believed that the basis for the existence of social ties is the "exchange of women" during the marriage ceremony. He argued that the marriage act itself does not actually occur between a man and a woman, but between two groups of men, with the woman functioning as one of the objects of the exchange, not as one of the partners between whom goods or services are exchanged. In further discussions, B. Malinowski and C. Lévi-Strauss presented a consensual view, claiming that the cycle of reciprocity between a man and a woman, initiated by marriage, is only a secondary manifestation of a broader cycle of reciprocity, for—by marrying a woman—a man enters into a whole cycle of dependency with her family. The same dependency occurs with a woman. As a result, through the marriage, an affinity relationship is established between men and women belonging to two different groups. A network of mutual obligations and relationships is formed, which, according to Lévi-Strauss, is the basis for the existence of all social bonds. See Nowicka (2003), p. 352.

individuals enter into a bond of marriage with the approval of the remainder of society. In every society, both a 'primitive' one and a more diverse one, the relationship is defined by a whole set of rules which may be referred to as matrimonial law. The researcher argued that it is within this relationship that the place of law and its connectivity with other norms of conduct can best be explored.

> Marriage in all communities becomes an almost unworkable arrangement unless there develops a specific type of emotional attitude between the two partners. [...] You cannot sanction devotion, loyalty, fidelity in the deeper sense of the word, mutual recognition of each other's value and of the mutual duties arising from it. (Malinowski 1934, p. xlix)

This means that the study of the institution of marriage in a given society should be combined with research into the norms governing premarital life and with an analysis of other aspects of social life, such as character formation and upbringing, exchange of tribal services, transfer of power, kinship.

## 3.3 Marriage: An Institution or a Social Contract?

It is a disputed matter whether marriage should be considered an institution, a personal status, a type of contract between two people, a religious bond or a social pledge. An example of such a dispute can be observed in a discussion that took place in the 1960s on the pages of *The Journal of Ethiopian Law* between George Krzeczunowicz and Jacques Vanderlinden. The latter's article on the sources of Ethiopian law from the thirteenth to the twentieth centuries (Vanderlinden 1966a, pp. 227–639) triggered the debate. The article, though appreciated in the community, raised many objections from George Krzeczunowicz, who, like Vanderlinden, focused his studies on the history of Ethiopian law. In the next issue of the journal, Krzeczunowicz formulated accusations against Vanderlinden's work (Krzeczunowicz 1966, pp. 621–627). The same issue of the journal contained the French scholar's response to the claims about his alleged inaccuracies (Vanderlinden 1966b, pp. 635–639).

One of the criticisms raised by Krzeczunowicz was that Vanderlinden treated marriage as a type of contract between two people, while—according to the former—the relationship should be treated as an institution, since the main purposes of marriage (having and raising children, culturally normalised sexual relations, and running a joint household) are not proprietary in nature and are regulated by rules that apply to everyone. A contract, on the other hand, is a proprietary agreement, where the rules that apply are individually determined. The arrangements between both parties regarding the value of the dowry and the nature and cost of engagement gifts are considered by Krzeczunowicz as regulations. These arrangements, however, do not fall within the scope of the marriage itself and apply only to the period before the wedding ceremony. Taking all this into account, according to Krzeczunowicz, marriage should be treated as an institution.

Vanderlinden had a different opinion; justifying his treatment of marriage as a contract, he indicated other cases in Ethiopian law that, being not proprietary in nature, are nevertheless treated as contracts rather than institutions. Following this line of thought, Vanderlinden also pointed to a number of marriage provisions in the Ethiopian Civil Code that are not obligatory in nature and, on the contrary, allow for some degree of freedom in their interpretation.

The debate outlined above referred to provisions in the Ethiopian Civil Code introduced in 1960 under Emperor Ḫaylä Śəllase I (1930–1974). However, this does not change the fact that the discussion raises a broader issue related to the definition of marriage. Since the argumentation cited by George Krzeczunowicz is closer to Ethiopian thinking (as will be shown in the fourth chapter), marriage will be discussed here as an institution.

## 3.4 The Characteristics of African Customary Marriages

As demonstrated in the previous section of this chapter, it is difficult to clearly define marriage. One civil case before a British court (Hyde vs. Hyde of 1866) defined marriage as "[...] a voluntary union for life between one man and one woman, to the exclusion of all other" (quoted after Cotran 1967, p. 15). Using this definition as an example, we can see that it does not match the definition of African marriages, especially when it comes to those performed under customary law. First of all, in traditional African societies, the union is rarely voluntary, especially when it comes to the brides. Secondly, it does not have to be a union between one man and one woman, as polygamous practices (both polygyny and, more rarely, polyandry) are common on the African continent. And thirdly, due to the existence of legal procedures facilitating the dissolution of marriage, it is often not a lifelong union.

It would be an oversimplification to say that there is such a thing as a 'typical African marriage' (for the same reason that one does not speak of a single African law), but—according to Eugene Cotran—customary marriages encountered in Africa share several common features.

First is the aforementioned polygamous nature of marital relationships. Cotran (1967, p. 17) even claims that polygyny is characteristic for African marriages, since "[...] all customary laws in Africa, without exception, allowed, indeed encouraged, a man to have as many wives as he pleased". This is not true, as there are numerous ethnic groups in Africa in which it is a woman who can take more than one partner (e.g., the Lele, the Pende, the Bunda).[5] Cotran's observation may also apply to customary marriages in Ethiopia, although it should be remembered that efforts to prohibit polygamy date back to at least the fifteenth century and Emperor Zärʾa Yaʿəqob (1434–1468) (Tamrat 1972, pp. 242–243; Perruchon

[5] It should be emphasised that polyandry was much rarer than polygyny. Cf. Zajączkowski (1980), p. 68.

1893, pp. 10–12, 38, 94). In addition, it was extramarital unions rather than polygamy that were characteristic of Ethiopian society, as shown by Reidulf K. Molvaer (1995).

The second distinctive feature of African marriages is the role played by the families of the future spouses at every stage of the relationship, starting with finding a suitable male or female candidate, since (as mentioned earlier) an African marriage is not a voluntary union between two people, but rather a union of two families. It is the family members, not the future spouses, who negotiate the amount and type of matrimonial dues and engagement gifts. It is also the duty of family members to mediate between the quarrelling spouses and discuss the terms of their divorce. In this case, Cotran's theory is applicable both to Ethiopian customary laws and to the legal codes in the Ethiopian Empire. For example, in the twenty-fourth chapter of the Fətha Nägäśt, there are two large subsections describing precisely who acts on behalf of the bride-to-be or groom-to-be and based on what rules (Tzadua and Strauss 1968, pp. 134–142).

Another distinctive feature of marriages in Africa is the complexity and number of rituals involved in the wedding ceremony. The rituals vary in nature and length across various cultures, but from a legal point of view, it is difficult to distinguish which are part of the legal procedures and which have only a social dimension. In this respect, Ethiopian customary marriages also fit Cotran's theory, as each of the ethnic groups has rituals associated with the marriage ceremony, and—in many cases—it is difficult to determine the extent to which the rituals are purely cultural or reflect legal requirements.

A fourth distinctive feature of African customary marriages is the part of the betrothal process that was mistakenly referred to by early scholars of African cultures as the "brideprice" (Cotran 1967, p. 17). The term implied that the bridegroom in fact buys a wife, just as he buys other things he needs in the household. With the development of research on the African family and the emergence of theories about what this due paid to a woman's family actually is, the term began to fall out of use. Currently, some researchers believe that it is a kind of compensation for a family losing one of its members. Others believe that it is a safeguard for the woman to ensure that she is treated well by her husband's family, for in the event of divorce, the woman usually kept her family's gifts (e.g. Cotran 1967, p. 18).

Both of the aforementioned theories can be equally supported. For the purposes of this study, however, the legal dimension of matrimonial dues is important. According to both Eugene Cotran and Alfred Radcliffe-Brown (Radcliffe-Brown and Forde 1950), gifts offered by the groom to the bride's family were one method of legalising the marriage. If the gifts were accepted by the bride, then the marriage became legitimate. European travellers who visited the Ethiopian Empire in the nineteenth and twentieth centuries[6] related examples that support this hypothesis.

---

[6] The most extensive descriptions are to be found in Bruce (1790), Huyn and Kalmer (1935); Rey (1935) and Walker (1933).

Another characteristic feature for marriage customs is the emphasis on having children as the goal of marriage. Although in most cultures and religions, procreation is seen as a vital aim of marriage, according to Cotran, it is particularly important in African cultures. This is evidenced by such practices as polygamy, rituals related to male and female fertility performed during marriage ceremonies, and by such institutions as the levirate and sororate, the practice of inheriting widows and female marriages.[7] The fact that, during matchmaking, one of the most important issues discussed is to which family the children from the future marriage will belong is another piece of evidence of the importance of this aspect among African marriages. This also finds confirmation in Ethiopia.

The sixth feature of African traditional marriages is said to be the low status of women compared to that of men. It is arguable whether this is characteristic of African customary marriages only, given that until recently a similar situation could be observed in some European societies. However, Cotran argues that the practices mentioned above (polygamy, the levirate, wedding gifts), the lack of a requirement for a woman's consent to marry, and her relatively limited power over her children and property, demonstrate that the wife's low status is characteristic of African customary marriages.

A final feature indicated is the ease with which divorce can be obtained in Africa. Earlier researchers have argued that a husband can send his wife away for any reason and whenever he wishes. Cotran's research does not support this. He does, however, point to two important features that distinguish divorces in Africa from those in Europe. The first is the need for mediation between the spouses before the final separation takes place. The mediators should be members of both families. If mediation fails, the divorce can be conducted without a court procedure and only on the basis of an agreement between the spouses. The second distinctive feature is that customary laws generally do not provide a clear definition of the reasons why a marriage should cease. In determining the conditions of divorce, the number of children within the relationship is usually considered. The wealth of the wife's family is also important, since—in the event of divorce—they would have to give back the equivalent of the gifts received. Above all, however, other possible solutions that could prevent divorce are sought. The last feature noted by Coltran only partially characterises marriages in Ethiopia, where the grounds for divorce are clearly defined in most customary laws of the ethnic groups. These include infidelity, infertility, physical or mental illness and conspiracy against the spouse. However, lengthy mediation is carried out before divorce takes place, which is in line with Cotran's theory.

[7] These are legal marriages between women with the aim to maintain family continuity (the married woman was to be a surrogate mother who would bear a male heir) or to create new ties with other families if a male heir is lacking. Marriages of this type are known in such ethnic groups as the Fon, the Igbo and the Lovedu. For more on the topic, see Greene (1998), pp. 395–412.

## 3.5 Changes in the Institution of Customary Marriage in Africa

Cotran's research was focused on former British colonies in Africa and only to a small extent describe the situation in Ethiopia, but even a cursory discussion on the evolution of the institution in other regions of Africa is important for understanding the processes that took place in Ethiopian legislation in the 1960s.

For Cotran, changes occurring in customary marriages resulted from both direct and indirect reasons. As sources of the latter, he mentions contacts with European cultures and the influence of monotheistic religions. Among the direct factors, he includes:

- the decreasing influence of the family on the choice of spouse. The spouses-to-be decide for themselves whom they want to marry. The consent of both sides is more important than their material and social status
- wedding gifts being replaced by their equivalent in cash, or this part of the pre-wedding ceremony being completely renounced
- the rituals associated with nuptials being partly or completely abandoned, especially among the urban population. Among the disappearing rituals, Cotran mentions the symbolic abduction of the bride and her ceremonial defloration
- women's emancipation.

The most obvious immediate causes of changes in the institution of customary marriages are legal reforms. According to Cotran, the most significant ones were introduced during colonial times and just after African states gained independence.

Contrary to Britain's civilising mission to which all its colonies were to submit, the British administration generally avoided interfering in local law, provided that it functioned correctly or did not significantly collide with the British understanding of justice and morality. A sphere that did not fit into the latter and thus had to be reformed along European lines was that of marriage. Colonial legislators, unable to shape the nature of customary marriages, attempted instead to demonstrate the superiority of marriages performed in colonial offices over those performed before a local official or clergyman. For example, under the colonial-era Ugandan Penal Code, a woman married in a customary ceremony was not considered a legal wife. Consequently, she could not refuse to testify against her husband at court.

Major changes in legislations relevant to the institution of marriage took place after African states gained independence. The reforms aimed at creating unified laws that would apply to all citizens, regardless of their ethnicity. This objective could have been achieved in three ways. One involved discarding all laws introduced under colonialism and reverting to the customary laws predating subjection to a foreign power. This was difficult insofar as in many cases customary laws were never written down and, to be implemented, had to be codified first. Even so, a number of governments opted for this method of normalising civil law, including Tanzania, Kenya, Malawi, Zambia, Swaziland, Botswana, Lesotho, Sierra Leone, eastern Nigeria, Mali, Niger, Senegal, Burkina Faso (Cotran 1967, p. 27; Boye et al. 1991, pp. 343–349).[8]

The second method involved the unification of different customary legal provisions. This way was, in a sense, a necessary continuation of the first, but most of the countries mentioned above did not go through the stage of codifying customary law. The only exception was Tanzania, where the government decided to launch a Unification Project with the initial aim of creating a single, common civil law. In order to carry out the unification process as quickly as possible, the original objective was quickly abandoned and a strategy of convincing all ethnic groups to submit to the law prepared by the legislators was adopted. As a result, many Tanzanian citizens did not follow the unified law at all, considering it foreign, or had not heard of it at all.

The last approach was to skip the unification of customary law, and to create an entirely new law, which, however, was based on the foundations of customary law. This was applied by Ghana and Uganda. Ethiopia, in turn, has chosen this same path, but by modernising the state rather than by regulating any post-colonial legacy.

## 3.6 Types of Marriages in Ethiopia

Ethiopia is inhabited by over seventy ethnic groups (Central Statistical Office in Ethiopia 2007, online), whose customary laws regarding marriage differ from each other on many issues. For example, among the Amhara, marriages are not permitted between members of the same family who are separated by less than seven degrees of consanguinity, while under Afar customary law it is possible for even close relatives to marry (see Savard 1970). Among the Oromo, only exogamic relationships are permitted and marrying the wife of a deceased brother is allowed (Tafla 1987, pp. 121, 177 & 377).[9] As a result of this practice, a man can have many wives, though, according to Oromo law, he cannot divorce any of them.

Separate regulations also apply to the amount and type of wedding gifts. Among the Amhara, wedding presents (*ṭäloš*), such as jewellery, clothing and animals, are given by the groom directly to the bride, while among the Tigrayans it is the groom who receives gifts (*gäzmi*) in the form of money and clothing from the bride's parents. In turn, among the Oromo, Somali, Gurage, Kafficho and Anuak, it is possible to give the wedding gifts in instalments (Jembere 1998, p. 76).

The differences between the various laws can also be seen in the provisions regarding the reasons for the dissolution of a marriage. According to Abera Jembere, divorce is usually permissible under customary laws if mediation by the family

[8] A similar political approach was adopted by the Republic of South Africa; however, there the legislators had to also additionally tackle racist apartheid law. For more on this, see Bennett (2000), pp. 1–24.

[9] For an extensive description of the types of marriages among the Oromo, see Fantaye Efeta (1983).

members of the quarrelling spouses fails. Only with the Tigrayans is divorce possible on the basis of specific allegations.[10]

The systems of customary law among the different ethnic groups living in Ethiopia differ significantly between each other, but there are various similarities. The most important include the necessity to obtain the consent of both parties to the marriage, the need to pay a pre-nuptial fee (in the form of gifts), and the presence of rituals associated with each stage of the nuptials, from matchmaking to the party held on the day following the wedding.[11]

The above cursory overview of marriage rituals clearly shows the diversity—not only in this regard—of cultures in Ethiopia. However, as mentioned earlier, the Amharic culture has had a profound influence on the cultural and social development of Ethiopia, including the development of the institution of marriage and related Ethiopian legislation. Thus, the present study will be focused on the types of marriage encountered among the Amhara people, while the discussion on the institutions of other ethnic groups will be limited. Obviously, some Amhara ceremonies or rituals may have been borrowed from other cultures.

## 3.7 Types of Marriages Among the Amhara People

Among the Amhara, there are three main types of marriages: *sərat*, *dämoz* and *qal kidan bäqurban*. The most popular is the marriage of the *sərat* type (referred to also as *särg*, literally ‘the ceremony’). This is a civil marriage, which until recently was often preceded by a long period of engagement.[12] Until the mid-twentieth century, marriages of this type were usually arranged by the families of the future married couple, and their consent was not obligatory. Furthermore, until the wedding day, the man was not allowed to meet his future wife or any of her relatives (Ullendorff 1962, p. 179). The wedding itself would take place when the girl achieved sexual maturity, i.e., at the age of 12 or 13 (Lvová 1997, p. 577).[13]

---

[10] The claims made by Abera Jembere have to some extent been confirmed by the results of studies conducted by other researchers of Ethiopia, according to whom the reasons for divorce are clearly defined (Abera Jembere 1998, p. 76).

[11] It should also be remembered that, in addition to marriages concluded in accordance with customary laws, there are also religious marriages—Christian and Muslim. The latter are always concluded in accordance with Sharia law and are granted by *qadi* (judges), who were given this right on the basis of a 1942 proclamation. However, it is often the case that Muslims living in Ethiopia opt out of this type of marriage in favour of civil unions performed in registry offices. See Lvová (1997), p. 580.

[12] Previously, the engagement ceremony often took place when the future bride and groom were still children (Ullendorff 1962, p. 179).

[13] Early marriages in Ethiopia have been discussed in Haile Gabriel Dagne (1994), pp. 35–38. In 2003, the Ethiopian government passed a law banning marriage for people under the age of eighteen. Three years later, Mekonnen and Aspen (2010) conducted a study on the effectiveness of the social campaign related to the implementation of this law.

The course of the ceremony varies according to the financial means of the bride and groom's families, but the various rituals remain the same. Once the two parties agree on the terms of the marriage, a contract is drawn up and signed in the presence of the elders.[14] Each of the families designates a guarantor of the relationship, referred to as 'the father of the marriage' (*yänägär ʾabbat*, literally 'the father of the speech').[15] It is his task to ensure that both parties comply with the signed agreement (Marein 1949, p. 99).[16] On the day of the marriage, the bride and groom are led before the *šum*[17] and—in the presence of more than two witnesses[18]—a marriage act is signed and a *fəṭəm* oath[19] pronounced. A wedding that lasts many days ensues, taking place in the bride's father's house.[20] More or less one week later, yet another wedding reception takes place, this time in the house of the groom. It is referred to as *məlaš* (Pankhurst 1992, p. 103) and only after this event has ended does the marriage become fully official and legally-binding (Nicolas 2011, p. 89).

During the wedding, yet another ceremony takes place, in which exclusively women participate—the bride, all her friends and the groom's mother. During this ceremony, the woman receives her 'bread name' (*yädabbo səm* or *mərat səm*).[21] From that moment onward, members of the husband's family would address her using only that name, while members of her family would continue to use the name the woman had received at birth. In previous times, when the wedding was over, the *mize* ('the best man') would carry the bride to her husband's house. The woman was accompanied by her friends, each carrying a piece of bread (*dabbo*). Once there, the *mize* would continue carrying the bride on his shoulders until her mother-in-law

[14] Such negotiations may last even a few months, cf.: Walker (1933), pp. 23–41; Nicolas (2011), pp. 90–107.

[15] According to J.I. Eadie (1924, pp. 75–79), *yänägär ʾabbat* is the lawyer of the girl's family. However, this explanation seems to be an oversimplification, perhaps stemming from a desire to facilitate the reader's understanding of the role that the 'father of the marriage' played during premarital negotiations. His role is also highlighted by Walker (1933, pp. 25–27).

[16] For examples of marriage contracts concluded in the eighteenth and nineteenth century, see Crummey (1988), pp. 315–327.

[17] An explanation of the Ethiopian terms used in this book can be found in the dictionary at the end of the publication.

[18] The sources are not in agreement on the number of witnesses who attest to the legitimacy of a wedding ceremony. Harry M.H. Hyatt (1928, p. 207) states that there should be a minimum of two witnesses, while Nathan Marein (1949, p. 98) writes of a minimum of five witnesses.

[19] *Fäṣmi* in Tigrinya. This oath is always taken when the one making it wishes to emphasise that he accepts the obligations imposed on him and the promises he has made. It usually begins with the words: "*Nəgus yəmut...*" ["Let the emperor die if..."]. See Ullendorff (1962), p. 187.

[20] An extensive description of the course of the wedding can be found in Hyatt (1928), pp. 201–206; Huyn and Kalmer ([1935]), pp. 172–173–157; Walker (1933), pp. 27–32; Leslau and Kane (2001), pp. 11–15. Among the Amhara, the bride and groom receive presents not only from the family, but also from the invited guests. For more on the type of gifts received, see Salamon (1994).

[21] In Amharic, *yädabbo səm* literally means 'bread name', while *mərat səm* signifies the sister-in-law's name (*mərat*—'sister-in-law').

revealed what bread name she had chosen for her. The bride's friends would give the bread to the groom's mother, who would distribute it to the other guests.[22]

Nowadays, the bread naming ceremony is no longer so common and can only be observed in rural areas. What occurs during the ceremony has also changed. The choice of the bread name is made not only by the woman's mother-in-law, but by all relatives and close friends of the bride and groom. Guests are divided into groups that include the bride and groom's families, the *mize*, friends of both the bride and groom, and close neighbours. Each group chooses a name for the bride. According to tradition, the name should be composed of two parts, one of them being *wärq* (literally 'gold').[23] The *mize* then demands that each group provide a name of their choice, along with an explanation. The final name which becomes the bride's bread name is chosen through voting conducted by all those gathered in the house. At the end of the ceremony, the *mize* distributes the bread to the guests. When accepting the bread, each recipient is required to pronounce the bride's new name, which is meant to symbolise her acceptance into her husband's family.

The wedding night is awaited with some tension, both by the young couple and the bride's family and especially by the latter, because this is when it becomes apparent whether they lied during the pre-wedding negotiations about the girl's virginity.[24] The act of defloration takes place in the home of the newlyweds (*čagula bet*). Then the *mize* hangs a white cloth as a sign that the bride was untouched (i.e., a virgin).[25] Next, the groom is seated on the shoulders of the *mize*, while the guests gathered at the event begin to dance and sing a traditional Amharic song: *bər ᵓambar säbärälachəhu* ('[the groom] has broken the silver bracelet') (Yemane 2004, p. 188). This ceremony is called *yähəgg mägsäs sərat* (Kane 1990, p. 33). It is worth noting that the name of the ceremony contains two words signifying 'law' in Amharic—*həgg* and *sərat*.[26] The second term refers to customary law, while the first—according to Ethiopian worldview—to natural law. The use of both terms emphasises the

[22] The women did not receive a bread name only in the case of a marriage by abduction (*ṭäläfa*). See Elias Yemane (2004), p. 184. The custom of distributing bread among wedding guests was also present in ancient Greece and ancient Rome. See Ringrose (1911), p. 8; Kocurek and Wigmore (1918), p. 288.

[23] A woman's new name should reflect her character or beauty. In turn, the presence of the word 'gold' in the name is supposed to indicate that the new member of the family is someone important to those accepting her into the family. For examples of bread names, see Elias Yemane (2004), p. 185.

[24] The girl's virginity is important not only to confirm her parents' truthfulness (and therefore their honor), but also because, being her first man, her newly married husband is certain that the child she bears will be his.

[25] In the old days, during the act itself, the groom's best men were present in the marital home, and they were tasked with holding the bride down during the sexual act. In fact, it was in accordance with custom for the bride to try to break away and scream during intercourse. Cp.: Molvaer (1995), p. 105; Prouty (1986), p. 36.

[26] The third part of the ceremony's name comes from the verb *gäsäsä*, which means 'to break the hymen'. Noteworthy, there is also a phrase *həgg gäsäsä* meaning 'to deflower' (Kane 1990, p. 1956).

importance of the bride's virginity during marriage negotiations. According to Amharic customary law, its absence could be sufficient reason to annul a marriage.

The next day, the white cloth that the *mize* had hung out the previous night is taken to the bride's parents. If the girl was not a virgin, the parents would be shamed as *gud fäla* (literally 'a strange ferment'; Yemane 2004, p. 188) and their social position would suffer. In such a case, the bride has to return to her parents, who would be forced to give back all the gifts received before and during the wedding ceremony. Since the beginning of the twenty-first century, this custom has disappeared and instead of a cloth, the parents are gifted with flowers or *bərəlle ṭäğ* (a type of bulbous vessel for mead) to express gratitude for having raised their daughter to be a decent girl (*cäwa ləj*) (Yemane 2004, p. 188).

After the wedding, the young couple resides in the home of the groom's family. It is not until 2 or 3 years after the wedding that the newlyweds can ask the parents to assign them land on which to build a house. If the bride had not yet reached puberty, she would return to her father's house after the wedding. She would move to her husband's house only after she reached the appropriate age (Lvová 1997, p. 577).[27]

It is currently increasingly rare for *sərat*-type marriages to be arranged.[28] They are not preceded by a long period of engagement, and the people involved go directly to a judge (*dañña*) or magistrate's office to get married.

Another type of marriage is the *dämoz* ('salary') relationship. This is a kind of fixed-term contract in which a woman agrees to perform the duties of a wife in exchange for appropriate remuneration (either financial or in the form of material goods).[29] The contract can be terminated at any time during the relationship, and the spouses are not obliged to pay any compensation. Once the contract expires, it can be renewed, or the man and woman agree that the contract will continue at certain times (e.g., every 6 months).[30]

Marriages of this type were often contracted by men who were away from home for a large part of the year (such as merchants and soldiers). Children born in *dämoz*-type unions have the right to inherit on the same terms as children from other marriages, but the wives do not. Women in these unions also do not have the right to administer their husbands' property, but if the man's death occurred before the expiration of the contract, they could claim payment of the wages due them for the entire period of the marriage (Marein 1949, p. 99).

Even though Edward Ullendorff (1962, p. 179) wrote that relationships of this type were not accepted either by the Ethiopian Orthodox Church or by the state

[27] For more on the marriages of underaged girls in Ethiopia, see Haile Gabriel Dagne (1994), pp. 35–38.

[28] For more on contemporary arranged marriages, see Fafchamps and Quisumbing (2005), pp. 347–380; Nicolas (2011), pp. 90–120.

[29] According to Eadie (1924, pp. 76 & 79), in 1924, the wife's *dämoz* salary amounted to 5–30 *bərr*.

[30] Unions of this type were common among the people of the Arabian Peninsula before the advent of Islam. *Zawaj al-muta*, or temporary marriage, is also permitted by Shiites. For more on this topic, see Zyzik (2003), pp. 89–91 and Wiebke (1982), p. 37.

elites,[31] the Ethiopian legislation does take them into account. In 1949, Judge Nathan Marein (1949, p. 99) described cases in which the Supreme Court awarded alimony benefits to a woman who entered into a relationship of the *dämoz* type.

The most binding type of relationship is the *qal kidan bäqurban* marriage (also referred to as *ᵓaklil*, literally 'crown'). This is a religious marriage that cannot be dissolved. The ceremony involves a man and woman receiving holy communion (*qurban*) together. Marriages of the *qal kidan* type were entered into most often by Ethiopian aristocracy and the clergy, for whose members it was the only possibility to get married. Ethiopians generally avoid *qal kidan* marriages precisely because of its indissolubility and the fact that even after the death of a spouse, a dispensation must be obtained before remarrying. This is why a church marriage is most often entered into by older members of society (Marein 1949, p. 99; Lvová 1997, p. 578; Ullendorff 1962, p. 179).

The marriage ceremony in the church begins with a holy mass, during which the bride and groom are anointed with holy oil,[32] while a wedding cloak referred to as *mäqʷanäṣäfiya* is placed over their shoulders, which is meant to symbolise their unity as a married couple. The priest then takes the groom's hand and places it in the bride's hand, blessing them with the sign of the cross. After binding the spouses with a symbolic marriage knot, the priest informs them of the duties of a husband and wife using the following words:

> [...] Blessed son and dear brother...accept your bride... you will be kind and helpful towards her because you have *taken the place of her parents*...if you abide by what you have been told, the Lord himself will help you, blessing your property, gives you numerous children, granting yow a long life and happy days".
>
> Blessed and gifted sister...you are requested to abide even more by *your obligation*. To day you have been united and made a single being with him. He will be *your master* therefore you have to honor and respect him. You will *not rebel against his advice and orders*; and you will greet him with joy and shining face, never grumble while in his presence nor waste your property, always be *submissive* to what the Lord will dispose for him, as the Lord commands you to obey your parent. You will live with him, always respecting him and, in the same way Sara lived with Abraham replying to him: "My Lord". (quoted after Allehone Mulugeta 2000, pp. 1336–1337)[33]

The ceremony ends with the joint reception of holy communion (Hyatt 1928, p. 207)[34] and the circling of the church three times by the bride and groom and their guests (Fritsch 2008, p. 315).

---

[31] Eleonora Lvova (1997, pp. 577–584), who conducted research in Ethiopia in the 1990s, confirms that *dämoz*-type marriages still exist in Ethiopia in rural areas, even though they are increasingly less frequent. Lvova also describes a case of a *dämoz* marriage, which lasted 25 years.

[32] Anointing involves making the sign of the cross on the forehead, chin, cheeks and the outside and inside of the hands (Fritsch 2008, p. 315).

[33] According to Allehone Mulugeta (2000, p. 1336), the content of the oath indicates discrimination against women in marriages.

[34] Emmanuel Fritsch (2008, pp. 309–327) also mentions a ritual referred to as *täklil* ('coronation'), which takes place during the wedding ceremony. If it is the first marriage for each of those getting married, then crowns are placed on their heads to resemble saints and to remind them of the seri-

*Blatten geta* Mahtämä Sillase Wäldä Mäsqäl (1982, p. 581) described in *Zəkrä nägär* the marriage ceremonies among the Ethiopian aristocracy in the mid-twentieth century. He writes that the marriages of dignitaries' children were arranged not only by their parents, but also by the imperial couple themselves.[35] On the wedding day, the bride and groom wore richly decorated clothing embroidered with gold thread. The parents of the bride and groom also dressed in a similar fashion. Often the bride and groom's clothes were their dowry from their parents or from the imperial couple themselves. Just as often, the ruler gave the future couple seventy mules and one hundred horses decorated with gold, silver and bronze as a wedding gift. Such gifts were most often given to members of the imperial family, who also received socks made of expensive fur, shoes made of material embroidered with gold thread, a fur toque, a fur waistcoat, gloves, gold jewellery (earrings, armlets and anklets, rings), a gold cross, a hat, a cloak and a green umbrella decorated with gold.[36]

The wedding ceremony itself for members of the Ethiopian aristocracy was no different from the one described above, although it was followed by a ritual unknown among the emperor's ordinary subjects. On the day following the wedding, the best man and bridesmaid would visit the parents of the bride and groom to congratulate them on the happy event. The parents of the bride and groom were expected to return the favour with the gift of a length of cloth or a small sum of money (Mahtämä Śəllase Wäldä Mäsqäl 1982, p. 586).

Ethiopian priests can only marry before ordination and even after the death of their wife they cannot remarry. The wedding ceremony takes place on a non-fasting day. Apart from family and friends, the wedding is also attended by the *yänäfs ᵓabbat* ('spiritual father') of the groom, who is the equivalent of the 'father of the marriage', present during a ceremony of the *sərat* type. After the ceremony in the church, the guests would make their way to the bride's house (Hyatt 1928, p. 209). During the wedding reception, the priest present at the event gives a sermon, after which he blesses not only the bride and groom but also the bread (*dəfo dabbo*) specially prepared for the occasion (Fritsch 2008, p. 322).

The types of marriages discussed above are the most frequently encountered among the Amhara. In addition, there are also three others, described by Helen Pankhurst in the book *Gender, Development and Identity. An Ethiopian Study*. The first of these is the marriage of the *sämanya* ('eighty') type.[37] It is described as "a

---

ousness of the sacrament of marriage. For more on the wedding mass in the Ethiopian Orthodox Church, see Fritsch (2008), pp. 309–327 and Kessis Kefyalew Merahi (1998), pp. 37–49.

[35] Quite often, children of nobles were sent to the imperial court not only to serve but also to get an education. They were treated by the imperial couple as their foster children (cf., e.g., Bairu Tafla 1972).

[36] Mahtämä Śəllase Wäldä Mäsqäl (1982, pp. 583–585) also mentions wedding presents which courtiers received from the imperial couple.

[37] According to E. Firtsch (2008, p. 321), the name of this type of marriage refers to the biblical Eve, whom God was said to have created eighty days after the creation of Adam. Tsegaye Beru (2013, p. 342), on the other hand, claims that the term comes from the sum of 80 Maria Theresa

marriage between equals", during which the man and woman sign a kind of marriage contract that has to be authenticated by two witnesses. Some researchers[38] equate this type of marriage with the *sərat* relationship, although, unlike the latter, this marriage does not have to be arranged. Frequently, the term *sämanya* signifies all types of relationships that are not of the *dämoz* type or marriages by abduction (*ṭäläfa*).

Of the two further types of marriages, the first one, *qäṭäro ᵓasər* ('ten [years] of work'), was most often encountered in rural areas, but it has already disappeared. This type of marriage was performed when the bride had not yet reached puberty and could not live with her husband, or there was a shortage of workforce on the bride's father's farm. In such a case, the groom would work on his father-in-law's farm until his wife was mature enough to leave the family home.

The last type encountered among the Ethiopians is marriage by abduction (*ṭäläfa*).[39] While this may seem shocking, it should be remembered that not all marriages by abduction involved violence and the unwillingness of one of the parties to marry. Frequently, all relationships not arranged by families or to which the families objected were referred to as *ṭäläfa* marriages. It also happened that kidnappings were arranged by the two families when they could not afford to organise a wedding ceremony in accordance with custom (Pankhurst 1992, p. 105; Augustyniak 2009, p. 103).[40] Marriage by abduction was also encouraged when the nuptials, according to tradition (of the *sərat* type), would not have been appropriate, for example in a situation when the bride was a divorcee or widow. In such a case, *ṭäläfa* enables avoiding the costs associated with the wedding and the embarrassing ceremonies linked to confirming the bride's virginity. According to Eleonora Lvová, the abduction could last from 3 months to 5 or 6 years. After this period, the young would enter into a *sämanya* wedding (Lvová 1997, p. 579).[41]

Whatever the reasons for abduction were, the act itself is a transgression against the law, a violation of all relevant procedures. Among both the Amhara and the Oromo, abducting a girl means disrespect for the whole family, especially the father of the kidnapped. His displeasure may be even greater if the abductor had previously sent his matchmakers. The father's explicit non-agreement to his daughter's

talars (the official form of payment in Ethiopia until 1894), which had to be paid in the case of infidelity of one of the spouses or divorce.

[38] E.g., N. Marein, E. Lvová, E. Fritsch.

[39] Marriage by abduction was also present in other cultures. For more on this, see Kocurek and Wigmore (1918), p. 281.

[40] According to Huyn and Kalmer ([1935], pp. 177–178), marriage by abduction occurred exclusively in the Oromo ethnic group. In the early twentieth century, this type of marriage was "ridiculed" and the abduction itself became just a "kidnapping game". The authors' words are contradicted by research conducted by Andrea Nicolas (2011, pp. 120–139) between 1999 and 2002 among the Oromo.

[41] Successive Ethiopian governments have sought to ban marriages by abduction, underage nuptials and unions of the *qäṭro ᵓasər* type. However, this law has not been enforced.

marriage during their first visit is a clear signal to the family of the matchmaker that this decision is final and further meetings are pointless (Nicolas 2011).

An abduction usually happens when the girl is not accompanied by her family members. After the deed, the groom-to-be and his two companions hide the kidnapped girl. The father of the abductor will then be informed of the whole incident while the culprit takes cover not only from the anger of the kidnapped girl's family, but also from the law enforcement officers who may arrest him in connection with the case.[42]

While the kidnapper is in hiding, it is his father's task to find mediators among the village elders to act on his behalf. If the boy's father was not involved in the kidnapping, he himself can act as one of the mediators, but if he even only knew of the planned act, it is the kidnapper's uncle who may act on his behalf. The mediators, before going to the kidnapped girl's home, determine the next steps and the amount of cattle that will be offered to the girl's family during the mediation.

On the first day of the mediation, at dawn, the groom's mediators set off for the kidnapped woman's parents' house. The group consists of an even number of elderly men and "[...] two cows that have not calved and two bulls that have not yet ploughed the field" (Nicolas 2011, p. 126). If the kidnapper previously sought the girl's hand in another way, the group of mediators includes the same men who were previously his matchmakers. Their aim is to bring the cattle into the homestead of the abducted girl's parents. If successful, this will signify the family's consent to the marriage. Sometimes, in order to facilitate the operation, the kidnapper's family contacts some neighbours of the kidnapped girl's parents to persuade the girl's father to accept the cattle. If the abduction did not take place with the knowledge and informal consent of the girl's family, the recipients will defend themselves from accepting the gift by closing the farmyard gates or chasing the stranger's cattle out of the homestead. If they succeed, the mediators will return the next day to try again.

The attempt to bring cattle into the homestead should not be made more than twice. Therefore, on the second day, the kidnappee's family accepts the animals. The abductor's mediators remain at the gates, and upon being asked to state the purpose of their visit, they reply that they have come to reconcile the two parties. As a sign of favouring the elders' intentions, the kidnapped girl's mother anoints the cattle she has received with butter. The bulls that have never ploughed the ground (meaning they are uncastrated) symbolise the groom, while the cows symbolise the bride. Their anointing by the woman is a symbolic blessing of the young couple. Since the wife cannot perform the anointing without her husband's consent, her act will signal to the mediators of the future groom that the girl's father is also in favour of the marriage. Anointing the animals also means that the next stage of the marriage negotiations may begin, which will focus on the type of reparation to be given for the moral wrongs suffered by the abductee and her family. It may also so happen that after the anointing ceremony, the kidnapped girl returns to her family home as

[42] According to Nicolas (2011, p. 125), one can be sentenced to 15 years in prison for participating in or assisting an abduction.

the consent for marriage has been given and there is no reason to keep the girl in hiding.

Two rounds of negotiations take place within 2 weeks of the abduction. During the first, it is important for the groom's mediators to show their deference and contrition to the bride's family at every stage of the negotiations. However, this does not mean agreeing to all kinds of concessions. During the second round of negotiations, for the first time in the entire process, the elders will be addressed directly by the girl's father. After listing one by one the wrongs he has suffered, he will demand reparation from the kidnappers. It is important that both parties reach a satisfactory compromise, as the absence of the girl's family at the wedding ceremony will make the marriage illegal.

The wedding takes place one or 2 weeks after the last round of negotiations. It is more modest compared to the wedding that would take place in the case of a *sərat* union and usually lasts only 1 day. If both families live in the same locality, guests move from the bride's family home to the groom's house during the wedding. If the bride and groom live far away from each other, the wedding reception takes place in the groom's household and it is at the same time a *məlaš*, i.e., a repeat wedding.

## 3.8 Divorces and Their Causes

In the discussion on marriage among Ethiopians, it is repeatedly noted that divorce can be obtained quite easily. This may have been due to the fact that most Ethiopian marriages were arranged and therefore there was no emotional bond between the spouses. Today, the high number of divorces is seen as mainly due to the emotional immaturity of the partners and the fact that Ethiopian women are becoming increasingly independent, not only economically, and aspire to more than just being a housewife (Meskerem Lemma 2015).

Regarding the possibility of obtaining a divorce among the Amhara, of the above-mentioned marriage types only the *qal kidan bäqurban* cannot be dissolved. In the case of a *dämoz* marriage, the very premise is that it will cease after a mutually agreed period. In the case of *sərat* marriages, divorce may occur when attempts to reconcile the feuding spouses fail.[43] Separation must be by mutual consent and, on divorcing, the spouses are obliged to return goods received and acquired during the union.[44] Once the marriage has ended, both parties may enter into further relationships.

[43] The research conducted by Abate and Shiferaw (2008) prove that the mediators are reluctant to negotiate divorce cases and tend to side with men, which contradicts the provisions of the current (proclaimed in 1995) Ethiopian Constitution (Article 35). Consequently, many women bypass the traditional courts, going directly to the state courts.

[44] It is often the case that a provision concerning the division of property in the event of divorce is already in the marriage contract.

Regarding the division of property after divorce, under the current law, joint property will be divided equally between the spouses, while the assets they owned before marriage will remain theirs. Ethiopian courts also take into account customary laws in their divorce decrees. If customary law dictates the return of the wife's dowry, then the divorced man has to return it or its equivalent.[45]

Amharic customary law strictly defines which of the divorcing spouses is given custody of the children. Traditionally, children up to the age of three were left in the care of their mother, while the father was obliged to contribute to their upkeep. After the age of three, boys were taken into the custody of their father, while girls remained with their mother. According to Nathan Marein (1949, p. 20), who described the laws in Ethiopia in 1949, the official child custody provision did not differ significantly from the Ethiopian tradition. Under current laws, children are in the custody of their mother until they reach the age of seven, while the father is obliged to pay alimony. In the case of a daughter, such an obligation ceases when the girl marries, and in the case of a boy, when he reaches the 'age of maturity'.

As mentioned earlier, Ethiopia is inhabited by almost eighty ethnic groups. The types of marriages observed among the Amhara have been described above. However, it should be remembered that over the centuries, the traditions of the various ethnic groups have influenced each other and unions of a similar nature, though under different names, can be observed among different groups.

It is also worth mentioning that apart from the Amhara, mostly Christian, the largest ethnic group is the Oromo, some of whom are Muslim. In addition to state law, Oromo Muslims are also bound by Sharia law, which allows polygamy. As a result, the Oromo also have other types of marriage that do not exist among the monogamous Amhara.[46]

From a European perspective, the multitude of forms of marriage encountered in Ethiopia may have posed quite a challenge to legislators. In the following chapters, the development of Ethiopian legislation in this area will be examined.

## References

Abate M, Shiferaw W (2008) Customary dispute resolution in Amhara region: the case of Wofa Legesse in north Shewa. In: Pankhurst A, Assefa G (eds) Grass-roots justice in Ethiopia: the contribution of customary dispute resolution. Centre Français d'Études Éthiopiennes, Addis Ababa, pp 107–121

Mulugeta A (2000) Women, state and the family; issues of legal pluralism and challenges to family law. In: Yimam B (ed) Proceedings of the XIVth international conference of Ethiopian studies. Institute of Ethiopian Studies, Addis Ababa University, Addis Ababa, pp 1334–1358

Augustyniak Z (2009) Marriages in Ethiopia. Studies of the Department of Languages and Cultures 43:99–115

[45] For a detailed description of Amharic customs related to divorce and division of property, see Walker (1933), pp. 42–48.

[46] Among the Oromo, non-Islamic polygamy is also very common.

Bennett TW (2000) The reform of customary marriage law in South Africa. Recht in Afrika 1:1–24
Beru T (2013) Brief history of the Ethiopian legal systems—past and present. Int J Leg Inf 41(3):335–388
Boye AK, Hill K, Isaacs S, Gordis D (1991) Marriage law and practice in the Sahel. Stud Fam Plan 22(6):343–349
Bruce J (1790) Travels to discover the source of the Nile, II. J. Ruthven, Edinburgh
Central Statistical Office in Ethiopia (2007) Population and housing census. https://www.stats-ethiopia.gov.et/census-2007-2/
Cotran E (1967) The changing nature of African marriage. In: Anderson JND (ed) Family law in Asia and Africa. Frederick A. Praeger Publishers, New York and Washington, pp 15–33
Crummey D (1988) Three Amharic documents of marriage and inheritance from the eighteenth and nineteenth centuries. In: Beyene T (ed) Proceedings of the eight international conference of Ethiopian studies, vol I. Institute of Ethiopian Studies, Frobenius Institut, Johann Wolfgang Goëthe Universität, Addis Ababa, Frankfurt am Main, pp 315–327
Dagne HG (1994) Early marriage in northern Ethiopia. Reprod Health Matters 2(4):35–38
Eadie JI (1924) An Amharic reader. Cambridge University Press, Cambridge
Efeta F (1983) Civil code and customary marriage. A case study with reference to the Seboo Oromo. BA thesis, Faculty of Law, Addis Ababa University
Fafchamps M, Quisumbing AR (2005) Marriage, bequest and assortative matching in rural Ethiopia. Econ Dev Cult Chang 53(2):347–380
Fritsch E (2008) Matrimony in the Ethiopian church. In: Marinčák Š (ed) Swätě Tajomstvá na Krest'anskom Východe. Center of Spirituality East-West, Košice, pp 309–327
Gluckman M (1965) Politics, law and ritual in tribal society. Basil Blackwell, Oxford
Greene B (1998) The institution of woman-marriage in Africa: a cross-cultural analysis. Ethnology 37(4):395–412
Huyn L, Kalmer J (1935) Abessinien—Afrikas Unruhe-Herd. Das Bergland-Buch, Salzburg
Hyatt HM (1928) The Church of Abyssinia. Luzak & Co, London
Jembere A (1998) Legal history of Ethiopia, 1434-1974. Erasmus Universiteit, Afrika-Studiecentrum, Leiden, Rotterdam
Kane TL (1990) Amharic-English dictionary, vol 1-2. Harrassowitz, Wiesbaden
Kocurek A, Wigmore JH (1918) Evolution of law: selected readings on the origin and development of legal institutions, vol 1-3. Little, Brown and Company, Boston
Krzeczunowicz G (1966) Putting the legal clock back? The law and its sources. Journal of Ethiopian Law 3(2):621–627
Kuper A (1997) The invention of primitive society. Transformations of an illusion. Routledge, London and New York
Lemma M (11 April 2015) Ethiopia: marriage vs modern day Ethiopians. The Ethiopian Herald, https://allafrica.com/stories/201504131744.html
Leslau W, Kane TL (2001) Amharic cultural reader. Harrassowitz, Wiesbaden
Lvová E (1997) Forms of marriage and the status of women in Ethiopia. In: Fukui K, Eisei K, Shigeta M (eds) Ethiopia in broader perspective. Papers of the XIIIth international conference of Ethiopian studies, vol III. Shokado Book Sellers, Kyoto, pp 577–584
Malinowski B (1934) Introduction. In: Hogbin HI (ed) Law and order in Polynesia: a study of primitive legal institutions. Harcourt, Brace and Co., New York, pp xvii–lxxii
Marein N (1949) Handbook to the laws of Ethiopia. Addis Abeba University, Addis Abeba
Mekonnen BM, Aspen H (2010) Early marriage and the campaign against it in Ethiopia. In: Aspen H, Teferra B, Bekele S, Ege S (eds) Research in Ethiopian studies. Selected papers of the XVIth international conference of Ethiopian studies, Trondheim, July 2007. Harrassowitz, Wiesbaden, pp 432–443
Merahi KK (1998) The order of marriage and social ethics. Organization for Social Services for AIDS (OSSA) in Ethiopia, Addis Abeba
Molvaer RK (1995) Socialization and social control in Ethiopia. Harrassowitz, Wiesbaden

Morgan L (1871) Systems of consanguinity and affinity of the human family. Smithsonian Institution, Washington DC
Nicolas A (2011) From process to procedure. Elders' mediation and formality in Central Ethiopia. Harrassowitz, Wiesbaden
Nowicka E (2003) Świat człowieka—świat kultury. Systematyczny wykład problemów antropologii kulturowej. Wydawnictwo Naukowe PWN, Warszawa
Pankhurst H (1992) Gender, development and identity. An Ethiopian study. Zed Books, London
Perruchon J (ed) (1893) Les chroniques de Zar'a Yâeqôb et de Ba'eda Mâryâm rois d'Éthiopie de 1434 a 1478. Émile Bouillon, Paris
Prouty C (1986) Empress Taytu and Menelik II. Ethiopia 1883-1910. The Red Sea Press, Trenton
Radcliffe-Brown A, Forde D (eds) (1950) African systems of kinship and marriage. Oxford University Press, London
Rey CF (1935) The real Abyssinia. Seeley, London
Ringrose H (1911) Marriage and divorce laws of the world. The Musson-Draper Company, London
Salamon H (1994) Making point with knives: wedding gifts and intergroup relations. In: Marcus HG (ed) New trends in Ethiopian studies. Papers of the XIIth international conference of Ethiopian studies. The Red Sea Press, New York, pp 966–973
Savard GC (1970) Cross-cousin marriage among the patrilinear Afar. In: Proceedings of the third international conference of Ethiopian studies, vol III. Institute of Ethiopian Studies, Haile Sellassie I University, Addis Ababa, pp 89–98
Tafla B (1972) Marriage as a political device: an appraisal of socio-political aspect of the Menelik period 1889-1916. Journal of Ethiopian Studies 1(10):13–23
Tafla B (ed) (1987) Aṣma Giyorgis and his work. History of the Gāllā and the kingdom of Šawā. Franz Steiner, Stuttgart
Tamrat T (1972) Church and state in Ethiopia, 1270-1527. The Clarendon Press, Oxford
Tylor EB (1865) Researches into the early history of mankind and the development of civilization. John Murray, Albemarle Street, London
Tzadua P, Strauss PL (1968) The Fetha Nagast. The law of the kings. Faculty of Law, Haile Sellassie I University, Addis Ababa
Ullendorff E (1962) The Ethiopians: an introduction to country and people. Oxford University Press, London
Vanderlinden J (1966a) An introduction to the sources of Ethiopian law from the 13th to the 20th century. Journal of Ethiopian Law 3(1):227–639
Vanderlinden J (1966b) A further note on an introduction to the sources of Ethiopian law. Journal of Ethiopian Law 3(2):635–639
Wäldä Mäsqäl MŚ (1982) Zəkrä Nägär. Artistik, Addis Abäba
Walker CH (1933) The Abyssinian at home. The Sheldon Press, London
Wiebke W (1982) Kobieta w islamie. Wydawnictwa Artystyczne i Filmowe, Warszawa
Yemane E (2004) Amharic and Ethiopic onomastics. A classic Ethiopian legacy, concept, and ingenuity. The Edwin Mellen Press, Lewiston
Zajączkowski A (1980) Czarna Afryka wczoraj i dziś. Ludowa Spółdzielnia Wydawnicza, Warszawa
Zyzik M (2003) Małżeństwo w prawie muzułmańskim. Dom Wydawniczy Elipsa, Warszawa

# Chapter 4
# The Sources of Ethiopian Law

## 4.1 The Beginnings of Ethiopian Statehood

As mentioned in previous chapters, considering the multiplicity and diversity of cultures, there is no such concept as a single African law, although distinct common traits can be found in the legal systems functioning in Africa. For most African states, the time of intensified codification took place when the countries were the colonies of Western powers. The codification of law in Ethiopia, which is the subject of this book, proceeded in a different way and at different time.

Ethiopia occupies a special place among the African states. Historically, it is the only country in Africa that has resisted being subjugated from its origins to the present day (except for the period of Italian occupation between 1936 and 1941). From a linguistic and cultural point of view, Ethiopia is an ethnic mosaic with a mix of Christian, Muslim and indigenous African influences. From earliest times, Ethiopian culture has oscillated between orality, which is characteristic of African cultures, and written culture, which emerged in Ethiopia with the arrival of settlers from South Arabia. For any discussion on the development of legislation in Ethiopia, from rules propagated orally among the population of the Empire to the codification of these laws, at least a brief account of the history of the Ethiopian Empire is necessary.

The origins of the Ethiopian state can be traced back to the ancient city-state of Aksum. It was founded by the descendants of settlers from South Arabia (also known as Arabia Felix), who arrived on the African continent in the first millennium BCE. Among the existing statehoods in the Arabian Peninsula, four city-states stood out economically, politically and culturally: Ma'in, Qataban, Saba and Hadramaut (Bartnicki and Mantel-Niećko 1978, p. 1). Their success resulted from their agricultural and technical advancement combined with an intercontinental trade network. The states contended for a dominant position in the region, which would give them control over the trade route from the north of the peninsula, passing through all four states. The profits from the trade in gold, pearls, frankincense, coffee, spices and



Z. Augustyniak, *Marriage in the Ethiopian Empire*, Studies in the History of Law and Justice 33, https://doi.org/10.1007/978-3-032-26065-9_4

slaves were, along with agriculture, the basis of their prosperity, and the city-state that held power over the route controlled all trade in the region.

For a long time, the Kingdom of Saba was winning the struggle for power over the region. It was ruled by the *mukarribs*, who held secular, religious and military power. It was only between the fifth and fourth centuries BCE that the Kingdom of Saba began to be governed by secular rulers. It is also at that time that the most vigorous expansion took place, resulting from the desire to establish trade routes on the African continent. Africa was an important source of commodities unavailable on the Arabian Peninsula—ivory and rubberwood; thus, from the fifth century BCE onwards, Sabaean tradesmen began to resettle on the African Red Sea coast. The Sabaeans brought with them not only commercial activities but also their highly developed culture, both technical and intellectual, to Africa.

Of the many peoples who moved from the Arabian Peninsula, only two are known from historical sources: the Habashat and the Agazians (Agazi, Gaze). The former is evidenced in South Arabian inscriptions, while the latter people is mentioned in inscriptions from Adulis, left by an unidentified ruler of Aksum (Hable Sellassie 1972, p. 27). The name Habashat appears only once in inscriptions from the times of Emperor ᶜEzana (who ruled over Aksum in the fourth century), written in the Sabaean and Ge'ez languages.

Archaeological evidence found at various sites in the northern areas of present-day Ethiopia suggests that in the first millennium BCE, the region was strongly influenced by the culture of Arabia Felix, mainly Saba, which is often interpreted as a result of the presence of settlers from the South Arabian city-states, who modelled their settlements after South-Arabian patterns. The monuments discovered share the architectural style and building materials with those discovered in South Arabia; the inscriptions are carved in the same script, they feature the same figures and names of gods, and the place names are the same on both sides of the Red Sea (Phillipson 2012, pp. 19–44). Given all these similarities, the question arises to what extent the newly established culture was an imitation of that of the Arabian Peninsula. This question is also relevant to the issue of legislation. Was the legal code in force in the African settlements the same as that in the settlers' land of origin? Judging by the similarities in other aspects of life, this seems likely.

However, it should be remembered that the Sabaean settlers did not come to uninhabited areas. At that time, the area of the later Aksum state was inhabited by Cushitic people. Most probably, when the South Arabian colonies became established in terms of organisation and economy, they came into contact with the indigenous inhabitants of the African coast. The cultures—Semitic and Cushite—started to blend, with the former being the dominant factor. As a result, a new ethnic group, referred to as the Semitised Cushitic people, was formed. It is highly likely that during the period of mixing of the Semitic and Cushitic peoples, changes occurred similar to those that took place later in the Roman Empire, but with the difference that the newcomers did not reject local law (Glenn 2005, pp. 5–9). Thus, it seems that during this period, rules in force among the Cushites were incorporated into the legal system of the Sabaean settlements in Ethiopia, insofar as they did not conflict with it.

## 4.2 Law in the Kingdom of Aksum

Around the first century CE, the Sabaeans living in Africa finally gained independence from the Kingdom of Saba. A new state, Aksum, was established. The circumstances favoured development as trade routes passed through the new state, connecting South Arabia with the Kingdom of Meroe (Bartnicki and Mantel-Niećko 1978, p. 4), which at the time was becoming increasingly weaker. This allowed the people of Aksum to take over trade in ivory, rubber and spices. With economic growth came political and cultural development and territorial expansion westwards into what is now Sudan. Aksum established trade contacts with Greece, India and Ceylon,[1] and its rulers began using the title *nəguśä nägäśt*, meaning 'king of kings', and initiated the process of centralising power.[2] Most probably, the Kingdom of Aksum was dominated by Agazian people, as suggested by the traditional name of the region, *bəḥer Agᶜazi* ('the land of the Agazi'). The official language of the country was Ge'ez, which in the next centuries played an important role in shaping Ethiopian culture (Mantel-Niećko 1975, p. 39).

Little is known about the stratification of Aksum society, although archaeological excavations may provide some information. It can be assumed, based on the surviving inscriptions concerning land endowments, that the social status of an inhabitant of Aksum was strongly linked to the size of land owned (Munro-Hay 1991, p. 252). However, it remains unknown whether being a citizen of Aksum involved similar privileges as citizenship in ancient Rome. There is also no information on the modes of land inheritance or the institution of marriage. It can be assumed that polygamy existed in Aksum, although this assumption can only be made on the basis of records from later centuries. Nothing is known also about the law in force, although an inscription from Safra suggests that there was a legal code in Aksum.

The inscription from Safra, discovered by Abraham J. Drewes on 8 May 1955 (Drewes 1962, p. 30), was carved on a stone slab 24 centimetres wide, and the date of its creation is estimated as the second or third century CE. The inscription, written in Ge'ez, consists of four parts. According to Drewes, the inscription is exceptional not only due to its content, but also due to the language used to write it. Indeed, the text contains seventy-nine words, of which just over a third do not appear in any of the known dictionaries of the Ge'ez language. Despite these difficulties, A. J. Drewes managed to partially read the content of the inscription that deals with the obligations of the people of Aksum towards their ruler. The first text lists the foodstuffs (butter, honey, bread) and animals (cows and sheep) that were to be handed over to the ruler's court "selon la loi" [in accordance with the law] (Drewes 1962, p. 48). According to the inscription, these products were to be given at specific intervals and in the event of "d'établissement du camp" [the establishment of a camp]

---

[1] This is attested by coins found during excavations conducted in the Aksum territory.

[2] The first king of Aksum referring to himself as 'king of kings' was Sembrutes, who ruled over the country at the turn of second and third century CE (Lewicki 1969, p. 220).

(Drewes 1962, p. 48). This suggests that the inhabitants of the region did not donate the above-mentioned products to the royal court on a regular basis, but only when the sovereign stayed in the area. It was therefore not a kind of regular tax paid to the king, but rather a type of occasional tribute.

The next two parts of the inscription detail the amounts of gifts that should be given to the royal court. The second specifies the exact amount of bread due to the ruler from his subjects and the amount of bread that each Aksumite should donate for sacred purposes. The following part specifies the provisions concerning the cattle due to the king. The final section of the inscription deals with gifts to be given "don et l'habit" [on a regular basis] (Drewes 1962, p. 54), i.e., taxes. This tax due to the king consisted of one coin and one cube of butter. Those who supplied the royal court with wood and oil were exempt from the tax.

At the turn of the third and fourth centuries CE, Aksum had reached the height of its power and the rulers decided on the next major step, i.e., the adoption of Christianity. The baptism of Ethiopia took place around 333 CE (Iliffe 2011, p. 49) during the reign of Emperor ᶜEzana. His reasons for embracing Christianity are not fully known, but it probably served both the political and economic interests of Aksum. A common monotheistic religion helped centralise power, and adopting the same ideology as the Byzantine merchants with whom Aksum traded extensively was not insignificant.

The adoption of Christianity is also an important caesura for the development of Ethiopian legislation. Although no direct sources survive to confirm this, the close cultural and political ties between early Aksum and South Arabia—well attested in epigraphic material (Drewes 1962) and in archaeological and historical analyses (Phillipson 2012)—make it plausible that early Aksumite norms reflected legal principles known in the Sabaean sphere. It can therefore be assumed that, as in the states of southern Arabia, polygamous unions were widely accepted in Aksum, while the enforcement of the law was handled by the *mukarribs*, who held political and sacerdotal authority. This type of power was based on the charisma of the ruler who does not constitute law, but is the guardian of the patterns of behaviour observed by the entire community.

After the Sabaean population blended with Cushitic people living on the African continent, the legislation of the Sabaean colonies saw the merging of the legal provisions of the two cultures. When reconstructing the development of law in the early Aksumite period (first-fourth century CE), three conceivable scenarios are to be considered. The new rules of conduct applicable in the colony could have been established with consideration for social patterns specific to the Cushite population. It cannot be excluded that the Cushites adopted Sabaean patterns. However, the most likely seems a compromise, wherein the two sets of laws were merged into one, with the assumption that the patterns most applicable to given socio-political conditions would be applied. As for the laws related to the institution of marriage, they were convergent for both groups as the Cushites also preferred polygamous unions.

With the advent of Christianity in Aksum, the laws derived from the new monotheistic religion were also added to the body of laws already in place. Ethiopian legal scholars refer to these principles by two terms: *həg ləbuna* and *fətha fəṭärätawi*

(Jembere 1988, p. 27). The former term can be translated as 'moral law' and, in its broadest sense, means the ability to distinguish between right and wrong, while the latter term signifies 'law of equity', i.e., the observance of the patterns of behaviour prevalent in a given society, as outlined in chapter one, and the punishing of those members of the community who did not follow the patterns. Ethiopian legal scholars believed that both concepts—moral law and natural justice—developed in parallel after Ethiopia adopted Christianity, and the only difference between the two was that the principles of moral law were taught during evangelisation, while the teaching of natural justice was passed on within families from generation to generation. Thus, it can be assumed that the law in Aksum was based on two pillars: customary law, which derived from a natural sense of justice, and canon law, derived from the Old Testament. Later on, Ethiopian legislation was enriched by another source of law, which was the *Senodos*, a collection of canonical and liturgical texts of the Orthodox Ethiopian Church.

## 4.3 Christian Dogmas and the Old Testament

In accordance with Ethiopian oral tradition, the one who evangelised Emperor $^{c}$Ezana was Frumentius, a young merchant who was taken prisoner as he travelled from Tyre to 'India' (Phillipson 2012, p. 92).[3] Upon arriving at the court of Aksum, Frumentius became the teacher of $^{c}$Ezana, who was very young at the time. Many years later, when the imperial teacher was ordained in Alexandria as the first bishop of Aksum, Frumentius baptised the Emperor. However, the adoption of Christianity in Ethiopia was not as rapid a process as Ethiopian historiography describes it. In the fourth century, Christianity was only one of several religions present at $^{c}$Ezana's court. Historical sources indicate that more than a century after the alleged conversion of the Emperor and the entire court to Christianity, $^{c}$Ezana's successor made an offering consisting of fifty captives to Mahrem, the local god of war. In all likelihood, $^{c}$Ezana sought to extend imperial patronage to all religions, although he might have valued Christianity most highly, as he displayed symbolism associated with the religion on Aksumite coins.[4] In addition, between the fifth and seventh centuries, the Holy Bible was translated into Ge'ez. It can be assumed that this was also when the legal provisions contained in the Bible enriched the legislation of Aksum. As for those related to the institution of marriage, according to Old Testament teachings, polygamous unions were forbidden and the union of one man with one woman was considered a marriage. However, it must be remembered that Christianity was only one of the religions professed in Aksum and even among the aristocracy

[3] The term 'India' was used to refer not only to the Indian Peninsula but also the area of South Arabia and regions on the African continent east of the Nile.

[4] Perhaps, however, the reason for placing Christian symbols on the coins is more prosaic. At the time, Aksum was trading extensively with both Rome and Byzantium. It is possible that adherence to the same faith greatly facilitated trade contacts with these countries.

polygamous marriages certainly occurred. Polygamy was also widespread among Aksum's subjects.

The most important rules taken over from the Old Testament are the Ten Commandments. These set the standard of behaviour for the people of Aksum. The legal rules contained in the books of the Old and New Testaments were later reflected both in the sixteenth-century Ethiopian legal code known as the *Fətḥa Nägäśt* and in the criminal and civil law codes developed in the 1960s.

## 4.4 Senodos

Another important source of Ethiopian law based on the dogmas of Christianity was the *Senodos,*[5] which is a collection of canonical and liturgical writings of the Ethiopian Orthodox Church (Bausi 2010, 623). In 1901, an Italian researcher of Ethiopian theology and history, Ignazio Guidi, proved that the Ethiopian *Senodos* was a translation from Arabic of the liturgical texts used by the Melchite community of Egypt.[6] Further research proved that the Senodos is often quoted in writings attributed to Emperor Zärᵓa Yaᶜəqob (1434–1468), allowing Guidi to hypothesise that the collection may have been composed earlier than the fifteenth century (as previously assumed). It was not until forty years later that another Italian researcher of Ethiopian history, Carlo Conti Rossini, confirmed Guidi's hypothesis by finding quotations from the *Senodos* in manuscripts from the fourteenth century, which dated the collection to the late thirteenth and early fourteenth centuries. Further research confirmed that the translation from Arabic was made during the reign of Emperor ᶜAmdä Ṣəyon I. At that time, other texts important for the Orthodox Ethiopian Church were also translated: 'Didascalia Apostolorum',[7] 'Testamentum Domini',[8] 'Testamentum Domini Nostri Jesu Christi in Galilea'[9] and 'The Letter of Clement' (also known as the 'First Letter to the Corinthians').[10]

[5] The older form of writing this word is *Sənodos*. The word comes from the Greek and means 'assembly, council'.

[6] The Melchites now constitute the second largest Catholic community in the Middle East. It was originally a contemptuous name, referring to a group of Christians who sided with the Church and the Byzantine Emperor at the Council of Chalcedon in 451 CE. Over time, it was adopted as the name of the Christians who make up the Melchite Catholic Church, bringing together Catholics living in Arab countries (mainly Syria, Lebanon and Palestine). They retain the Byzantine liturgy, celebrated mainly in Arabic.

[7] A collection of ecclesiastical ordinances written in Greek in the first half of the third century for Christian converts in northern Syria. See Quasten (2003), pp. 737–738.

[8] The term 'Testamentum Domini' is used to refer to ancient Christian liturgical and legal or apocryphal writings whose authorship is attributed to, among others, the apostles John, Peter, and Matthew. See Wysocki (2013), pp. 743–744.

[9] An apocalyptic text written in Ge'ez. See Wysocki (2013), p. 743.

[10] One of the oldest patristic writings, contemporary with some parts of the New Testament. It is attributed to Clement I of Rome. The immediate reason for writing the letter was said to be some

The majority of the texts in the *Senodos* are rules of canon law, which cover almost all aspects of ecclesiastical life, from the rules concerning the election of the bishop, to the description of the ecclesiastical hierarchy and the types of ordination, the liturgy of the Eucharist, the rituals associated with the celebration of Christian festivals, and the enumeration of penalties to which those who do not observe canon law are subject.

The second collection relevant to the present study is a series of texts on the observance of patterns of behaviour and lectures on Christian morality, attributed either to various historical figures, such as St Clement or Hippolytus of Rome or to the apostles. Also included in the *Senodos* are the writings of the Church Fathers, canons produced during the meetings of ecumenical councils in the fourth century and meetings of local councils of Church representatives.

In-depth research into the Ethiopian *Senodos* was undertaken by Alessandro Bausi. He has shown that the collection of canon law from the thirteenth century is found in at least 38 manuscripts. In addition, three manuscripts are known that are copies of some of the manuscripts just mentionned, while two more have been lost. The *Senodos* itself can be divided into three parts:

- a section consisting of writings attributed to either the apostles or St Clement;
- canons written at regional councils and canons written at the Council of Nicaea;
- a section comprising homilies and treatises by the Church Fathers.[11]

Based on the linguistic analysis of the *Senodos* texts, Alessandro Bausi identified those that could have been added to the collection during the Aksumite period:

- *Epistle 70* written by Cyprian of Carthage[12];
- *The Epistle of the Apostles*[13];
- Two epistles written during the synod meetings in Gangra (now Çankırı in Turkey) and Antioch (now Antakya in Turkey)[14];
- Doctrinal works, extracts from sermons, letters and catechesis by St Peter;

disturbances in the Corinthian community. See Dressler (2003), pp. 774–775 and Bausi (1992), p. 16.

[11] For a list of titles and the number of texts included in each part of the *Sənodos*, see Bausi (1992), p. 17.

[12] St Cyprian of Carthage (AD 210?- 258) is the author of 81 letters, which are an important source for the history of the African and Roman Church.

[13] An apocryphal work, written in the mid-second century in Asia Minor. *The Epistle of the Apostles* is a kind of encyclical addressed to all the Christian communities of the time, concerning the life and teachings of Jesus, his prophecy for the future of the Church and all humanity.

[14] During the Synod in Gangra (ca. 340 CE), condemnation was announced of the proponents of extreme asceticism and the teaching of Eustathius of Sebaste, who rejected the institution of marriage and the family as unworthy of a Christian. In turn, the Council of Antioch (ca. 341 CE) produced 25 canons that were included into almost all the law books of the Eastern churches. It was at this synod that the later famous formula of faith, based on the Nicene symbol, was also composed. For more on this subject, see 'Council of Antioch (1998).

- *Baptismal Order*[15];
- A collection of prayers;
- *71 canons*;
- *Traditio Apostolica*, i.e., a compilation of Old Greek texts;
- *Collectio Antiochena*, which was included in the *Senodos* almost in its entirety.[16]

As in other cases of canonical-liturgical collections of the Eastern Churches, the *Senodos* was created to provide a foundation for the Christian tradition. In the Roman Catholic Church, the legal rules of the institution were either developed during synods or promulgated by the Pope. According to Alessandro Bausi, in the Middle Eastern churches, due to the proximity both politically and culturally to Islam, it was insufficient to rely on bishops' decrees and synodal arrangements. It was necessary to refer to pseudo-epigraphic literature that would prove that Christianity, more than Islam, was the basis of law in a given society (Bausi 1992, pp. 19–20). Moreover, in Ethiopia, with the introduction of the *Senodos*, rulers gained an additional argument to confirm the decisions they made. The rulers could thus rely not only on their own judgement, but also on the writings of the Church Fathers when making judicial decisions.

## 4.5 The Acts of Emperor Caleb

Because of the scarcity of information on the development of Aksumite legislation during ᶜEzana's reign, it is not clear if the laws in force in the state were created by the ruler himself or derived either from the books of the Old Testament or from the common law tradition.[17] More information on the development of law comes from the reign of Emperor Caleb.

Caleb (also known as Ǝllä 'Aṣbəḥa) decided to conquer Felix Arabia with Byzantine support. The first expedition (in 523 CE) proved to be a military failure, but the next one, two years later, ended in an undisputed victory. From a political point of view, this expedition was intended to support the South Arabian Christians persecuted by the Judaised ruler of the area, Dhu Nuwas. Economically, however, its aim was to prevent the Persians from taking control of the trade route between the Mediterranean and the Indian Ocean. At the turn of the seventh and eighth centuries, it was Muslims—rather than Persians—who took over this trade route and,

[15] In this case, the word 'rite' signifies a liturgical book containing texts and regulative norms used in the celebration of the Sacrament of Baptism.

[16] These are writings produced during the meetings of ecumenical councils. The canons are arranged chronologically and form a series. The collection also includes canons from the Council of Constantinople I (381 CE) and the Council of Chalcedon (451 CE). See Bausi (2010), p. 624.

[17] These sources are limited to inscriptions and travelers' accounts. One can find information about the decrees issued by the rulers, sentences (among which execution, confiscation of property and resettlement are the most frequently mentioned) and deeds of grant of property. See Sergew Hable Sellassie (1972), pp. 68–113.

by occupying the Dahlak Island and the gulf of Massaua, deprived Aksum of profits from trade with the Arabian Peninsula.

Nevertheless, Caleb is also known as a ruler who significantly strengthened his state: during his reign, Aksum developed considerably culturally and economically, as well as administratively.

The end of Caleb's reign marks another significant development of the Ethiopian state and law. With Caleb's abdication, the religious and secular authorities were definitively separated. Under King ᶜEzana, the ruler was at the same time the head of the Church. This tradition was abandoned when Caleb's renounced the throne. The ruler handed over the crown of the Church to the Basilica of the Holy Sepulchre and removed himself to the hermitage of *Abba* Pänṭälewon. This became the symbol of the separation of secular and ecclesiastical authority.[18]

Thus, it may be inferred that the law in Ethiopia emerged from the dogmas of Christianity, the regulations and moral guidelines contained in the Old Testament, the writings of the Church Fathers and the laws introduced by the Christian rulers of the country. It must be remembered, however, that the emergence of Christianity in Ethiopia did not eradicate other beliefs and associated social patterns. Some of the people of Aksum still adhered to moral principles and patterns that were followed before the advent of Christianity. Thus, before discussing the successive stages of the development of law in Ethiopia, the second pillar of Ethiopian legislation should be presented: customary law (or rather laws, considering the multiplicity of ethnic groups living in Ethiopia).

## 4.6 Custom as a Source of Law

There is no single definition of customary law. Often different terms are used to describe customary law, such as primitive law, folk law, the law of the people, unofficial law, local law (Abdo and Abegaz n.d., p. 3). All these terms are used to highlight the opposition between customary law and the law of modern Western states. For the purposes of the present study, customary law is considered to be the set of norms and rules of conduct that exist in a particular group or community, that are accepted by that group or community, and that are treated as binding law. As already noted, the prevailing norms and rules of conduct by definition have not been imposed on a community, but have been established by that community, and all members of the community have agreed to abide by them.

The purpose of customary law is not only to define the rights and obligations of the members of a community. Customary law also creates a mechanism for resolving disputes without the use of an institutionalised judicial apparatus. This was important for two reasons. Firstly, reporting a crime often required an expedition of

[18] *Abba* Pänṭälewon was one of the religious authorities of the time. Ethiopian tradition has it that he was one of the Nine Saints who arrived in the late fifth century from Rome to Ethiopia to evangelise the people of Aksum. Cf. Sergew Hable Selassie (1970).

several days as institutional courts were only found in regional capitals or larger cities; and secondly, in the case of a conflict in a micro-community, the most important issue was (and still is) not to remove the culprit from the community (which is often the focus of institutional justice), but to punish him in such a way as to show the other members of the community that his act violates the prevailing pattern of behaviour (Abdo and Abegaz n.d., p. 5). If a member of the community were to be disposed of after each transgression committed, the community's existence could soon be significantly threatened. Therefore, customary law is primarily geared towards mediation between the victim and the offender, and the punishment imposed may be severe but short-lived. The only situation in which the culprit can be sentenced to death or banishment is if his or her behaviour threatens the entire community.

Conflict resolution in communities using customary law was handled by elders. Since the rules of customary law were often not written down but remembered through the generations, the eldest members of the community were the ones who were approached for mediation.[19] In communities of this type, the elders also had the right to promulgate new norms and rules of conduct and to do matchmaking for marriage purposes. New rules were introduced when the existing customary law did not provide a solution. It should be remembered, however, that the introduction of a new law had to be agreed upon with the members of the community and the rules were never contrary to the moral law mentioned in the earlier parts of this chapter.

The customary laws of various ethnic groups living in Ethiopia differ in both form and content, and are limited only to the specific area inhabited by the group recognising the law. How important the use of customary law was in the legislative process can be seen from the fact that the highest normative act of the state, the 1930 Constitution of the Ethiopian Empire, allowed the use of traditional law in the processes of the lower courts.[20]

Nowadays, Ethiopian jurisdiction makes equally abundant use of customary law provisions in resolving conflicts in minor cases. In particular, customary law provisions are used in passing judgement in family law cases, especially those concerning marriages, divorces and the determination of paternity or inheritance rights. In addition, customary law is used in matters relating to land ownership (Civil Code 1960, pp. 93–134, 137–187, 191–203).

Although the various sets of customary law had a tremendous impact on the development of Ethiopian legislation, few of them have been studied in depth. This is primarily due to the scarcity of sources as customary law operated in societies in which—for the most part—the oral tradition played a predominant role. However, the increase in research interest in the history of legislation in Ethiopia has meant that the customary law of some ethnic groups has been studied to some degree. In the following section, the most important elements of customary law operating

[19] Legal provisions were often memorised in the form of proverbs; numerous examples are quoted by Maḫtämä Śəllase Wäldä Mäsqäl (1953).

[20] The current constitution of Ethiopia also allows for the co-existence of common law and state law. See Augustyniak (2014), p. 31.

within the Amhara, Tigray and Oromo ethnic groups will be presented. These groups have been chosen because of the profound influence their laws have had on the development of Ethiopian legislation and their customary laws are relatively well-described.

The following overview is based primarily on research conducted by Abera Jembere between 1974 and 1990, and those in 2004–2005 by Ethiopian researchers, anthropology and law students at Addis Ababa University. The results of these studies have been presented in a book edited by Pankhurst and Assefa (2008). As noted earlier, the customary laws of various ethnic groups living in Ethiopia vary considerably and it would be difficult to present them in their entirety, thus, only the three areas of issues relevant to this book have been described, namely:

- local legal institutions;
- methods of resolving conflicts[21];
- the functioning of local customary courts in contemporary Ethiopia.[22]

## 4.7 Customary Law Among the Amhara

The Amhara ethnic group inhabits the central highlands of Ethiopia. For many years, the Amhara were the dominant group, making up about a third of the country's population. According to the 2007 census, the number of people claiming to belong to the Amhara group is 19,878,199, representing almost 31% of the country's population (Central Statistical Office in Ethiopia 2007).[23]

Amharic customary law was not written down; its rules were passed down orally from generation to generation. Due to its dominant role in the history and culture of the Ethiopian Empire, Amharic customary law was applied throughout most of the country. Some of its provisions (e.g., rules related to inheritance, the institution of family arbitration) were even included in the 1960 Civil Code (1960, pp. 137–187).

The legal institutions dealing with conflicts consisted of the *ᵓabbat*, *yägobäz ᵓaleqa*, *čəqa šum* and *yäzämäd dañña*. The first of these literally means 'father'. This institution was established when there were no government representatives in an area. It was found both in the countryside (*mändär*) and in larger administrative units, such as a district (*kəfəl hagär*), province (*wäräda*) and county (*awraya*). The *ᵓabbat* was elected at a meeting of all the residents from among the local elders. He had to be a widely respected person with authority, charisma and life wisdom.

[21] Magic was also used in the resolution of conflicts within local legal institutions (e.g., the *qallu* among the Oromo or the *leba šay* among the Amhara), but in this chapter the magic ceremonies and rituals related to the detection of the perpetrator of a crime are not described due to their low impact on the development of Ethiopian legislation.

[22] The following descriptions of customary law are intended to provide a general presentation of the characteristics of the customary law of each ethnic group.

[23] Newer data are not available as the results of 2014 census have not been published yet.

Depending on the number of inhabitants and the size of the village, the local community could elect between one and seven *ᵓabbats*, who were collectively responsible for creating new laws and upholding existing ones. They could rule on both criminal and civil matters.

Immediately after the election of the *ᵓabbat* or *ᵓabbatoch*, another meeting of all the residents was called at which the newly elected judge or judges were sworn in.[24] At the meeting, the new appointees would announce to the residents a pre-determined list of rules for good neighbourly coexistence, which required the approval of the whole community.[25] The meeting ended with the words: "May your flock be guarded by my flock". This phrase had a double meaning for the Amharic people. The first indicated that as long as there was unity among the members of the community, the intervention of the *ᵓabbat* was not needed. The second meaning of the sentence included a provision of customary law: "If you steal cattle from my herd, I will do the same to you".

The *yägobäz ᵓaleqa* ('leader of the wise') was chosen by the members of a community to be their military leader. He had the right to mobilise all men of conscription age in the event of a military clash caused by war or rebellion against the ruling administrators. In times of peace, the *yägobäz ᵓaleqa* and his team were in charge of policing the community and bringing the guilty before the magistrate.

The *čəqa šum* was the village chief. His office was hereditary in the province of Uello, while in the provinces of Gonder and Gojjam the office was rotated among senior government officials holding lands granted to them by the emperor. In addition to dealing with administrative matters such as collecting taxes, announcing government decrees to the inhabitants, the *čəqa šum* was in charge of conducting divorces and punishing those committing minor offences against the law (assaults, burglary). He was subordinate to the provincial administrator (*wäräda dug*), the head of the municipality (*mälkäña*) and the district chief (*ᵓabägaz*) or the imperial official in charge of collecting taxes in the province (*gult-gäži*).

Among the Amhara, there was also the institution of family arbitration conducted by the *yäzämäd dañña* ('family judge'). Its purpose was to bring about a compromise between two disputing parties. Arbitrators were chosen whenever a conflict arose among community members. Family arbitrations were aimed at resolving a dispute amicably so that one did not have to consult an *ᵓabbat* or a local court, whose verdicts could further aggravate relations between the conflicted parties. Admittedly, approaching imperial officials directly was not forbidden, but the general perception was that it was far more beneficial to both the aggrieved party and

[24] In order to notify all the villagers in the region of an upcoming gathering, bonfires were lit on the surrounding hills at sunset. Whoever of the villagers spotted such a bonfire would light a torch in front of their house, which was a signal to the other villagers. The gathering was held the next morning (Jembere 1988, p. 47).

[25] Typically, these were rules related to keeping people safe ("do not leave your farm unattended", "watch out for strangers", "bring anyone who breaks the law before the authorities") and helping your neighbour ("help whoever is in need") (Jembere 1988, p. 48).

the community as a whole to resolve the conflict with the help of local legal institutions. This approach is aptly reflected in an Amharic saying: "Even a swarm of bees would not leave their hive and go to a new one before they settle down on a nearby tree or fence" (Jembere 1988, p. 49).

Among the Amhara, the system of punishing those who had defied the established law was multistage and aimed at reverting the erring person back onto the path of appropriate conduct rather than on administering punishment. If members of the community violated the existing law, they were first admonished by their family and relatives. If they disobeyed, they were reprimanded by the whole community. If this too was of no avail, the guilty party had to appear before an *ᵓabbat* who, on behalf of the whole community, warned them of the consequences of the actions. If the culprit continued to behave contrary to the accepted rules, the *ᵓabbat* could require them to prepare a party for fellow residents as reparation. The third offence of the same kind resulted in social ostracism—first subtle, then open.

The extent to which the conflict resolution procedures among the Amhara have changed since the collapse of the Ethiopian Empire in 1974 can be observed in the results of the field research conducted in 2004 by Melaku Abate and Wubishet Shiferaw (Abate and Shiferaw 2008, pp. 107–121), anthropology and law students at Addis Ababa University. In their opinion, there are three terms in the Amharic language to describe institutions devoted to resolving conflicts and based on customary law: *šəmagələnna* (arbitration), *ərq* (mediation) and *gälagay* (conciliator). The first two terms are used interchangeably to refer to formalised procedures aimed at reconciliation between the disputing parties, while the third term is used to describe any means that lead to both parties giving up litigation.

There are two possibilities of informing the relevant informal institutions of grievances: an accusation can be made after mass, in the presence of the entire community, or the aggrieved person can report directly to the representatives of the elders. If the first option is chosen, then family members or neighbours of both conflicted parties engage in a search for a mediator to help resolve the conflict. The elders are usually contacted directly only when murder is involved. The direct intervention of the elders is to prevent further bloodshed.

In the case of a murder, representatives of the elders start by getting both parties to seek reconciliation. If both parties agree, then experienced mediators are selected from among the community members to undertake negotiations. Sometimes the murderer goes to the church and rings the church bell as a sign of remorse for his shameful act.[26] When the local community hears the ringing of bells, it means that negotiations between the two sides should begin.[27] Due to the nature of the case,

---

[26] As long as the murderer is on the church premises, the family of the murdered person cannot kill him or her.

[27] According to the researchers' informants, the ritual of ringing bells is nowadays practised increasingly less frequently in villages, while in towns it is no longer practised at all (Abate and Shiferaw 2008, p. 108).

they usually last quite a long time. Priests are often present during the negotiations and play an important role in the reconciliation process of both parties. This is due to the fact that the victim's family must swear an oath on the *tabot* that they shall not seek vengeance.

As mentioned earlier, customary law was used to resolve not only family law cases, but also those involving criminal law and commercial law. The mediators appointed to handle cases had no legal training whatsoever and were chosen solely on the basis of their character traits: charisma, wisdom and reason.[28] The hearing involving the mediator, both parties to the conflict and their witnesses usually took place outdoors, often on land belonging to a church or in a local marketplace. The place and time of the start of the hearing were decided by the mediators, although taking into account the suggestions of the conflicted parties. In the course of the hearing, first the witnesses were questioned, then the mediators questioned both sides of the conflict and tried to reach a compromise. After lengthy discussions with both parties and with each other, the mediators publicly announced the verdict. If both parties accepted, the sentence became binding. If one of the parties disagreed with the verdict, it could not be appealed, as no such legal mechanisms existed. If the losing party did not comply with the verdict, he or she faced social ostracism, which could include being banned from participating in public gatherings and festivals. Mediators did not receive any remuneration for their assistance. The conflicted parties only had to bear the costs of organising a feast, which was held at the end of a successful trial.

If the trial ended successfully for the aggrieved party, he or she received compensation, the type of which depended on the type of crime committed. If the case was less grave, a public apology was sufficient, whereas if it was serious (e.g., murder) financial compensation was involved.

In cases ending with an apology as a reparation, the person apologising had to carry a 'stone of repentance', usually hung around his/her neck or shoulders. When the culprit reached the victim, he/she had to prostrate before him/her in a gesture of submission. The victim, on the other hand, would remove the stone from the culprit's shoulders in a gesture of forgiveness. Both parties would then take an oath never to act against each other again. In more difficult cases, the culprit had to prepare a *gan* of beer, butcher a sheep, goat or ox (depending on the gravity of the offence committed) and throw a party in his/her own home for the victim and the mediators.

If the perpetrator committed murder, he/she had to pay the victim's family what is referred to as the 'blood price', which is about 3000 *bərr*. The conflicted parties then had to walk over a gun lying on the ground and fire one shot each at the church gate. This ritual was meant to symbolise the erasure of any resentment towards the opposing side of the conflict.

[28] They were also selected due to the nature of the case.

## 4.8 Customary Law Among the Tigray

The number of people who identify themselves as belonging to the Tigray ethnic group is 4,324,933, representing 6.1 per cent of Ethiopia's population (Central Statistical Office in Ethiopia 2007). The Tigrayans, who also constitute the most populous ethnic group in Eritrea, are closely related linguistically and culturally to the Amhara—they speak Tigrinya, which, like Amharic, is a Semitic language, and are mostly members of the Ethiopian Orthodox Church. Tigray is the third most homogeneous region in Ethiopia, after the Afar and Somali regions.

As with the Amhara, the customary law of the Tigrayans was passed down orally from generation to generation. Most of the laws referred to criminal cases, land tenure, marriage, divorce, inheritance and resolving conflicts. Some of the Tigrayan customary law codes were not written down until the late nineteenth and early twentieth centuries. About seven groups of customary law texts are known to have been kept either in church libraries or with elders. Their content and the order in which they were written down was examined by Friederike Kemink (1991), who conducted research on customary law in the Hamasen area.[29] Listed in order of their creation, these are as follows:

### *4.8.1 Wala Sobattä ᵓAnsäba*

A set of laws written down on 16 December 1907 in Audi Berhanu. It was binding for seven communities living in the north-east of the Hamasen province: the area between the Anseba and Gerger rivers, the Hamasen highlands and the area inhabited by the Bilen (Belen) ethnic group. The sense of community that led to the creation and observance of the common code of customary law resulted not from a belief in a common ancestor, but rather from territorial proximity and common political interests.

When the code was written down in 1907, several changes were made to the existing provisions, including those relating to the institution of marriage. One provision, known as *mäkänäyat* (in Amharic—*demoz*), banned temporary marriage,[30] and introduced the definition of marriage as a union between two people who have a community of property and the right to inherit from each other.

[29] Hamasen—the historic province of Eritrea, which extended to the area around Asmara. In 1996, the province was divided into five administrative regions: Maekel, Debub, Gash-Barka, Anseba and the Northern Red Sea Region (Kemink 1991, pp. 55–72). For more on the customary law codes in force in western Eritrea, see Elliesie (2015), pp. 169–180.

[30] For more on the types of marriages in Ethiopia, see Augustyniak (2009), pp. 99–113.

### 4.8.2 *Sərᵓat Adkämä-Mälga*

According to oral tradition, the set of laws was compiled in the second half of the fifteenth century, during the seventh meeting of community representatives in May Gif (now Tekala). According to the same tradition, the agreed code was partly written down and deposited in the library at the Debre Abune Yonas Monastery, but was destroyed during various armed conflicts. In order to ensure that individual regulations were not forgotten, the family elders of the Adkeme-Melga area met once every 3–7 years for a fortnight in May Gif to either confirm the usefulness of the legal provisions in question or to amend them. Thanks to these activities, the code was not forgotten and it was also possible to revise the provisions contained therein.

In 1912, an Italian official, Ilario Capomazza wrote down the Adkeme-Melga code dictated to him and published it in Italian. A Tigrinya-language version was not published until a decade later. In 1940, at the behest of the Italian governor of Seraye, Eugenio di Savoia-Genova, Eritrean dignitaries from Seraye met to discuss changes to the code of customary law. A year later, the manuscript with the written code was given to Carlo Conti Rossini, who was to prepare it for publication. However, due to the Second World War, work on publication was delayed and the first volume of the code was not available to readers until 1948. The second volume was published in 1953, by Lanfranco Ricci, already after C.C. Rossini's death.

### 4.8.3 *Sərᵓat Nay Habsällus Nay Gäbrä-Krəstos Nay Däkqätäšäm*

The alleged authors of this body of law are *däǧǧazmač* Habsällus and his son Gäbrä Krəstos, who lived in the eighteenth century. The code was revised by the *däǧǧazmač* Ḫaylä of Sezzega (d. 1876), who for this purpose convened a meeting of the elders of the various regions in the village of May Guayla, near Sezzega. *Däǧǧazmač* Ḫaylä forced the residents of Leggon Čäwan and Kebese Čäwan in southern Hamasen to give up their customary law in favour of customary law from the north. However, after his death, these communities reverted to their own laws. Another modification of the code took place during the first years of the Italian colonial occupation. Accordingly, two meetings were held in the village of Addi Quansi (in 1901 and 1915), where the laws were written down. A modified version was adopted in 1926 and was used until the end of the Italian colonial period.

### 4.8.4 *Sərᵓat Adgäna Tägäläba*

According to oral tradition, this code was written in the eighteenth century. Shortly after Eritrea was made an Italian colony, the decision was made to modify and standardise many of the customary laws operating in the Akkele Guzay area. To this end, 28 provincial administrators and 83 experts in customary law, who had been delegated by the inhabitants of each village, met several times in the villages of Segeneyati, Addi Qeyyeh and Senafe under the leadership of *Ras* Täsämma ᵓAsbäroma. After a year and a half, they promulgated a code of civil law applicable to communities living in the Akkele Guzay area. The code came into force on 6 January 1945 and was published in the Asmara Judicial Gazette.

### 4.8.5 *Həggi Nay Läggon Čäwan*

According to oral tradition, the legislation was promulgated in 1494/95. Subsequent meetings at which the code was supplemented took place in 1657/58 [1650 A.M.], in 1899/1900 [1892 A.M.] and between 1941 and 1952, when Eritrea was administered by the British. The Läggon Čäwan Customary Law was published twice: in 1918 and in 1945.

### 4.8.6 *Həggi Sähärtän, Lamzan, Wäqärtän əna Ḍamban*

At the beginning of the twentieth century, representatives of the elders of the Seherten, Lamzan, Weqerten and Damban villages in Methaz Reᵓesom decided that they would no longer follow the *Habsällus-Gäbrä Krəstos* code, but would create their own. According to one source, the elders made this decision because they felt disrespected by not being invited to a meeting where changes to the code were to be discussed. The lack of evidence that the communities in these villages had their own customary law in the nineteenth century or earlier may confirm the above.

### 4.8.7 *Sərᵓat Karnäšäm*

There is little information on the circumstances under which the people of Karnäšäm decided to create their own legal code. It is known that this took place at the beginning of the twentieth century at a meeting in the village of Zager. Until then, the inhabitants of Karnäšäm had followed the *Habsällus-Gäbrä Krəstos* code. As the Karnäšäm code is similar to the Seherten, Lamzan, Weqerten and Damban codes, it can be assumed that it originated under similar circumstances (Kemink 1991, p. 57).

Like the Amhara, the Tigrayans had legal institutions whose task it was to uphold the law and to punish those who disobeyed it. Among the legal institutions still in place were the local elders (*bayto*) and the institution of *čəqa šum*, also existing among the Amhara.

*Bayto* is the Tigrayan term for a meeting of the elders of the various clans. The meeting was convened when there was a need to change the law or introduce a new rule, probably every couple of years. If the legal issue concerned people outside the community, three representatives of the *bayto* met with representatives of the community from which the defendants came to discuss the legal issue in question. After discussions within the assembly, the content of the new law was agreed upon and accepted by the whole assembly, who then swore to abide by it. Often, the new law (or set of laws) was named either after the creator of the concept behind a particular law, or after the region in which it was to be observed, or after the group that was to observe it.[31]

All those who rented land and paid taxes (*gäbbar* in Amharic) had the right to participate in the *bayto*. Three members of the assembly were delegated to *bayto* meetings at the provincial (*wäräda*) level. In turn, three representatives of the provincial assembly were seconded to the district-level (*ᵓawraya*) meetings. At the latter meetings, laws were discussed that would later apply to all residents of the district. Before a legal provision was approved at the *bayto ᵓawraya* meeting, *bayto wäräda* representatives who wanted a legal change would travel with the provincial administrator to another province or district seat to present arguments for the new law. When the law was voted at the district meeting, its content was presented to the district administrator, who in turn informed the provincial administrator of the introduction of the new law, and his approval was needed for it to take effect. If there was a problem with the interpretation of a particular law, the opinion of the members of the *bayto ᵓawraya* was binding.

Among the Tigrayans, the office of the village chief was held for life. The *čəqa šum* had executive and judicial authority over the area he governed. He passed judgements in civil and criminal cases, based on the customary law in force in his region. His judgement had to be confirmed by the *məsläne*, or deputy municipal administrator. If either party in the trial contested the decision, then the case was referred to the *wäräda* court. In turn, cases in which the death penalty was pronounced were referred to the Supreme Court, unless both parties to the conflict reached an agreement on the payment of reparations.[32]

In the event of a dispute, one arbitrator each (usually a man, although older women were sometimes chosen) was selected by both parties to the dispute to act as judges in the case, together with the *čəqa šum*. The hearing took place in the public square and both sides usually presented their arguments in person. The exception were women, who could not represent themselves. Their husbands or male members of their families spoke on their behalf. Before the hearing began, both parties took an oath (*feṣmi*)[33] that they would respect the court verdict. Anyone breaking the oath risked receiving a fine, the amount of which could sometimes equal the compensation for murder. Both parties would then appoint a person to ensure proper

[31] In some areas, only the residents of specific villages, known as *ᵓaddi həggi* or *ᵓaddi həggi wägän*, and their representatives had the right to amend legislation (Kemink 1991, p. 57).

[32] Within Eritrea, the usual amount of compensation was 1000 *bərr*.

[33] *Fätm* in Amharic. This is the same oath that is taken during the *särg* wedding ceremony, described in the second chapter of the book.

conduct during the trial, for example that both parties appeared in court on time.[34] Any adult male who owned his own household could become such a guarantor, provided he was relatively wealthy and had the approval of all members of the community. In some cases, he also had to be the relative of another guarantor. Married but not wealthy women could not become guarantors. However, such an option was available to women who were financially independent and not necessarily married. This was, however, a rare case.

Once the hearing started, the judge presented the essence of the conflict and formulated the accusation. It was the defendant's duty to present evidence that the plaintiff was guilty of failing to comply with the rules, resulting in damage. The evidence in the case could be the testimony of a witness, the testimony of the culprit (or one of his associates) or an oath taken by them. It was characteristic for the course of the trial that both parties would bet (*wərrəd*). This meant that one of the parties offered to pay the judge a certain amount of money if their testimony turned out to be false. This forced the opponent to take the bet and offer an even larger sum. The opponent had the right not to take the bet, but this meant a loss of credibility, both in the eyes of the judge and the rest of the community (not to mention depriving the judge of additional income). On the one hand, the *wərrəd* deterred both parties from making false statements, but on the other, it was cause for abuse as the wealthier person could use betting as a means to gain favour with the judge, especially if the latter did not counteract the making of higher and higher bets. Moreover, the abuse of *wərrəd* could distract from the substance of the conflict.

After hearing both sides and considering all the evidence, the judge would issue a sentence. The losing party was obliged to pay the court costs, including the judge's fees. If the losing party disagreed with the verdict, it could be appealed to the district judge, or to a higher authority, which was the provincial administrator.

Field research conducted by Shimelis Gizaw and Taddesse Gessesse in 2004 (Gizaw and Gessese 2008, pp. 217–235) in the provinces Adigrat, Mekele and Adi Keyih confirmed that in contemporary Ethiopia resolving conflicts through the application of CDR is still preferred,[35] mainly because the processes conducted by state courts last a lot longer and are much more expensive.[36] The researchers also indicate the minor importance of religious courts, both Muslim and Christian, which in their view play a purely nominal role, although priests of the Ethiopian Orthodox Church take an active part in meetings of councils of elders during CDR trials (Gizaw and Gessese 2008, p. 218).

---

[34] The institution of a guarantor was important not only in court cases, but also, for example, in sale-purchase transactions, where the guarantor was supposed to ensure the transaction was conducted correctly.

[35] CDR = Customary Dispute Resolution, i.e., common law dispute resolution.

[36] According to the researchers' informants, the exception is theft cases. Those accused of such a crime prefer to be tried by state courts, which have much worse statistics when it comes to detecting this type of crime than CDR courts (Gizaw and Gessese 2008, p. 224).

Customary courts in Tigray only deal with cases involving individuals, as conflicts between legal entities are resolved by state courts, and customary courts are prohibited from passing judgment on such cases.[37]

Due to the many conflicts between the Tigrayans and the neighbouring Afar and Rayyaa, a legal institution called the *ᵓabbo Gäräb* ('father of the [river] Gereb') was established in the Wajirat and Rayya provinces. This is an advisory body consisting of a group of elderly men from both ethnic groups who resolve conflicts between the Tigrayans and the Afar based on written rules of conduct previously agreed upon by both groups. Only men with charisma, known for their eloquence and with a high degree of trust within their communities are selected to be *ᵓabbo Gäräb*. It deals only with the most serious crimes (murder, rape, conflicts over access to water and pastures), leaving minor matters to the councils of the elders of the respective groups.

In murder cases, the proceedings are conducted by both the *ᵓabbo Gäräb* and the Ethiopian state courts. Interestingly, for a CDR trial, the offender is released from custody after signing an appropriate statement. The proceedings conducted by an *ᵓabbo Gäräb* begin with negotiations between the elders and the family of the person murdered.[38] The men stand in front of the family of the murdered person dressed in festive *šammoch*, which is meant to symbolise a plea for mercy for the criminal. If the family of the murdered tentatively agrees to forgo bloody revenge in favour of reparations, the members of the *ᵓabbo Gäräb* can sit down and enter into detailed negotiations. During the talks, the council members try to prove that the blood spilled was not 'black', meaning that the murder was not premeditated. If the negotiations are successful, another date is set for a meeting at which the culprit should appear. In order to prove their regret for the deed committed, the offender must appear before the family of the murdered person dressed in a type of garment called a *wacco*, sewn from black wool, and prostrating beg the victim's family for forgiveness. The family of the murdered person symbolically forgives the murderer by saying *kab näbsə, nab gäbsə*, i.e.: "Let us take barley grains instead of a soul". After the symbolic forgiveness, financial reparation will still be necessary. Its amount ranges from 5000–20,000 *bərr* depending on the financial resources of the guilty party.

In addition, the guilty party must pay 1000 *bərr* as a penalty for the crime committed. The sum is divided 50/50 between the provinces (*wäräda*) of the murderer and his victim. In the province of Irob (northern Tigray), a trial concluded by an agreement between the parties is celebrated with a feast called *kukhta* or *sola*, organised by the guilty party. During the feast, a bull is slaughtered as, according to custom, eating the bull's meat together seals the agreement. During the feast, the

[37] The importance of customary law for Tigrayans can be seen from the fact that in Eritrea (with a 50–60% Tigrayan population), community courts were established in 2004 to adjudicate on minor court cases (minor crimes, tenancy, marriage). The judges of these courts are nominated by the government but are expected to apply customary law when adjudicating. For more, see Saleh Mohammad and Hirt (2015), pp. 153–168.

[38] In the province of Irob (northern Tigray), those members of the *ᵓabbo Gäräb* who are related to one of the conflicted parties cannot participate in the proceedings.

elders observe whether each member of the victim's family has received and eaten a piece of meat. If they have not, they will likely seek revenge. In addition, a marriage is arranged between people from both families, with the aim of ultimately reconciling the parties and preventing any possible revenge.

In the case of crimes other than murder, the elders do not usually demand financial compensation, although there are exceptions to this rule. It may happen that the guilty party has to hand over—for a certain time—some of their cattle or sheep to the victim's homestead. During this time, the injured party has the right to use the milk or wool of the animal, although it is not allowed to kill it. After an agreed period of time, the animals are returned to the culprit's homestead.

There is no possibility of appealing against the *ᵓabbo Gäräb*'s judgment and the court's decision is made public, together with the reasons behind it, i.e., quoting the provisions of customary law that have been applied. In this way, the provisions of customary law are passed on to the next generation and the local community knows what laws are still in place and what the penalties are for non-compliance.

The non-acceptance of the *ᵓabbo Gäräb*'s sentence resulted in social ostracism. Under the Ethiopian Empire, the guilty party could expect their home to be destroyed by villagers and their cattle to be taken from them. However, according to the Ethiopian constitution of 1995, such action would have been a violation of the perpetrator's rights, so nowadays social ostracism consists of not paying the guilty party visits and not inviting them to weddings, funerals and other social ceremonies. Ostracism also involves declining to help under any circumstances.

## 4.9 Customary Law Among the Oromo

The Oromo are the largest group of Cushitic peoples inhabiting north-east Africa. The Oromo inhabit southern Ethiopia and adjacent areas of northern Kenya and western Somalia. Some Oromo adhere to Sunni Islam, some to Christianity, while others remain of the traditional faith. The basis of their economy is livestock farming and agriculture. The Oromo language belongs to the Cushitic group. According to the 2007 national census, 25,363,756 people belonging to the Oromo ethnic group live in Ethiopia (Central Statistical Office in Ethiopia 2007).

Among the Oromo, customary law is closely linked to the *gadaa* system (Legesse 1973; Pankhurst and Assefa 2008). This is an age-class system (*lubaa*) in which a group of men belonging to one class hold full political, administrative, military, economic and religious power. The transfer of power to the next group takes place after 8 years in the course of a festive ceremony. However, before the new group of *gadaa* can assume power, they must prove themselves to be worthy. Their readiness is shown by declaring war on any of the neighbouring communities. The difficulty is that it must be a community that no previous *gadaa* group has fought against.

Every Oromo boy must join his first *gadaa* group exactly 40 years after his father (in power at the time) did, regardless of his age. There are seven *gadaa* classes (two of which have two stages each), and each one lasts from eight to twenty-seven years.

The most important class is the fifth one—the *gadaa* ('government')—which lasts eight years, after which the whole system is named. During this time, men belonging to this class rule over the entire community.[39]

The men of the *gadaa* group made most decisions about the functioning of the community together in meetings called *lubaa*. However, individuals from the group were elected to perform special functions. The most important position in the group was that of *abbaa gadaa* ('the father of the *gadaa*'), who was the leader of the group and presided over meetings of the legislative council called *čaffee*. The position was usually hereditary and the son of a *gadaa* leader, who had ruled the previous forty years, was elected as the new leader of the group. The *abbaa gadaa* was also responsible for overseeing the performance of rituals related to social life and the passing of men through age classes. The group leader also had a decisive say regarding the introduction of new laws.

An equally important position was that of the *abbaa bokkuu* ('the father of *bokkuu*'), whose title was derived from the name of a stick, a type of short mace ending in a heavy head, used for fighting. The mace was a symbol of power, which was passed on to the *gadaa* group that was taking over.

The *abbaa seera* ('father of the law') worked closely with the *abbaa gadaa*. It was his responsibility to memorise Oromo customary laws and quote them during *čaffee* meetings. Because the *abbaa seera* knew all the laws, in some Oromo communities he presided over the election of a group leader. To become *abbaa seera*, a candidate had to demonstrate oratorical skills, knowledge of customary law, as well as of the history and customs of the group, heroism and the wisdom that would enable him to resolve conflicts peacefully in the future.

The last of the important functions in the *gadaa* group was that of *abbaa k'orro*, who acted as an intermediary between the representatives of the state authority and the leaders of the minor Oromo communities.

Traditional Oromo legal institutions vary from region to region. As there are many Oromo communities, only the institutions found in the Borena Oromo (other names: Boran, Boorana) community in southern Ethiopia and northern Kenya are presented below.

The most important of the institutions is the *gumi gaayoo* ('crowd in the *gaayoo* square') meeting, which is held four years after the subsequent *gadaa* group takes power. During the meeting, new laws are discussed and (occasionally) legal disputes are resolved. The meeting should be attended by representatives of each of the community groups found in Boren. In addition, in theory, any member of the community could attend the *gumi gaayoo* assembly, either as a listener or as a voting member. However, each community had its own rules regarding attendance.

Since among the Oromo, the symbol of justice is a type of grass called *margo*, gatherings of clan representatives were held in open spaces where this plant grew, at some distance from human settlements and near a large tree. Each of the Borena clans would send a delegation of five people to become members of the *čaffee*

[39] For more on the *gadaa* system among the Oromo, see Legesse (1973).

council. New or amended legislation was first brought to the council by delegates and then discussed. At the end of the meeting, the accepted laws were again read out and the members of the assembly once again approved them.

Less important than the *gumi gaayoo* meeting was that of the *lubaa gadaa*, or reigning group of the *gadaa*. These were not held on a regular basis, but when there was a need to introduce a new law that would apply only to the community to which the *lubaa gadaa* belonged, or to amend an existing law. They would then gather under a large tree that grew near the *abbaa gadaa*'s house. The discussions usually lasted 15 days and were accompanied by many rituals.

One of the rituals involved bringing a proposal to amend the law. A proposal was submitted to the *lubaa gadaa* by the *abbaa bokkuu*. The members of the group would then sit on stools, pull out their maces, which they had hidden in the folds of their robes called *buluko*, and begin the discussion. Each member of the assembly could voice his opinion for or against the motion. When speaking, they would stand in front of the other members of the assembly, holding the *buluko* in the left hand and a whip in the right, which they cracked whenever wanting to emphasise an important thought. Before the next person was allowed to speak, the previous speaker was given extra time to summarise the speech and possibly recall what they had forgotten to say.

If any member of the congregation shouted *Kebe!* ('I am stopping!'), then the council meeting was adjourned. The *lubaa gadaa* meetings ended when an agreement was reached to introduce a new law. The next day, the *abbaa qorro* would kill a bull and soak his mace in the animal's blood. The *abbaa bokkuu* would then exclaim *Sere tumma!* ('I have created a law!') while hitting the ground with his mace. Following this action, the other members of the congregation would exclaim 'We accept it!'.

In the event of a conflict between two community members, a court was convened. Three members of the *lubaa* assembly were appointed to the court. In addition, both parties to the dispute delegated three assessors (*shene*) each, so each case was adjudicated by nine judges. If either side in the dispute claimed that the *shene* chosen by the opponents was their personal enemy or a relative of their adversary, then the opponents had to replace the assessor. Meetings were held in a place referred to in Oromo as *terre* ('court') and any member of the community could attend.

After the judges started the trial, both parties to the conflict were questioned by lawyers of their choice (*abbaa alenga*). As with the *lubaa* assemblies, if one of the judges shouted 'Kebe!' the court session was interrupted. At the end of the hearing, the judges gave their verdict. It was final if the *lubaa* judges were in agreement. However, if there was no agreement, then two more *lubaa* judges were added to the panel and the verdict became final by majority vote.

The verdict of the judges could be appealed by both parties. Frequently, the conduct of the appeal process was referred to the court of another community. This was done through two assessors of the appellant referring the case to the *lubaa* judges of the other community. Referring to these judges guaranteed impartiality in sentencing, but at the same time caused a lot of trouble because the assessors of each side presented as the aggrieved party. Consequently, in the early twentieth century, at a meeting called *oddaa* (after the huge sycamore tree under which the elders meet), the *gumi gaayoo* assembly passed a number of resolutions related to appealing judgements (Jembere 1988, p. 53):

- If the judgment was delivered by three *lubaa* judges, there should be five *lubaa* judges from the same community involved in delivering the judgment in the appellate process. If the judgment in the first instance was delivered by five *lubaa* judges, there should be seven in the court of appeal.
- One of the *lubaa* judges who sat on the bench in the first instance court should refer the case to the judges in the court of appeal.
- Each of the conflicting parties should select three assessors.
- The assessors and the *lubaa* judges (nine to thirteen in total) make up the panel of judges in the appellate process. The judge of the first instance court shall act only as the speaker of the case.
- The verdict of the appellate court shall be announced by the most senior *lubaa* judge, who also presides over the court. The verdict of the court of appeal is final.

According to Borena Oromo customary law, if someone has committed a crime, it is the duty of the aggrieved party to bring the offender before a magistrate. If the aggrieved party fails to do so, any member of the *lubaa* assembly may take the initiative on this matter. The accused must name his lawyer or adjourn the trial by calling out '*Kebe!*'. In such a case, a new court date is set and if the accused does not admit guilt, the aggrieved party can bring their lawyer. If the aggrieved party does not come forward, the *lubaa* representatives adjourn the trial until the aggrieved party or someone close to him/her is brought before the court. The injured party is then asked to present witnesses in the case. Before the witnesses give evidence, they must take an oath before the *lubaa gadaa*.

If the aggrieved party wins the trial, compensation is awarded. More often than not, as punishment, the *lubaa gadaa* decree the number of cattle that the accused must kill to feed the victim's family. If the offence was more serious, the judges would order members of the community to go to the accused's homestead to take as many cattle as they liked, kill them and eat them. If the accused had no cattle, then they were flogged or warned of what might happen if such an offence was committed again.

In modern Ethiopia, the *gadaa* system mentioned at the beginning of this section no longer functions in many provinces of the Oromia region,[40] as a result of which the Oromo have created a legal institution referred to as *Jaarsa Biyyaa* ('the elders of the community').[41] This is a group of the elders in the clan (*gosa*), subclan (*balbala*) or village (*ganda*), which deals with the resolution of conflicts involving both individuals and collectives. *Jaarsa Biyyaa* deal with the criminal, civil and com-

[40] Research conducted by Hinnant (1977) and Yacob Arsano in 1994/1995 (Arsano 1997) suggests that the *gadaa* system and all related legal institutions have survived among the Borena Oromo and the Guji Oromo.

[41] Among some Oromo groups, this gathering bears the name *Jarsa Araaraa* ('the elders of reconciliation').

mercial law cases based on the particular clan's customary law or (in the case of villages) the customary law of the Oromo (*seera Oromo*).[42] As in previous cases, only men who have charisma and are respected by the rest of the community can belong to the group of mediator judges.

As mentioned earlier, the *Jaarsa Biyyaa* institution does not function only at the clan and village level, but also at higher levels, such as the *sadan* (a community of three villages), the *shanan* (a community of five villages) and the *seglan* (a community of nine villages). *Jaarsa Biyyaa* institutions are hierarchical and those at higher levels act as courts of appeal. Thus, if a case reaches a higher level, then—respectively—three, five or nine judges are involved in the process.

A case can be brought to the *Jaarsa Biyyaa* tribunal in two ways: either by the aggrieved party (or their family member) seeking the support of the judges, or the judges themselves calling both parties to explain the essence of the conflict. The latter occurs even if the conflicted parties do not want the tribunal to be involved. Its members, however, consider it their duty to mediate the case in order to prevent an escalation of a conflict that could harm the peaceful existence of the entire community. However, if the *Jaarsa Biyyaa* do not respond quickly enough, members of the public can express their disapproval by saying '*Jaarsa Biyyaa hinjiruu?*' ('Are there no elders in this community?').

Having accepted the case, the tribunal sets the date and place of the trial. It usually takes place outdoors in the main square called the *aradda*. As indicated earlier, the trial is judged by three to seven members of the tribunal, who choose a chief judge (*abbaa murtii*, literally 'father of the court') and two prosecutors (*lamii qoraa*) from among themselves. Before they begin their deliberations, the judge and the prosecutors must publicly take an oath called *kakuu* before the *Waga Lafaaf Sami* ('God of Earth and Heaven').[43] The oath is to ensure the impartiality of the judges and the fairness of the trial. The *lamii qoraa* then sit on either side of the *abbaa murtii*. All three must hold the *halangee*, a type of whip that symbolises the truth, in their hands. If in the course of the trial one of the prosecutors, usually an elder, wishes to raise an important point, he says '*Koottu*' ('Come here/look here'), to which the other prosecutor should reply '*Dhufee*' ('I have come'). No aspect of the case can be raised until such ritual exchange has occurred. Thereafter, time is given to both sides of the conflict to make their case. After this stage, the prosecutors and the observers of the trial question both sides. Participants in the process who wish to question either party or express their opinion on a particular subject must ask the *abbaa murtii* or *lamii qoraa* for the right to speak by saying '*Nagumgumachisi*' ('Let me speak'). The members of the *Jaarsa Biyyaa* decide whether or not to take the speaker's suggestion into consideration, although they cannot prohibit anyone from expressing it. Moreover, all participants in the trial

[42] Field research on the functioning of CDR in the Oromia region was carried out in 2004/5 by Abdella and Amenew (2008), pp. 169–183.

[43] The content of the oath is to be found at the end of this book, in the Annex.

have the right to suggest to the judges the type and amount of punishment to be awarded the accused.

If after questioning the accused continues to plead innocence,[44] the chief judge orders both conflicted parties to leave the meeting and retreat into two different places. The judges, together with the litigants, then discuss the arguments presented by both sides and try to agree on a verdict. If this fails, the court meeting is adjourned. The date of the next sitting is set according to a rule referred to as *bultii* (postponing the issue to another meeting day).

On the appointed day, the members of the *Jaarsa Biyyaa* gather to once again hear the arguments of both sides, but this time the parties are heard separately, in two different locations. After hearing one side's testimony, the tribunal members repeat what they have heard and then proceed to question the other side. This process is called *cokoo*. If this time the accused pleads guilty, a penalty is set, depending on the seriousness of the offence committed. If the offence was not serious (e.g., slander, insult), the accused must make a public apology to the victim. If, on the other hand, the offence was more serious, the accused must pay compensation to the victim or slaughter a sheep, goat or buffalo and give the meat to the victim and their family.

If the *cokoo* procedure fails, the judges call witnesses who testify under oath. In turn, the victim is asked to provide evidence of the accused party's guilt (*raga*). If the witnesses' testimony is unreliable, no sufficient evidence is provided and the accused still does not admit guilt, then the court summons the suspect's family: the father, mother, eldest brother and wife, who, together with the accused, must publicly take a *kakuu* oath affirming the defendant's innocence.[45] Family members who take this oath are referred to as *fitensa*. Members of the Oromo community take this type of oath very seriously, recognising that there are serious consequences for breaking it, not only from the other members of the community, but also from God, who may curse the perjurer.

Once the defendant and their entire family have taken the oath, the judges declare the defendant not guilty and close the trial by blessing both parties to the conflict. If, on the other hand, any member of the family is absent when the oath is taken, or the family does not wish to take the oath, then the defendant's oath is invalid. For the judges, this is a sign that the defendant is being untruthful and he/she is immediately convicted.

The means of seeking justice presented above are used in all types of conflicts, except for criminal cases involving bodily harm or murder. In such cases, a procedure called *gumaa* is applied. There are three types of *gumaa* depending on the circumstances surrounding the crime (*gumaa adii*, *gumaa barruu* and *gumaa gurratti*).

---

[44] In Oromo communities, it is expected that the accused admit their guilt personally.

[45] The content of the oath is to be found in the Annex.

In the case of *gumaa* murders, a tribunal called the *Rayya Anbaa* conducts the trial and delivers the verdict. This is a group made up of clan elders whose members are not related to either the victim's family or the murderer's family.

The chapter presents the genesis of the Aksum state and hypotheses on the origin of Aksum law. Then, the sources of law were discussed that influenced the development of legislation in the Ethiopian Empire, as will be demonstrated in the following chapters. The first of the sources that shaped the development of law in Aksum (and later in the whole Ethiopian Empire) were the rules of conduct derived from Christian teachings, which were based on passages from the Old Testament. Later, these principles were supplemented with those of the *Senodos*. Another factor that impacted the development of law in Aksum were the laws of Emperor Caleb, who established a symbolic separation of state and church.

Equally important to the development of Ethiopian legislation were the customary laws of both the Sabaeans, who came from the Arabian Peninsula, and the Cushitic peoples living on the African Red Sea coast, whose culture blended with that of the newcomers to form the basis of Ethiopian culture.

Ethiopian legislation has also been to a significant degree influenced by elements of customary law of the three largest ethnic groups of Ethiopia, as outlined above. As the analysis shows, a common feature of customary laws (and the associated legal procedures) in all three groups is that local legislation is geared not to punish the offender, but to forgive and bring about reconciliation with the wronged party. The customary laws of the Amhara, Tigray and Oromo prioritise the welfare of the community over that of the individual, at the same time without neglecting to provide redress for the harm suffered by the aggrieved party. This approach coincides with Christian teachings, which preach a desire to forgive oppressors rather than to seek bloody revenge.

## References

Abate M, Shiferaw W (2008) Customary dispute resolution in Amhara region: the case of Wofa Legesse in north Shewa. In: Pankhurst A, Assefa G (eds) Grass-roots justice in Ethiopia: the contribution of customary dispute resolution. Centre Français d'Études Éthiopiennes, Addis Ababa, pp 107–121

Abdella A, Amenew B (2008) Customary dispute resolution institutions in Oromia region: the case of Jaarsa Biyyaa. In: Pankhurst A, Assefa G (eds) Grass-roots justice in Ethiopia: the contribution of customary dispute resolution. Centre Français d'Études Éthiopiennes, Addis Ababa, pp 169–183

Abdo M, Abegaz G (n.d.) Customary law. Teaching material. Faculty of Law, Addis Ababa University

Arsano Y (1997) The impact of state intervention on land and traditional leadership in Borana. Research report submitted to the ISS. Institute of Social Studies, The Hague

Augustyniak Z (2009) Marriages in Ethiopia. Studies of the Department of Languages and Cultures 43:99–115

Augustyniak Z (2014) Konstytucja Cesarstwa Etiopskiego z 1930 roku—pierwszy krok ku modernizacji państwa czy próba wprowadzenia monarchii absolutnej. In: Kraska-Szlenk

I, Wójtowicz B (eds) Current research in African studies. Papers in honour of Mwalimu Dr. Eugeniusz Rzewuski. Elipsa, Warszawa, pp 25–38
Bartnicki A, Mantel-Niećko J (1978) Geschichte Äthiopiens: von der Anfängen bis zur Gegenwart. Akademie-Verlag, Berlin
Bausi A (1992) Heritage and originality in the Ethiopic Sinodos. Journal of Ethiopian Studies 25:15–33
Bausi A (2010) Senodos. In S Uhlig (ed) Encyclopaedia Aethiopica, vol 4. Wiesbaden, Harrassowitz, pp 623–625
Central Statistical Office in Ethiopia (2007) Population and housing census. https://www.statsethiopia.gov.et/census-2007-2/
Civil Code (5 May 1960) Civil code of the empire of Ethiopia. Negarit Gazeta, Addis Ababa
Council of Antioch (1998) The editors of encyclopaedia Britannica. Encyclopedia Britannica. https://www.britannica.com/event/Council-of-Antioch
Dressler H (2003) Clement I, Pope, St. In: Carson T, Cerrito J (eds) New Catholic encyclopaedia, vol 3, 2nd edn. The Catholic University of America, Washington DC, pp 773–775
Drewes AJ (1962) Inscriptions de l'Éthiopie antique. E.J. Brill, Leiden
Elliesie H (2015) Social construct and system in Tigre tradition: a contribution to Eritrean customary law. In: Voigt R (ed) Tigre studies in the 21st century/Tigre-Studien im 21. Jahrhundert. Rüdiger Köppe, Köln, pp 169–180
Gizaw S, Gessese T (2008) Customary dispute resolution in Tigray region: case studies from three districts. In: Pankhurst A, Assefa G (eds) Grass-roots justice in Ethiopia. The contribution of customary dispute resolution. Centre Français d'Études Éthiopiennes, Addis Ababa, pp 217–235
Glenn HP (2005) On common laws. Oxford University Press, Oxford
Hable Selassie S (1970) A history of Aksum: the successors of Caleb. In: Conference on current research trends in Ethiopian history. Haile Sellassie I University, Addis Ababa, pp 30–37
Hable Sellassie S (1972) Ancient and medieval Ethiopian history to 1270. United Printers, Addis Ababa
Hinnant JT (1977) The gada system of the Guji of Southern Ethiopia. University of Chicago, Chicago
Iliffe J (2011) Afrykanie. Dzieje kontynentu. Wydawnictwa Uniwersytetu Jagiellońskiego, Kraków
Jembere A (1988) Tatayyaq Muget: the traditional Ethiopian mode of litigation. In: Beyene T (ed) Proceedings of the eight international conference of Ethiopian studies, vol 1. Institute of Ethiopian Studies; Frobenius Institut, Johann Wolfgang Goëthe Universität, Addis Ababa, Frankfurt am Main, pp 245–262
Kemink F (1991) The Tegrenna customary law codes. Paideuma 37:55–72
Legesse A (1973) Gada. Three Approaches to the Study of African Society. The Free Press, New York
Lewicki T (1969) Dzieje Afryki od czasów najdawniejszych do XIV wieku. Wybrane zagadnienia. Wydawnictwa Uniwersytetu Warszawskiego, Warszawa
Mantel-Niećko J (1975) Etiopia. Podstawowe wiadomości o kraju, jego dziejach i historii badań. Skrypt dla afrykanistów i semitystów. Wydawnictwa Uniwersytetu Warszawskiego, Warszawa
Munro-Hay S (1991) Aksum. An African civilization of late antiquity. Edinburgh University Press, Edinburgh
Pankhurst A, Assefa G (eds) (2008) Grass-roots justice in Ethiopia: the contribution of customary dispute resolution. Centre Français d'Études Éthiopiennes, Addis Ababa
Phillipson DW (2012) Foundations of an African civilization. Aksum and the northern horn, 1000 BC—AD 1300. James Currey, Woodbridge
Quasten J (2003) Didascalia Apostolorum. In: Carson T, Cerrito J (eds) New Catholic encyclopaedia, vol 4, 2nd edn. The Catholic University of America, Washington DC, pp 737–738
Saleh Mohammad A, Hirt N (2015) Conflict resolution and customary law in contemporary Eritrea: case studies in the Saho community. In: Voigt R (ed) Tigre studies in the 21st century/Tigre-Studien im 21. Jahrhundert. Rüdiger Köppe, Köln, pp 153–168
Wäldä Mäsqäl MŚ (1953) Yäᵊabbatoč qərs [legacy of the forefathers]. Addis Ababa
Wysocki M (2013) Testamentum Domini. In: Gigilewicz E (ed) Encyklopedia Katolicka, vol XIX. Towarzystwo Naukowe Katolickiego Uniwersytetu Lubelskiego, Lublin, pp 743–744

# Chapter 5
# The Fətḥa Nägäśt and First Attempts at Codifying Law

## 5.1 The Fall of Aksum

In the sixth century, the Aksum state began to slowly go into decline. As a result of Persian expansion, Aksum lost control of the Red Sea trade route, which was a serious blow to its economy. Economic problems and the necessity to move the state capital deep into African territory had quite an impact on the weakening of the position of the Aksum rulers, which in turn resulted in the emergence of centrifugal tendencies in the country. In addition, the *History of the Patriarchs of Alexandria* mentions the invasion of foreign peoples, who not only plundered the country, but also persecuted Christians (Burmester and Khater 1970).[1] As a result of both internal weaknesses and external factors, Aksum ceased to exist around the seventh century.

Associated with the fall of Aksum is the legend of a bloodthirsty queen named Judith (also known by the names Gudit or Ǝsato). Leading a huge army, she sacked the country, razing it to the ground and destroying Aksum's churches. The story of her conquests and 40-year reign is repeatedly related in books on the history of Ethiopia (see Sergew Hable Sellassie 1972, pp. 225–232; Andersen 2000, pp. 31–63; Kaplan 1992, pp. 44–47); thus, only a fragment of one of the chronicles will be cited below,[2] as it contains a short description of a customary court Judith was subjected to. This was supposed to have been the main reason for her resentment towards the residents of Aksum.

According to the chronicle, Judith came from an aristocratic but poor family. Poverty forced her to prostitute herself on the streets of Aksum. Stricken by her beauty, a young deacon asked what she would like to receive in return for the

[1] For more on the causes behind the fall of the Aksum state, see Hable Sellassie (1972), pp. 205–237.

[2] The text comes from the unpublished *Chronicles of Ethiopia*, compiled (from manuscripts in Ethiopian monasteries and churches) by *Qesä Gäbäz* Täklä Haymanot from Aksum. See Hable Sellassie (1972), p. 228.



Z. Augustyniak, *Marriage in the Ethiopian Empire*, Studies in the History of Law and Justice 33, https://doi.org/10.1007/978-3-032-26065-9_5

opportunity of spending the night with her. Judith replied that she wished to have golden shoes. Since the deacon was not wealthy enough to buy the proper material, he snatched a piece of a gold curtain hanging in one of the churches. The residents of Aksum quickly found out about the theft. Upon realising that the severed piece was large enough to make a woman's shoes, they ordered every female resident of Aksum to place her foot on the fabric. Soon, it turned out that the severed piece was the size of Judith's foot. The elders asked, "Who is the man who gave these to you?" and when Judith answered the question,

> [...] the elders and the learned people of the country assembled to pass correct judgement and they said, 'What can a boy under twenty years do when he sees such a beauty. She is the one who put him under temptation to do that. He is innocent of guilt and his age will protect him (from being condemned). She is the only one and solely responsible for the desecration and she made shoes from the curtain of Sion.' They condemned her to cut her right breast and be exiled from the country. The decision carried, they exiled her and chased her to the Red Sea which was the boundary of Egypt. The son of the king of Sham called Zenobis found her (…).[3]

This report may give some insight into how the legal institutions in Aksum emerged, although it should be noted that there are no contemporary Ethiopian sources that could confirm it. In the times of the Kingdom of Aksum, the king had both legislative and judicial powers. Most probably, kings passed judgements only in matters of highest importance, leaving smaller issues to local courts. In the latter case, verdicts were passed by the elders of a community, who invoked the provisions of customary law. The tradition quoted above also suggests that the institution of customary courts must have been so important that the elders also had the right to deal with crimes involving members of the clergy, who should theoretically have been under the jurisdiction of the church. Moreover, the sentence presented in the above passage indicating Judith as guilty of a crime committed by a deacon may correlate with the weaker position of women in customary courts, as discussed in previous chapters.

## 5.2 The Law in Ethiopia During the Reign of the Zag$^{w}$e Dynasty

The fall of Aksum did not mean the end of Aksum civilization. Certain patterns of this culture were adopted by the Cushite Agew people living south of the city-state. Between the tenth and twelfth centuries, a Christian state was established in Lasta, headed by a ruler who did not originate from Aksum. Soon the rulers from Lasta established a new dynasty, the Zag$^{w}$e.

There is sparse information on the dynasty of Ethiopian rulers descended from Lasta. There is no agreement among historians of Ethiopia about the duration of

[3] For the Ge'ez original text and its English translation, see Hable Sellassie (1972), pp. 228–229.

their reign. Calculations, based on genealogies, range between 130 and 370 years. It is known that the last ruler of the Zagʷe dynasty ruled until 1270. It can therefore be assumed that the dynasty was in power between 900 and 1270 CE (Phillipson 2012, p. 228). Little is also known about how the kings of the Zagʷe dynasty seized power in the state. There are no contemporary Ethiopian sources, and only oral traditions describe the takeover.[4] The lack of information about the history of the Ethiopian state at that time can be partly explained by the fact that later Ethiopian historiographers considered the Zagʷe dynasty usurpers, thus they were not interested in commemorating their history.

For the above-mentioned reasons, little is also known about the development of legislation at the time, although certainly the contribution of the Lastan rulers to the development of legislation was enormous. As Bairu Tafla writes, "[...] the Zagʷe Dynasty [...] produced some of the most distinguished rulers who might have contributed no less to the laws and traditions of the Kingdom than the Aksumites" (Tafla 1991, p. 98). There is no doubt that rulers of the Zagʷe dynasty relied on Christianity in both internal and external politics (Bartnicki and Mantel-Niećko 1978, p. 13); thus, it can be assumed that in establishing subsequent laws, the rulers used the provisions of canon law and Christian doctrine.

One of the few pieces of information regarding the legislation at the time is provided by the text *Gädlä Yəmrəḥannä Krəstos*, a hagiography of Emperor Yəmrəḥannä Krəstos, the twelfth ruler of the Zagʷe dynasty, according to the traditional list of kings. The text states that the king issued a decree regulating the inheritance of family property, the contents of which also applied to the succession of the Ethiopian throne:

> If there are two or three brothers, born of the same father and mother, and if one becomes rich and the other poor, let the poor man share the property of his rich brother. For both are the fruits of the same womb (quoted after Tadesse Tamrat 1972, p. 60).

According to this decree, each of the sons of the reigning ruler held rights to the royal crown which, contrary to hagiographic descriptions, meant that the problem of succession was usually solved by force. The same source contains information about the ruler's decree forbidding his subjects from practicing magic and participating in witchcraft (Sergew Hable Sellassie 1972, p. 250). The author of the hagiography of Yəmrəḥannä Krəstos also mentions that the ruler, who was a very pious man, ordered his people to abandon polygamy in favour of monogamy (the observance of which would lead to salvation), as previously advocated by the patriarch of the Ethiopian Orthodox Church, Sinoda II (1032–1047) (Tadesse Tamrat 1972, p. 243).

---

[4] According to one of the traditions, which was probably intended to legitimise the Zagʷe dynasty, the dynastic change resulted from the marriage of the daughter of the last ruler of Aksum to a general of his army who came from Bugna in Lasta. This story is also one of the first accounts of political marriages in Ethiopian history (Tamrat 1972, p. 54). The historical sources from the reign of the Zagʷe dynasty are discussed extensively by Marie-Laure Derat (2010, pp. 159–195).

One of the most famous rulers from the Zagʷe dynasty was Lalibäla, who lived in the late twelfth and early thirteenth centuries and, according to Ethiopian tradition, forged twelve monolithic churches in the rocks with the help of angels.[5] Due to these deeds, as well as his pious nature, Lalibäla became one of the saints of the Ethiopian Orthodox Church. Little is known about his secular activities, including those related to legislation. The few available Arabic sources indicate that Lalibäla introduced a tax system in which the amount of tax due depended on the wealth of each subject. The same sources confirm that Lalibäla was the supreme judge, and in order to fulfil the duties associated with this function he constantly travelled around the country (Sergew Hable Sellassie 1972, p. 270). His hagiography, on the other hand, mentions the decrees he issued ordering the relinquishment of land to the Church, as well as decrees on compensatory land grants (Pankhurst 1967, p. 10; Phillipson 2012, p. 242).

Lalibäla was the last great king in the Zagʷe dynasty. Most likely, a nephew named Näᵓakkwəto Le'ab ascended the throne after him, but many members of the dynasty, who would have preferred to see Lalibäla's son Yətbaräq on the throne, were dissatisfied. Moreover, in the second half of the thirteenth century, a new dynasty joined the struggle for power, with its members claiming to be the only legitimate successors to the Aksum throne. In Ethiopian historiography, they are known as the Solomonic dynasty.[6] Soon, rulers of this dynasty seized power as a result of wars and conspiracies, culminating in the assassination of the last Zagʷe dynasty ruler, which took place in a church.

## 5.3 Ethiopian Legislation During the Reign of Emperor ᶜAmdä Ṣəyon I (1314–1344)

The first ruler in the new dynasty was Yəkunno Amlak (1270–1285), who is credited with concluding *siso mänəgəsət* i.e., an agreement between the ruler and the Ethiopian clergy, regulating the distribution of arable land (Bartnicki and Mantel-Niećko 1978, p. 23). One third of the lands was to belong to the emperor, one third to the Ethiopian Orthodox Church, and the last part was to be given to the farmers. This division not only strengthened the economic position of the Church, but also was fundamental for the interdependence between secular and ecclesiastical power, also in matters of law. Indeed, the Emperor established the position of *əččäge*, the head of the Ethiopian monks, and the position of *aqabe säᵓat*, who gained the right

[5] For more on the Ethiopian legend linked to the construction of the churches, see Pankhurst (1967), pp. 8–12.

[6] The name of the dynasty was meant to emphasise the descent of its members from the King of Israel, Solomon, who, according to Ethiopian traditions, had a son with the Queen of Sheba. The son, named Mənilək, was said to have been the first ruler of Ethiopia. For more on the tradition, see Budge (2000).

to settle religious disputes within the Orthodox Ethiopian Church and to issue legal verdicts (Bartnicki and Mantel-Niećko 1978, p. 23).

No document of a legal nature has survived from the reign of Yəkunno Amlak, except for the contents of an agreement reached between the emperor and the clergy, as well as a treaty concluded between the emperor of the Solomonic dynasty and the last representative of the Zagʷe dynasty, Näᵓakkwəto Le'ab. Little is also known about the emperor's internal and external political activities. All that has been passed down is that the ruler established Tegulet, in northern Shehua, as his main residence, and sought to centralise power.

Much better documented is the reign of the eighth ruler in this dynasty, ᶜAmdä Ṣəyon I (1314–1344). Although Ethiopian historiography focuses primarily on his victories against the Muslim sultanates, the emperor was also credited with the development of law in Ethiopia. It is from his time that one of the first Ethiopian legal documents dates. This is the *Śər'atä Mängəśt* ('Laws of the Empire'), a text described by Heinrich Scholler and Bairu Tafla as "an early Ethiopian constitution" (Bairu Tafla and Scholler 1976, pp. 487–499). Although it is difficult to determine its exact date (some of its parts were written later, during the reigns of Emperors Śärṣä Dəngəl and Fasilädäs), the very fact that it was composed in the first half of the fourteenth century reflected a desire to create a unified state administration and to organise rules of succession to the throne. According to Jacques Vanderlinden (1966, p. 229), the *Śər'atä Mängəśt* demonstrates the existence of the continuous legislative activity of the Ethiopian Empire, which began in the fourteenth century and culminated three hundred years later. An additional reason for writing or compiling the text, according to Heinrich Scholler and Bairu Tafla, was the need for a source that could be referred to in case of doubt about the conduct of a ceremony.

The text, written in Ge'ez, contains many archaic, vague words, making its translation difficult. Moreover, there are numerous loanwords, not only from Amharic, but also from Somali, Agew and other languages, the knowledge of which is necessary to fully understand the contents of the book (Varenbergh 1915/1916). Three manuscripts containing the *Śər'atä Mängəśt*, dating from the late eighteenth and early nineteenth centuries, are kept at the Institute of Ethiopian Studies in Addis Ababa. None of them is an independent book, but rather they are attached to other works of Ethiopian literature. One of the manuscripts is bound together with a copy of *Kəbrä Nägäśt* ('The Glory of the Kings'), while the other—with *Tarika Nägäśt* ('The History of Kings') (Bairu Tafla and Scholler 1976, p. 488).

*Śər'atä Mängəśt* consists of five parts, containing the rules of court ceremonies, the ranks and titles of magnates, judges and priests, and their associated functions. The text also includes a description of court ceremonies, such as the coronation of the emperor and his wife, the nuptials of princesses, and a description of funeral ceremonies of members of the imperial family.

The first part contains a list of the dignitaries who, along with Mənilək I, son of the Queen of Sheba and King Solomon, came from Jerusalem to Ethiopia. The text states that the newcomers included twelve law students and that the law in Ethiopia had its origin in the laws and regulations of ancient Israel (Bairu Tafla and Scholler 1976, p. 490).[7]

The second part, omitted from the translations done by both Joseph Varenbergh, as well as those by Heinrich Scholler and Bairu Tafla, contains a geographic description of the Empire with a list of provinces and cities.

The third part, the most relevant to the present study, contains a description of court rituals. The articles dealing with the institution of marriage or refer to women members of the imperial family will be presented below.[8]

One of the first articles in this part concerns the coronation of the emperor's wife:

> § 3. When the Queen is crowned, on a Sunday, she would be decorated before hand, and would seat herself on a small throne to the right of the King, while the latter sat on a large throne. The Tsirag-Massare, Like-Debterra, Kese-Hats and Like-Maemeran would give benediction, and would put the crown on her head, and there would be cheering. Then the Queen's maids would sing, and bring her out on a divan to the sound of Deb-Anbessa and Nessre-Kana being carried by the two Tseha-Sergotche (Bairu Tafla and Scholler 1976, pp. 491–492).[9]

The same article also states that when the queen accuses someone of a crime or is being accused of something, the judges are to be summoned to her home.[10] This seems to indicate that during the reign of ᶜAmdä Ṣəyon I, the court's deliberations were closed to the public when a member of the imperial family was accused of committing an offence. The wording of the article also suggests that the queen could preside over the court's deliberations on her own and issue verdicts in consultation with a panel of judges.

The next article that refers to women from the imperial family is linked to rituals related to the marriage of the emperor's daughters.

> § 6. When there were weddings for the princesses on Sunday, they would make them sit before the King; after that they were decorated with gold and purple and with crowns on their heads. The bride-groom would come; they would decorate him with clothes of honour and then, mounting a horse, he would leave with his wife. The army would mount their horses, and follow him, singing with the sound of Nessre-Kana and Negarit (big drum); and would go with her (the bride) and put her into the place which the King had directed.
>
> § 7. Also, in the case of the daughters of the Queens, they would veil the arwa sora (tent) and would furnish the floor with Bessate (carpets) and the bride-groom would come. He would go out on the 10$^{th}$ day and the King would decorate him (Bairu Tafla and Scholler 1976, p. 492).[11]

---

[7] For the history of Mənilək I's visit to the court of King Solomon, see Sellasié (1930), p. 10.

[8] The third part of *Śər'atä Mängəśt* also provides valuable information about the court titles held by aristocrats in charge of legal matters in the Ethiopian Empire. Thus, a judge held the title *liqe mäṭaňoč*, while a person responsible for formulating legal prescriptions bore the title *ǧan täšäkami* (Tafla and Scholler 1976, p. 491).

[9] Quoted here is the English translation by Tafla and Scholler (1976). The "standard" version of the text was edited and published in 1915–1916 by Varenbergh (with a German translation).

[10] Literally, to 'the empress' tent', as in the times of ᶜAmdä Ṣəyon I the emperor did not have a permanent residence, but travelled around the country with his court.

[11] For the original text, see Varenbergh (1915/1916), p. 17; German translation—32.

Although the above description of the wedding ceremonies of princesses is rather concise, it can be inferred that weddings were usually held on Sunday, and the blessing was given by the ruler himself, who also allotted the young couple's place of residence. It is not clear, however, why the fiancé stayed in the tent for ten days and what decoration or title the emperor bestowed on him. It may indicate that these ten days were meant to be the period during which the marriage should have been consummated.

The following article refers to a situation in which the princesses want to accuse "their enemies".[12] In such a case, the daughters of the king go to the *säqäla* ('the elongated house'),[13] where the *raq masäre*[14] and judges (*wämbär*) would submit the accusations on their behalf. In turn, when the princesses were accused, the whole procedure would take place in their tent.[15] In light of this and the previous article, the information that court hearings involving members of the imperial family were held behind closed doors can be seen as confirmed. The eighth article also shows that, unlike the queen, the princesses were not allowed to present their own case in court.

The remaining articles in the third part of the code deal with state administration and the legal duties of individual members of the imperial court. According to article 10, the emperor appointed three *bitwäddäd*s, one of whom, along with eight *azmač*s, was in charge of the judiciary process. Twice a week—on Wednesdays and Fridays—the panel of judges reported to the ruler, while on the other days they were in charge of conducting trials and issuing verdicts. The article also notes that any subject could report directly to the emperor, but most likely his case would be sent back to a lower court (Bairu Tafla and Scholler 1976, p. 493).

Article 15 concerns accusations made by and against *əččäge*. In both cases, the trial was held in the home of a bishop, to whom the imperial house provided a day's supply of bread, *ṭäǧǧ* (mead) and beef for the duration of the trial. The next article describes the rituals involved in the sentencing of judges (Bairu Tafla and Scholler 1976, p. 494).

Article 17, most likely added during the reign of Emperor Śärṣä Dəngəl (1563–1597), describes the procedure involved in presiding over a provincial court. The right to pass judgment was vested in the *bitwäddäd*, and in his absence it was passed on to the *blatten geta*. If the aggrieved party reported to both imperial officials, they would have the trial conducted by the *azmač* in accordance with the law "instituted before the time of Mənilək I's reign" (Bairu Tafla and Scholler 1976, p. 495), which may suggest that the sentences were issued in accordance with the customary law operating in the area, or among the ethnic group in question.

---

[12] See previous footnote.

[13] Literally "a shed built on a rectangular plan"; this might perhaps refer to the building where the magistrates' tribunal composed of the administrators of the imperial provinces held office.

[14] The article on accusations levelled against princesses was probably added or revised in the fifteenth century, as the title *raq masäre* was not introduced until the reign of Zärᵓa Yaᶜəqob.

[15] For the original text, see Varenbergh (1915/1916), p. 17, German translation—33. English translation: Bairu Tafla and Scholler (1976), p. 492.

The fourth part of *Śər'atä Mängəśt* concerns the relationship between the Church and the State. The legal proceedings in cases involving the clergy are described in four articles. The second article of the section regulates marriages of the clergy. Before the *Śər'atä Mängəśt*, according to the injunction issued by the *abunä*, priests had to make unanimous judgments on church marriages, and they could not have a dissenting opinion from the head of the Church. In addition, only the *abunä* had the right to dissolve a marriage contracted by a clergyman, and spouses could not obtain a divorce under secular law (Bairu Tafla and Scholler 1976, p. 498). This part of the code also indicates that secular courts could not pass judgment in marriage cases. Although the text does not specify whether this provision applied to all types of marriages, it can be assumed that it referred only to unions contracted in accordance with Christian doctrine. In the case of marriages contracted under customary law, most probably customary courts were referred to.

The last part of the code, described as 'judiciary' by Heinrich Scholler and Bairu Tafla, specifies the order in which members of the imperial court issue legal opinions and verdicts.

> The first ones to comment were Yeshalekkotch, next to them the Seyoume Messe would comment, next to him the Bejerond of the Ambessa-Bet (lion house) next to him the Bejerond of the Zufan-Bet (throne house), after him the Like-Meqnoise, next to him the Balamba-ras, after him the Fit-Awrari, next to them the Gerra-Azmatch and Kegne-Azmatch, after them the minor Blatten-Getta, next to him Tsehafte-Tezaz (verdict scribes) and the Azzajotch, after them the Rak Massare (ceremonial master), next to him would comment the Pashas and Dej-Azmatches of Damot, Gojam, Amhara, Begemder and Semen. Next to them would comment the Dej-Azmatch of Tigre […]. Next to him could comment the Akabe-Seat, next to him the Blatten-Getta, next to him the Ras. Finally, the King would give verdict and all would be finished (Bairu Tafla and Scholler 1976, p. 499).

Although it took so many opinions to make a judgment, the final say in a case was held by the ruler himself, who was considered the supreme judge and could overrule the judgment of any arbitrator. The emperor's status as the highest judicial authority is reflected in an Ethiopian proverb dating from the reign of ᶜAmdä Ṣəyon I: "A case decided on by a king and a thing cut by a sword are the same" (Scholler 1976, p. 521).

Throughout the history of the Ethiopian Empire, the incumbent ruler was considered the "the sole and final fountain of justice and equity" (Scholler 1976, p. 521). Judges, in passing judgments on behalf of the emperor, had to strictly adhere to the letter of the law, and could not interpret it, contrary to Muslim jurists when interpreting the laws in the Quran. It should be remembered that as in earlier centuries, during the reign of ᶜAmdä Ṣəyon I, the law in Ethiopia was based primarily on canon law, Christian doctrine and select provisions of customary law. Occasionally, however, judges had to pass judgment in a case without precedent. Unable to find relevant laws, the judges reported to the emperor, who, having familiarised himself with the case, issued an appropriate judgment. The emperor's decision, along with the reasons behind it, immediately became binding law, referred to as *aṣe śər'at* ('the emperor's law').[16] According to Abera Jembere, *aṣe śər'at* was usually used in civil cases, while criminal cases first used the provisions of canon law and then those contained in the *Fətḥa Nägäśt* code (brought to Ethiopia in the late sixteenth and early seventeenth centuries).[17]

From the analysis by Abera Jembere, it follows that some legal provisions on marriage and family stemming from *aṣe śər'at* were incorporated into the Civil and Family Law Code created in 1960. The most important of these are the following:

- If the marriage was contracted in accordance with local customary law, any property acquired during the marriage belongs to both spouses. However, in the case of divorce and division of property, the woman cannot take away things that serve only the man. In the same way, a man cannot take from a woman any things that only shc uscs.
- Except for a *qal kidan bäqurban* marriage, divorce can be ordered in all other types of marriages if negotiations conducted by family members on the behalf of the spouses fail, or if one of the parties strongly demands a divorce.
- If a woman is proven to have committed adultery, or if she leaves her home and spends the night away from her parents' home or the home of the father of the marriage (*yänägär ᵓabbat*), she not only loses her rights to any property acquired during the marriage, but is also deprived of her rights to her personal belongings. She can regain these rights if she presents a plausible reason for not staying in the family home or that of the *yänägär ᵓabbat*.
- Parents take complete responsibility for their children, until they are fit "to ride a horse" (in the case of boys) or "to wear the marriage cloak (*kabba*)" (girls).
- If the parents divorce, children up to the age of three are left in the custody of their mother, and the father is required to contribute to their upkeep. Boys above this age are placed in the custody of the father, while girls remain with their mother. The father does not have to pay child support for a daughter over the age of three if he chooses to raise her on his own (Jembere 1998, p. 91).

Based on the above records, it can be observed that in creating the *aṣe śər'at* the emperor applied the principle of equality before those of law and justice. This equality was independent of gender, although the exception to this principle is the provision stating that a woman would forfeit goods acquired during marriage if she spent the night away from home. The regulations say nothing about a punishment that would be meted out to a man for the same act. This is most likely due not only to Ethiopian morality, which valued men's moral liberty more highly than women's,

[16] Since the emperor could not be seen by his subjects, his verdict was announced by the *afä nəgus*. The court verdict, which became law, was announced by imperial heralds in the main squares of Ethiopian cities (Kropp 2012, p. 262).

[17] After the promulgation of the Penal Code and the Civil Code in the 1930s and 1960s, the *aṣe sər'at* ceased to be applied (Jembere 1998, p. 90).

but also to the lifestyle of Ethiopian men, who often left their homes for weeks or months at a time, either travelling to trade or summoned to join the army.[18]

## 5.4 The First Attempts to Create a Legal Code of the Ethiopian Empire

According to Ethiopian tradition, Emperor Zärᵓa Yaᶜəqob (1434–1468), the nineteenth ruler of the Ethiopian Empire, contributed the most to the development of Ethiopian legislation during what is referred to as the golden period of the Solomonic dynasty. The son of Emperor David II, he ascended to the throne as a mature man with a well-thought-out concept for ruling the state, the basis of which were to be maximally centralised power structures and the unification of the state management system. Meanwhile, in his external policy, Zärᵓa Yaᶜəqob sought to expand Ethiopia's borders and strengthen its position in the north (Bartnicki and Mantel-Niećko 1978, p. 57). During the 34 years of his reign, the Emperor succeeded in achieving all of his stated goals, one of which was the creation of the first legal code of the Empire, encompassing both canonical and secular law.

Wanting to base his rule on written law rather than oral tradition, the Emperor ordered the clergy of the Ethiopian Orthodox Church to create a code of laws. According to Abera Jembere (1998, p. 184), the result of the priests' work was the *Mäṣähafä Fäws Mänfäsawi* ('Book of Spiritual Cure'), written around 1450 and consisting of 62 chapters. The authors of the book used primarily Christian sources, such as the Old Testament, *Didəsqəlya*,[19] 'Letter of Saint Peter to Clement of Rome', the 'Canons of Hippolytus (Abudilus)', and the already mentioned *Senodos* (Jembere 1998, p. 184).[20]

Another view on the text's origin is presented by Michael Kleiner (2005). He claims that the codex was compiled by Michael, the Coptic bishop of the cities of Atrīb and Malīǧ.[21] According to Kleiner, the work was based on an Arabic book, *Kitāb aṭ-Ṭibb ar-rūḥānī* ('Book of the Spiritual Cure'). The book is composed of 47 chapters, each containing canons for specific sins and their corresponding types of

---

[18] There was no professional army in Ethiopia until the fifteenth century. In the event of a military threat, all men of draft age were required to present themselves with their own equipment to the district administrator or emperor.

[19] *Didəsqəlya* (or *Didascalia Apostolorum*)—an early Christian treatise dating from the third century (c. 230), which is the first known attempt to write down a code of canon law. The code contains both legal and spiritual provisions (Meinardus 1999, p. 46).

[20] The *Senodos* was also highly regarded by the emperor himself, who included excerpts from it in his writings on both the functioning of the state and spiritual matters. In addition, often the provisions contained in the book (along with legal provisions from the *Didəsqəlya* and *Mäṣḥafä Kədan*) were adopted and quoted as legal bases when justifying the sentences passed by the emperor (Bausi 1992, p. 16).

[21] Atrīb and Malīǧ are historical cities in the Nile Delta. The authorship of Bishop Michael is also confirmed by Ferenc (1985, p. 286).

repentance. However, each of the known Ethiopian manuscripts contains no more than 34 chapters (Kleiner 2005, p. 509). It is also difficult to determine the time when the work appeared in Ethiopia. According to Kleiner (2005, p. 509), this could have occurred between 1300 and 1620 ce.[22]

In the nineteenth century, researchers studying Ethiopian manuscripts—August Dillmann, William Wright and Hermann Zotenberg—established that apart from the above-mentioned codex, there was another book with the same title. Its authorship is unknown, although it shares many features with the text compiled by Bishop Michael. Both *Mäṣähafä Fäws Mänfäsawi* texts have a similar arrangement of their content. Each begins with an introduction consisting of three chapters. These describe the sources and purpose of confession, repentance and absolution; they also provide information for sinners on how to deal with their transgressions. In addition, they contain canons on punishments for particular crimes, although the choice of canons is not the same in each book. Another feature that distinguishes this book from Bishop Michael's text is the lack of some chapters and the less clear arrangement of the canons, which are not ordered according to their content. Besides, the book rarely lists the sources from which legal citations are taken (Kleiner 2005, p. 509).

Whether the *Mäṣähafä Fäws Nänfäsawi* was authored by clerics of the Orthodox Church of Ethiopia or compiled by Bishop Michael of Atrīb and Malīğ, the important point is that the code did not find wider application among the Ethiopians, mainly because of the incompatibility of its provisions (originating from late Antique and early Medieval Byzantine and Oriental sources) with the realities of the Ethiopian Empire at the time.

## 5.5 The Origin of the *Fətḥa Nägäśt*

According to Ethiopian tradition, after the failed attempt at introducing the *Mäṣähafä Fäws Mänfäsawi* as a book of Ethiopian law, Zärᵓa Yaᶜəqob decided to create another code. This time, the Emperor looked abroad for inspiration. He ordered that a suitable book be brought from Egypt. This task was entrusted to an Egyptian named Petros Abdä Säyd (cf. Paulos Tzadua 2005, p. 534).[23]

[22] Interestingly, the Arabic text was written around the same time and in the same place as the *Nomokanōn*, one of the sources of the *Fətḥa Nägäśt*, the first code of law in the Ethiopian Empire.

[23] On Ethiopian tradition linked to the appearance of the *Fətḥa Nägäśt* in Ethiopia, see Negussie (2010), p. 16. A rather fantastic theory regarding its authorship is presented by Huyn and Kalmer (1935, p. 248) who attribute it to Emperor Iyasu I (1682–1706), adding that "reformer Jassus' impetus for the creation of a general applicable legal code was derived only from the observation of the various iniquities in the country". This hypothesis is not supported by any other historical sources, and the attribution to Emperor Iyasu I of the reforming of the law can only be due to the authors' approval of the Emperor's earlier actions.

The story of the book's importation into the country is only partially confirmed by historical sources. The book was in fact brought from Egypt and translated into Ge'ez by an Egyptian named Petros.[24] However, it is certain the book was not brought to Ethiopia during Zärᵓa Yaᶜəqob's time. The philological analysis proves the translation into Ge'ez must have been done in the sixteenth century, that is at least a hundred years after the reign of Emperor Zärᵓa Yaᶜəqob, while information about the use of the law can only be found in the chronicles of Emperors Śärṣä Dəngəl (1563–1597), Susənyos (1607–1632), Iyasu I (1682–1706), Iyoᵓas I (1730–1755) Tevodros II (1855–1868) and Mənilək II (1889–1913) (see Paulos Tzadua 2005, p. 534).

A meticulous study of the text itself as well as of other historical sources indicates that the text that formed the basis of the *Fəṯḥa Nägäśt* was compiled in the thirteenth century by the Egyptian jurist Abū'l-Faḍāᵓ'il bin al-ᵓAssāl aṣ-Ṣafī,[25] probably commissioned by Cyril III ibn Laqlaq (1235–1243), the infamous seventy-fifth patriarch of Alexandria.[26]

In fact, Abū'l-Faḍāᵓ'il bin al-ᵓAssāl aṣ-Ṣafī was asked to reform the code of canon law not by Cyril III, but by his opponents, who, by enacting the new code, wanted to curb the Alexandrian patriarch's practice of simony and introduce rules ensuring that the Church's revenues were used for their intended purpose, rather than as Cyril III's private funds. The beginning of the reformative work was announced during a synod at the Harat Zuwaylah Church on the western outskirts of Cairo. Fourteen bishops were present, along with Abū'l-Faḍāᵓ'il bin al-ᵓAssāl aṣ-Ṣafī, who compiled a set of new rules shortly after the synod. The bishops enacted this code on third September 1238 (Swanson 2010, pp. 176–177). Some scholars argue that the compilation of laws created by Abū'l-Faḍāᵓ'il bin al-ᵓAssāl aṣ-Ṣafī was intended not to reform the canon law, but solely for the use of the *episcopalis audientia*, or courts in Egypt presided over by Coptic bishops.[27] This, apparently, is confirmed in the introduction by the author himself, who wrote that his text was to serve judges in their work (Paulos Tzadua 1973, p. 115).

Unlike the Muslims, Egyptian Christians did not have a codified legal system. Not wanting to rely solely on religious texts, they decided to look for other sources of legal regulations. Around 1100 CE, the Egyptian Melchites began to study Greek

---

[24] His name can be found at the end of one of the manuscripts containing the codex (see Tzadua 2005, p. 534). An interesting hypothesis, according to which the translator into Ge'ez was a European missionary, has been presented by Sand ([1968], pp. 7–9).

[25] Abū'l-Faḍāᵓ'il bin al-ᵓAssāl aṣ-Ṣafī lived during what is referred to as the golden age of Coptic literature. He is credited with the authorship of numerous theological and legal works. For more, see Graff (1944), pp. 567, 602–606.

[26] Cyril III is said to have been the creator of canons reforming canon law ('On Baptism,' 'On Marriage,' 'On Wills,' 'On Inheritance,' 'On the Priesthood'). A second series of canons was issued by Cyril III in 1240. These deal primarily with the clergy, and their purpose was strengthening the authority of the Patriarch of Alexandria. See Meinardus (1999), p. 51; Nessim Youssef (2009), pp. 115–125; Labib (1991), p. 553.

[27] Copts under Fatimid rule had the right to conduct civil litigation, mainly in relation to family law and succession (Sand 1980, p. 75; Meinardus 1999, p. 65; Tzadua 1973, p. 115).

and Byzantine legal texts and then translate them into Arabic. Many of them were adopted by the Copts, who made some amendments, mainly to adapt the law to their own religion. Moreover, Coptic scholars replaced the names of Byzantine rulers in the headings of the texts with that of Emperor Constantine I the Great (306–337).[28]

Abū'l-Faḍāᵓ'il bin al-ᵓAssāl aṣ-Ṣafī titled his text *Collection of Canons*, although it is commonly known as the *Bin al-ᵓAssāl's Nomokanōn*.[29] The year 1238 is considered to be the date of its creation.[30] The book was written in Arabic because, as of the ninth century, Coptic—as the language of literature—was supplanted by Arabic.

## 5.6 The Sources of the First Part of the *Nomokanōn*

The *Nomokanōn* was divided into two parts. The first, consisting of 22 chapters, refers to ecclesiastical law. The second one, made up of 29 chapters, concerns civil and criminal law.

The first part consisted of excerpts from the books of the Old and New Testaments and the writings of the Church fathers. Negussie Andre Dominic (Negussie 2010) presented an analysis of the biblical sources of the codex. In his opinion, the most frequently cited passages from the Bible were the gospels, accounting for more than half of all citations in the book. A significant number of the provisions came from other books of the New Testament—the Acts of the Apostles, the letters of St John, St Peter and St Paul (to the Romans, Corinthians, Galatians, Ephesians, Colossians, Thessalonians, Hebrews, Timothy, Titus). Other quotations in the first part of the *Nomokanōn* are from the Old Testament (the Pentateuch and the Book of Kings, the Books of the Prophets: Joshua, Samuel, Isaiah, Jeremiah Ezekiel, Daniel, Hosea, and the Books of Psalms and Proverbs) (Negussie 2010, p. 34).

Among the writings of the Church Fathers, which are cited in the first part of the code, the following can be distinguished:

- The *Didascalia Apostolorum*, cited 110 times[31];
- 'Letter of St Paul to Clement of Rome', cited 13 times;

[28] The change made by Coptic scholars should be seen as the source behind the Ethiopian tradition claiming that the book was brought to the Empire by Zärᵓa Yaᶜəqob. The Ethiopian ruler was nicknamed Constantine, from which might have emerged the mistake attributing the authorship of the book to him. See Sand (1980), p. 76.

[29] Many texts on legal issues produced during this period are called 'nomokanons.' These were texts of a scholarly rather than legislative nature. However, due to the esteem in which Abū'l-Faḍāᵓ'il bin al-ᵓAssāl aṣ-Ṣafī was held, his *Nomokanōn* was treated in Ethiopia not as a textbook, but as a code of law. See Sand (1968), pp. 7–9.

[30] According to the oldest known manuscripts, the Egyptian lawyer completed writing the codex in September 1238 (Sand 1980, p. 75).

[31] The number of citations have been provided after Negussie (2010),, pp. 36–38. Cf. Meinardus (1999), p. 46.

- 'Letter of St Peter to Timothy of Alexandria',[32] cited once;
- The Canons of the Synod of Ankara (314 CE), cited 6 times;
- The Canons of the First Council of Nicaea I (325 CE), cited once;
- The Canons of the Councils of Antioch (341 CE), cited 16 times;
- The Canons of the Councils in Laodicea (343–381 CE), cited 20 times;
- The Canons of the Council in Gangra (ca. 345 CE), cited 6 times;
- The Canons of the Councils in Carthage (419 CE), cited 8 times;
- The Canons of the Second Council of Nicaea[33] (787 CE), cited 69 times;
- The Canons of Hippolytus, Patriarch of Rome, cited 34 times;
- Canons of St Basil the Great, Bishop of Caesarea, quoted 96 times;
- Laws taken from the works of St Gregory of Nazianzus (1 quote) and St John Chrysostom (3 quotes);
- *The Canons of the Kings*, quoted 17 times[34];
- 'The canons promulgated by the Apostles, written down and distributed by Clement, a disciple of St Peter, to all his disciples and the faithful' (Paulos Tzadua 1973, p. 113; Negussie 2010, p. 37), cited 166 times.

Paulos Tzadua (1973, p. 113) also states that one source of the *Nomokanōn* were the canons of the Council of Serdica, but documents from this synod are not cited therein; thus, it is difficult to determine whether this was indeed the source of the codex.[35] Paulos Tzadua (1973, p. 113) also claims that the other sources included "the works of some of the Holy Fathers [...] and some of the Patriarchs of Alexandria", but without providing their names, perhaps meaning those bishops of Egypt who wrote commentaries on the 'Precepts of the Old Testament,' i.e., a compilation of moral principles and religious regulations contained in the Pentateuch, subjected to Christian interpolation, and being one of the four parts of *The Canons of Kings*.

Analysis of the theological texts presented above indicates that some of them had already been used in other books that served as a basis for creation of law in Ethiopia. For example, the Old Testament, the *Didəsqəlya*, 'The Canons of Hippolytus' and 'The Letter of St Paul to Clement of Rome' were the main sources on which the

[32] This source is not listed by Tzadua (1973, p. 115).

[33] Paulos Tzadua does not list the Second Council of Nicaea as a source for the first part of the *Nomokanōn*, while Negussie Andre Dominic does. Since the latter gives the number of quotations from the canons of this council found in *Nomokanōn*, I concluded that these canons were in fact one of the sources. Cf. Tzadua (1973), p. 113; Negussie (2010), p. 36.

[34] *The Canons of the Kings* are four books, legal and religious in nature, which contain regulations of canon law enacted at the Council of Nicaea. These books were to serve Constantine I the Great during the court hearings he presided over. A translation of the *Canons* into Latin (done by the Maronite Abramus Echellnsis) was published in a collection compiled by Giovanni Domenico Mansi, *Sanctorum Conciliorum nova et amplissima Collectio* (1758–98). Cf. Tzadua and Strauss (1968), p. XVI; Negussie (2010), p. 32.

[35] Ethiopian researchers do not provide any specific sources or authors of the regulations. See Tzadua (1973), p. 113.

*Mäṣähafä Fäws Mänfäsawi* code was based, while the canons of the Councils of Gangra and Antioch were among the sources of the *Senodos.*[36]

## 5.7 The Sources of the Second Part of the *Nomokanōn*

Much effort has gone into identifying the sources of the second part of Abū l-Faḍāᵓ'il bin al-ᵓAssāl aṣ-Ṣafī's work. It has been established that in this case he made little use of the theological works mentioned above. In this part of the *Nomokanōn*, the author relied primarily on *The Canons of Kings*, the authorship of which was attributed to the participants of the Council of Nicaea (for more, see Graff 1944, pp. 618–620). The collection consisted of four books. The last of these was fairly quickly identified as the (aforementioned) 'Precepts of the Old Testament,' i.e., excerpts from the Pentateuch accompanied by interpretations of the laws contained therein (Paulos Tzadua 1973, p. 113). This is the only book in *The Canon of Kings* which has a religious nature. Its other parts are secular and they originate from Byzantium (Sand 1980, p. 76). The first book is the 'Procheiron' (also known as 'Procheiros Nomos'), a vademecum of Roman law issued between 870 and 879 by Byzantine Emperor Basil I (867–886) and his sons, Alexander and Leo. The book contains the most important provisions of public and civil law in forty paragraphs. The Greek text was most likely translated into Arabic by the Melchites in the late twelfth and early thirteenth centuries, and it was this translation that was used by aṣ-Ṣafī when writing the *Nomokanōn*. It was identified as the first book of *The Canon of Kings* in 1859 by M. Amari, which was confirmed in 1883 by W. Riedel. Further research by Carlo Alfonso Nallino proved that the *Fətḥa Nägäśt* contains more than a hundred quotations from the 'Procheiron' (Sand 1968, p. 14).

Another text included in *The Canon of Kings* is 'The Syro-Roman Law Book', written between 476 and 480,[37] which was a compilation of the laws of the Roman Empire and the local laws of the Roman provinces. The work is cited ninety-eight times in the *Fətḥa Nägäśt*. 'The Syro-Roman Law Book' was translated into Syriac in 750 and into Arabic in 1100 (Sand [1968], p. 14). The latter became the basis for the second part of *The Canon of Kings.*

The third book of the *Canon* was the most difficult to identify, partly because the author of the *Nomokanōn* himself misstated his sources, and partly because the translator into Ge'ez confused the abbreviations used in the book (Sand 1968, p. 15). Both Reidel and Nallino assumed, based on philological analysis, that the third book was based on an Arabic translation of the canons promulgated after the Council of Nicaea. It was not until 1947 that Italian scholar G.A. Constanzo,

[36] Some manuscripts from the nineteenth century unified the legal provisions found in *Senodos* and those in the *Fətḥa Nägäśt*.

[37] The code is also known as 'Legislation of the Emperors Constantine, Theodosius and Leo' (Sand 1980, p. 77).

analysing the contents of the *Fəṭḥa Nägäśt* paragraph by paragraph, proved that at least twenty-four quotations in the *Nomokanōn* are from the *Ecloga*—the second (after the *Justinian Code* in the sixth century) codification of Byzantine law, proclaimed in 726 by Byzantine Emperor Leo III Isaurian (AD 717–741) and his son and co-emperor Constantine V Copronimus (AD 741–775). The *Ecloga* was intended to adapt the existing *Justinian Code* to the realities of the time. Moreover, the code was written in Greek rather than Latin, making it accessible to a wider audience and more useful for judges during trials ('Ecloga' 1998). The quotations in the *Nomokanōn* come probably from an excerpt made in the thirteenth century by the Melchites from an earlier Arabic translation containing the 'Nicene Canons', the writings produced during the Council of Nicaea.

## 5.8 Islamic Sources of the *Nomokanōn*

The text prepared by Abū l-Faḍāᵓ'il bin al-ᵓAssāl aṣ-Ṣafī, although based on Christian sources, contains nevertheless elements of Islamic law, as interpreted by the Malikite school.[38] This was due to the socio-political situation in Egypt, as mentioned earlier. Islamic influence can be seen primarily in the chapters on trade, divorce, charity legates, court rulings and court procedures (Sand 1980, p. 79). In some cases, the provisions of Islamic law overlapped with those of Roman law, thus it is difficult to identify on which code the author of the *Nomokanōn* relied. One such example is the Roman provision of *portio legitima*, concerning the non-receivable portion of a deceased person's inheritance ('Portio legitima' n.d. [online]), which does not differ from the Islamic provision on inheritance. Another example are the regulations regarding trade (Sand 1980, p. 79).

The influence of Islamic thought can also be seen in the construction of the codex and, more specifically, in the thematic arrangement of the book. The presence in the *Nomokanōn* of chapters on clothing and diet is closer to the concept of Muslim *fikh*[39] than Roman *ius civile*.

[38] The Malikite school—one of the four orthodox schools of Muslim law, whose founder was Malik ibn Anas of Medina. The primary sources of the Malikite legal system were the Quran, the *sunna* (the Prophet's way of conduct and behaviour) and the *'urf*, or the customary law of Medina. The Malikites developed the principle of *istislak* (general benefit) and applied the principle of *ijma*, or the consent of all jurists or of the whole group. See Cottart (1991), pp. 278–283.

[39] *Fikh*—the Muslim study of human law and duties, which includes both theoretical considerations and studies into what is permitted and what is forbidden. See Schacht (1991), pp. 886–891.

## 5.9 The Structure of the *Fətḥa Nägäśt*

According to the researchers cited above, there is no doubt that the Ethiopian *Fətḥa Nägäśt* is a literal translation from Arabic to Ge'ez of Abū l-Faḍāᵓ'il bin al-ᵓAssāl aṣ-Ṣafī's *Nomokanōn,* except for the initial part of the preface and the appendix (Sand 1980, p. 74).

It is understandable that a book that was to become the primary source of law in the Empire had to receive an Ethiopian preface. The appendix, the authorship of which remains unclear, is titled "The chapter on succession, on which the esteemed *Abba* Cyril, Patriarch of Alexandria, agreed with the bishops, chiefs and magistrates" (Paulos Tzadua and Strauss 1968, p. 313).[40] The passage is not found in earlier versions of the *Nomokanōn*, but it was also edited by Abū l-Faḍāᵓ'il bin al-ᵓAssāl aṣ-Ṣafī. It has been proven that this chapter is a literal translation into Ge'ez of a chapter from the canons of Cyril III ibn Laqlaq (Sand 1980, p. 78) which stands in contradiction to information found in the preface of the *Nomokanōn* (and in the *Fətḥa Nägäśt*). The appendix was based on the works of Abbas Qozmos (most likely referring to Cosmas III, who was Patriarch of Alexandria from 921–933) and on legal texts of unidentified authorship. The Amharic glossary added to the appendix, on the other hand, cites the works of Abba Gabriel as its source. This may be referring to another Alexandrian patriarch, Gabriel II ibn Tariq (1131–1145), who formulated the law of succession (Sand 1980, p. 78).

Similar to the *Nomokanōn*, the *Fətḥa Nägäśt* is divided into two parts. The first part, which consists of 22 chapters, deals with ecclesiastical and spiritual matters—the rights and duties of patriarchs, bishops, priests and deacons and the laity, the celebration of religious festivals, ministry and offerings to the church.

Part Two, dealing with secular affairs, consists of 29 chapters. Its provisions deal with such issues as commercial matters, donations, loans, judicial appointments, criminal matters, slavery and marriage. The book ends with the appendix discussed earlier.

## 5.10 Regulations Related to Marriage in *Fətḥa Nägäśt*

Particularly relevant for the present study is Chapter 24 of the code, titled "Betrothal, dowry, marriage and what follows them."[41] It contains six subsections:

---

[40] The title of the chapter does not provide an accurate portrayal of Cyril III's relationship with "his bishops, his chiefs and his magistrates". The laws created during that period and attributed to the Patriarch of Alexandria are in fact laws created by his opponents within the church. The purpose of introducing these laws was to limit the power of Cyril III, who used it for particularistic interests. For more, see Swanson (2010), pp. 175–177 and Burmester and Khater (1970), pp. 226–228.

[41] Provisions related to the institution of marriage are also found in other chapters of the *Fətḥa Nägäśt*. For example, in the chapter on slavery, there is a provision that a free woman may not

- [The purposes of marriage]
- Promise of marriage
- Betrothal
- The duty of the father towards his son concerning marriage
- Definition of marriage and matters concerning it
- The marriage which may be dissolved,

Although the chapter contains many quotations from the Old Testament, the provisions are derived from the 'Procheiron' described earlier, as mentioned by the translator into English, Abba Paulos Tzadua (Paulos Tzadua and Strauss 1968, p. 133).

The first subsection talks about the goals of marriage, the most important of which is to have offspring (Paulos Tzadua and Strauss 1968, p. 130; Fətḥa Nägäśt 1990 a.m. 1998, p. 206). Although the code allows multiple marriages (but not simultaneous, bigamy is prohibited), the first wife is the most important. The code states that:

> …[a second marriage] is inferior to the first. With respect to this second wife is prescribed in the canons that she shall not have the nuptial blessing, but upon her the penitential prayer shall be said.[42] […] the second marriage lowers the honored, namely the priests, from their honor; […] A third marriage is despicable and beyond this there is no lawful marriage among us (Paulos Tzadua and Strauss 1968, p. 132; Fətḥa Nägäśt 1990 a.m. 1998, pp. 206–207).

This provision stands in stark contrast to the practice of polygamy, which was widespread in Ethiopia during the reign of Zärᵓa Yaᶜəqob, who is credited with bringing the *Fətḥa Nägäśt* to Ethiopia.[43] Also other rulers, who certainly applied the code in passing their judgments, failed to follow the principles expressed in the first subsection. For example, Emperor Mənilək II (1889–1913) was married three times, to Alṭaš, Bafäna and Ṭaytu, and his grandson *Ləǧ* Iyasu married as many as ten women during his short reign (Augustyniak 2009a, pp. 56–61). Of course, most of the rulers' marriages were performed in civil ceremonies, but nothing in the *Fətḥa Nägäśt* confirms that the above-quoted provision refers only to unions performed in church.

The second subchapter, consisting of four parts, describes the cases in which a marriage cannot be concluded. It reiterates the provisions regarding the prohibition of bigamy and fourth and subsequent marriages. It is also forbidden to marry nuns,

---

marry a slave, nor live in his house, nor live with him, even if she has the consent of his master (Tzadua and Strauss 1968, p. 175).

[42] It is not explained why a penitential prayer is to be said during the ceremony for a woman who is in fact marrying for the first time. Perhaps the confusion is due to a mistranslation of the book's records, and it is more a prayer of thanksgiving. Cf. Fritsch (2008), pp. 318–321; Burmester (1967), p. 143.

[43] Despite his legendary piety, Emperor Zärᵓa Yaᶜəqob did not observe monogamy required by the sacrament of marriage. He was, however, very strict with his family members who did not observe this law. 'Amdä Mäsqäl, the Emperor's son-in-law, was accused of bigamy and sentenced to exile, although this might have been an excuse to remove him from the court, as an alleged leader of a conspiracy against Zärᵓa Yaᶜəqob. Cf. Tamrat (1972), pp. 240–243; Perruchon (1893), pp. 10–12, 38, 94.

women convicted of adultery, divorced women and widows, but only during the period of mourning for a previous husband (however, it is allowed to make matrimonial proposals to them during this time) (Paulos Tzadua and Strauss 1968, p. 137). Moreover, it is forbidden to marry a woman who has reached the age of sixty. This prohibition is understandable, since according to Christian teaching and the above-quoted chapter on marriage in the *Fətḥa Nägäśt*, the purpose of such a union is procreation, and it is unlikely that a woman of this age would be capable of giving birth to a child and raising it. Moreover, it is highly likely that this would not be the first marriage for such a woman, and subsequent relationships—as also noted earlier—were not welcomed.

Noteworthy is also the fifteenth point of this subsection, which prohibits forced marriage, citing kidnapping as one form of coercion (Paulos Tzadua and Strauss 1968, p. 138). The provision stands in stark contrast to the customary law of the Amhara, who accepted *ṭäläfa*, or marriage by kidnapping, as mentioned in the second chapter of the present study.

The 'Promise of Marriage' subsection also explicitly states what degree of consanguinity and affinity is permissible for marriage. According to one opinion quoted in the comment to the relevant prescription, four degrees of kinship are sufficient, in line "with the canons of the Apostles" (Paulos Tzadua and Strauss 1968, p. 134). However, according to the second opinion, the degrees of affinity should be six or even seven times removed. The final decision was to be made by priests on the basis of observation, taking into account, e.g., the size of particular Christian communities. The restrictions on marriage apply not only to relatives and affinities, but also to godparents and godchildren, as discussed in the second point of the subsection.

The subsection 'Betrothal' is divided into three parts. The first defines what a betrothal is and who can act as matchmaker for the bride-to-be. The code makes it clear that marriages should be arranged, and the wedding should take place 2 years after the betrothal. If the wedding ceremony does not take place after this period, the betrothal can be broken off (Paulos Tzadua and Strauss 1968, p. 138).

This part of the code also makes reference to marriage by kidnapping. The *Fətḥa Nägäśt* stipulates that if a betrothed woman is kidnapped and has sexual intercourse with her kidnapper and then manages to escape, she must return to her fiancé, provided he accepts her. If the man repudiates her, the woman must return and marry the kidnapper, provided he does not already have a wife (Paulos Tzadua and Strauss 1968, p. 139).

The second and third parts of the subsection deal with the gifts that the future spouses exchange during the engagement party. The code enumerates exactly which gifts and in what number should be returned in the event of a broken engagement or the death of one of the betrothed.

Part two of the subsection also provides information on the appropriate age for marriage. The law in the *Fətḥa Nägäśt* states that a man should be 20–25 years old, while a woman—12-15 years old.[44] Interestingly, there was a note added to the above provision:

> The age of twenty years is for the sons of wealthy families, who are supposed to be learned enough at that age. The age of twenty-five years is for the poor and unlearned young men. The same reasoning applies to the ages given for women (Paulos Tzadua and Strauss 1968, p. 140, n. 64).

As in the case of polygamy, this provision was in conflict with customary practice. The marriages of the children and grandchildren of Emperor Mənilək II, discussed below, may serve as examples.

The emperor, wanting to consolidate his grandson *Ləǧ* Iyasu's position at court before his death, arranged his marriage to Aster Mängäša (also known as Romanä Wärq), daughter of *Ras* Mängäš Yoḥannəs, and granddaughter of the previous emperor, Yoḥannəs IV (1872–1889). At the time, the bride was seven years old and the groom was five years older. Although this was a purely political marriage, it conflicted with the laws contained in the *Fətḥa Nägäśt*. Nonetheless, this did not hinder the union. Moreover, according to the *Ləǧ* Iyasu's chronicler, Gäbrä Ǝgziᵓabəḥer Elyas, the marriage to Aster Mängäša was the only "legitimate union" (Gäbrä Ǝgziᵓabəḥer Elyas & R.K. Molvaer 1994, 358) entered into by the heir-designate.

Similarly, the marriage of the youngest daughter of Emperor Mənilək II, later Empress Zäwditu (1916–1930), did not exactly conform to the rules set in the *Fətḥa Nägäśt*. Although the ceremony itself was held in accordance with the *Fətḥa Nägäśt*, Zäwditu Mənilək was seven years old when marrying her first husband, Ras Arᵓaya Śəllase, son of Emperor Yoḥannəs IV, then fifteen. This marriage was also a political one and it did not last long, as six years later *Ras* Arᵓaya died of smallpox (Zewde 2003, p. 134).

Subsection four is the shortest, and its title, 'The duty of the father towards his son concerning marriage', reflects the content. It also contains provisions for a woman who has reached the age of 25 and whose parents do not consent to marriage. In such a case, a woman, wishing to marry, can ask officials to provide her with a dowry according to the social status and wealth of her family. Moreover, if she is 'independent,' she can choose a husband on her own, without parental consent (Paulos Tzadua and Strauss 1968, p. 141).

The subsection entitled 'Definition of marriage and matters concerning it' is the longest and consists of three parts. The first contains the definition of marriage, which is to be the union of a man and a woman who unanimously declare their desire "[...] to live in harmony, to provide the means by which they may help each other in providing for their own needs, and to procreate offspring who will survive them" (Paulos Tzadua and Strauss 1968, p. 142). The wedding ceremony should take place in the presence of priests and witnesses.

[44] In the previous subsection of this chapter, it was mentioned that a betrothal between persons under the age of seven was prohibited.

The second part reiterates the provisions regarding the age of the future spouses and the consent to the union, which must be given by both the interested parties themselves and their parents or guardians. This section also indicates that no wedding can take place in secret, that is, without the participation of a priest and the recitation of a prayer for the spouses. During the wedding mass, the spouses should receive communion together, and their heads be decorated with crowns. If they do not receive it, their marriage will not be considered legitimate, because "it is the prayer which hands over the women to the man, and the man to the woman" (Paulos Tzadua and Strauss 1968, p. 142).

The above provision clearly indicates that the provisions in the *Fətḥa Nägäśt* regarding marriage refer to a *qal kidan bäqurban* union—a type of marriage that was only possible for Christians, as it required communion to be received by the spouses. The code does not include any provisions for unions between people of a faith other than Christianity. Only in the third part of this subsection is it stated that if a Christian wants to marry a person of another faith (male or female alike), they must get them to convert to Christianity. If they do not comply with this provision, they will be removed from the community (Paulos Tzadua and Strauss 1968, p. 144).

The third part is made up of 11 sections. The first is divided into five paragraphs, with each one referring to the subsequent marriage.

*Fətḥa Nägäśt* allows remarriage, but the ceremony is to be held without receiving communion and without a coronation (*qurban*). Instead of a mass for the couple, a prayer of absolution should be said. Before the marriage takes place, the future spouses, if they have children from previous relationships, should ensure that they will not be deprived of their inheritance in the event of a parent's death. It is also noted that if a priest remarries, he will be demoted. If he decides to marry a third time, he will be removed from the community and considered impure (Paulos Tzadua and Strauss 1968, p. 143).

A woman who wants to remarry must also comply with other, additional rules. As discussed above, a woman over 25 years old could choose her husband without the consent of her parents or guardians. However, if this would be her second wedding, she should ask her father for advice, even when she is financially independent. If the father is dead, the bride-to-be should seek advice from other family members. If the family is not satisfied with the woman's chosen candidate, the provincial administrator must approve the union. If the candidate chosen by the family is equal in social and property status to the woman's candidate, then the dispute will be resolved according to the bride's wishes.

According to the code, a third marriage shows a person's depravity and should be avoided. However, a footnote to this section provides a circumvention: if a man wants to marry again, he should fast strictly for 5 years.[45]

As already mentioned, the fourth marriage is a sign of promiscuity, and it should not be recognised as legitimate, with children from such a union having less rights

[45] The fasting provision does not apply to women. A woman who wants to marry for the third time is called "a dirty vessel in the Church!" (Tzadua and Strauss 1968, p. 143).

to inherit property and titles. Bigamy is also prohibited. A man who has two wives at the same time cannot attend Mass or receive communion. He will live outside his community until he decides to abandon his second wife, and if the bigamist is a priest, he will be stripped of his priesthood.

The above provision is another example of how statutory law diverged from the practice in Ethiopia. Various reports relevant to this aspect of Ethiopian culture indicate that *dämoz* marriages were popular among soldiers and merchants in the Empire. Under the code, a man with a wife married in church and a *dämoz* wife would be a bigamist. However, it was rare for men to stand trial for this. Moreover, children from a *dämoz*-type union had the same inheritance rights as children from a legitimate union (Augustyniak 2009b).

Section two of part three of *Fəṭḥa Nägäśt* describes marriages between Christians and representatives of other religions. As mentioned earlier, such marriages were possible as long as the dissenter converted to his partner's religion. If the marriage was performed without conversion, then the Christian woman was expelled from the community. She could return only if she abandoned her husband and showed repentance. She would then come back to the community "as an apostate converted from her impiety" (Paulos Tzadua and Strauss 1968, p. 144). If she underwent a purification ritual, she could remain among the other faithful and receive communion.

The code is silent on whether a man married to a representative of another religion faced a similar fate. What is known, however, is that if a father married his daughter to a dissenter against her will, he would be removed from his community. The man would be allowed to return to the community, as long as he separated his daughter from her husband and paid a fine corresponding to his property status.[46]

A father who gave his daughter away to a dissenter without knowing that he was not a Christian would also be banished from the community. This situation would be seen as his failure to fulfil his matchmaking duties, because he had not checked the social and property background of the candidate for a husband.

The third section deals with the period of time that must elapse between one marriage and another. A man may not marry again earlier than 1 year after his wife's death. If he does, everything he inherited from her shall be taken away. A woman, on the other hand, may not remarry before the expiration of 10 months after her husband's death. If she fails to meet this requirement, all of her husband's property will be taken from her "and she shall not be honored like other, respectable women" (Paulos Tzadua and Strauss 1968, p. 144).

The fourth and fifth sections deal with the management of joint property. According to *Fəṭḥa Nägäśt*, if a husband becomes impoverished because he spends all his property on wedding gifts, he has the right to use his wife's property. If she agrees to let her husband use her property and then revokes her decision, it is the man who is in the right.

The next four sections deal with the periods when one should refrain from sexual intercourse. As in most African cultures, there is a strict prohibition of sexual

[46] Social ostracism did not affect the daughter, who remained a member of the Christian community.

intercourse during menstruation and postpartum in Ethiopian law. According to the *Fətḥa Nägäśt*, children conceived during this time will be born leprous. One should also refrain from intercourse during fast and Holy Week, as the latter is supposed to be a time dedicated to despairing over the death of Jesus, while the fasting period is to be dedicated to prayer only (Paulos Tzadua and Strauss 1968, p. 145).

The tenth section describes the procedure to be followed by a wife accused by her husband of infidelity. If the husband had suspicions about the woman's faithfulness, he was to bring her before the church altar. The priest would pour water into a clay bowl and add a handful of earth from under the altar into it. The woman then had to swear on the Ark of the Covenant and the Holy Spirit that she would answer the priest's questions truthfully. After taking the oath, the priest would ask the woman the question, "Has a strange man committed adultery with you?" If the woman denied it, the priest would recite the following formula:

> If you are pure of what your husband suspects, drink then this water and no evil shall harm you. But if you have been foolish and have sworn falsely, let the curse of God be upon you and may you be taken a slave far from your family; let this water you drink spoil all your body and dissolve all your members and let your body be dissolved forever. (Paulos Tzadua and Strauss 1968, p. 147)[47]

As a sign of acceptance of any potential punishment, the woman would say the word "Amen" three times and drink the water given to her. If the woman lied, the water she drank would poison her body. If she was innocent, she was to give birth to a boy "of whom she will rejoice" (Paulos Tzadua and Strauss 1968, p. 147), while the husband would forget his accusations.

The same section describes a situation in which a husband has accused his newly married wife of not being a virgin on their wedding day. If his accusations proved false, the man was to be punished for his sinful words, and the accused woman remained his wife until her death. However, if the accusations were confirmed, the spouses would separate, and the woman cursed because she had disgraced her father's house and deprived him of his honour (Paulos Tzadua and Strauss 1968, p. 147).

The last section deals with restrictions on a woman's participation in Holy Mass. According to the law, a woman cannot cross the threshold of the church during menstruation and the postpartum period. She cannot take communion "even if she is the wife of the king" (Paulos Tzadua and Strauss 1968, p. 148), and a priest who would give her communion was to be demoted.

The duration of the ban on a woman entering a church depended on the sex of the child she had given birth to. If it was a boy, the ban lasted 40 days, if a girl—80. Restrictions on attending mass also applied to the midwife. If she had attended the

[47] The procedure associated with the 'ritual of bitter water' was taken from the Old Testament (the Fourth Book of Moses, Chap. 5, 11–31). According to one of the early Christian apocrypha ('Protoevangelium of James'), Mary was subjected to such a test. See Starowieyski (1980), p. 197. The absence of other sources confirming that such a procedure was in use in Ethiopia raises the suspicion that what is described here was intended only as a warning to potential adulteresses, rather than an actual ritual to which women suspected of infidelity were subjected.

delivery of a boy, she could not cross the threshold of the church for 20 days. If she had participated in the delivery of a girl, the ban was in effect for 40 days. Midwives were also forbidden to attend to an adulteress in labour (Paulos Tzadua and Strauss 1968, p. 148).

The sixth subsection is titled 'The marriage which may be dissolved'. The *Fəṭḥa Nägäśt* provides three main reasons why a marriage can cease to exist. The first is when one of the spouses desires to become a member of the clergy. Dissolution of marriage can also occur when the union has not been consummated. In view of the law, non-consummation of marriage refers not only to a lack of physical contact between the spouses, but also to a situation when the husband cannot give the woman a child, signifying he cannot fulfil the purposes of marriage, as discussed above. If a child does not come forth within 3 years of the wedding ceremony, the marriage can be dissolved (Tzadua and Strauss 1968, p. 149).

The third reason for the cessation of marriage is a situation when living separately, the parties would have "[a] life less burdensome and more agreeable" (Tzadua and Strauss 1968, p. 149), and such a burden might be a spouse's infidelity and violence in the relationship.

In the case of a woman's infidelity, the man must present proof of her adultery. If the evidence is verified, the marriage can be dissolved, and the man will receive all the wedding gifts and double the cost of the dowry. In addition, if the divorcing couple has no children, the man will receive one-third of the woman's outfits. If the divorcees have children, they will receive everything.

If a cheating wife is caught *in flagrante delicto*, the lover will also be punished, and will have to pay her husband the equivalent of the dowry the woman's father gave her during the marriage. If the wife's lover has a wife, the latter shall take all her dowry and betrothal gifts. If the couple has children, all property will belong to them, and its management will be handled by the cheater's partner.[48]

As for a man's infidelity, the text of the code itself does not mention what punishment awaits him, but in gloss 24 the following information is provided:

> It is right that the punishment for the adultery of the woman be greater than that of the man. This is so established because the adultery of the man is such that it is not necessary for the woman to be separated from him since the main aim of the law is to remove the difficulties which come upon men in their relationships.
>
> [...] And [it is right that the punishment for the adultery of woman be greater than that of man] because the lineage is maintained if the woman leads a honest life. If she commits adultery, the descent and the paternal lineage is corrupted. Also, the virgin spoils the form of her virginity by adultery, while for a man this is not so. (Tzadua and Strauss 1968, p. 153)

The same gloss contains information about what will happen if a man is caught committing adultery in his own home. In such a case, the cheater's wife will take

[48] This part of the code includes a definition of an adulteress: a woman who "[...] drinks against the advice of her husband with another man, or baths or jokes or goes to a hunting place or to a gathering while her husband is absent, or who passes the night out her home in another house". A similar description of an adulterer is not provided. See Tzadua and Strauss (1968), p. 152.

away the clothes she brought to the man's home after the wedding, pre-wedding gifts and one-third of the man's property.

In addition to the main reasons for divorce listed above, the *Fəṭḥa Nägäśt* lists five others.

One of them is when a woman is found "of a structure different from a woman's nature and not suitable for a man" (Tzadua and Strauss 1968, p. 150). The code does not define whether this refers to a woman's homosexuality or hermaphroditism. According to the law, a man can get divorced if he finds out about the woman's preference "on the first day of his contact with her, or on the second or third day [...]" (Tzadua and Strauss 1968, p. 150) and consults a priest on the matter. The woman would be forbidden to remarry, while her father or guardian would be excluded from the community and would not be allowed to cross the thresholds of the church and receive communion. However, if the husband knew about his wife's preference, but kept it a secret and had sexual relations with her, he will be excluded from the community (Tzadua and Strauss 1968, p. 150).

Another reason provided for dissolving a marriage is the fear that one of the spouses is possessed by the devil, which, most probably, also applied to all mental illnesses. According to the code, if this situation occurs during the marriage, the healthy spouse must be patient and accept this condition, i.e., the marriage cannot be dissolved. However, if the woman was possessed by the devil before the wedding, and her condition was concealed from her fiancé, the marriage may be dissolved and the man can take another wife. The dowry and everything the woman received from her father will remain in her possession. The cattle that belonged to her will remain hers, or she will receive a financial equivalent. The calves born from these animals and other products (such as hide) will be divided equally between the spouses. Slaves were also divided between them. In addition, if a man has used up some of his wife's belongings, he must reimburse her for them (Tzadua and Strauss 1968, p. 150).

A second opinion is given in the code regarding how to deal with cases in which the wife is not of full mental capacity. If the woman became ill after the marriage, the man can request the dissolution of the marriage, but he must give the woman the entire dowry and all the clothes he gave her. If the woman was ill before the marriage and the husband knew about it, at the separation he retains what he gave to his wife, leaving her only the clothing.

Another cause for divorce may be that one of the spouses has contracted leprosy. Two legal opinions are quoted under this point. According to the first, divorce is impossible in such a case. The second opinion, the "more just" one (Tzadua and Strauss 1968, p. 150), allows the cessation of marriage on the condition that the man returns the woman's entire dowry and properly provides for her. If he decides to stay with her, he must ensure she can lead a dignified life according to his means, since "what befell her was not by her or his will" (Tzadua and Strauss 1968, p. 150).

Another discussed case is the imprisonment of one of the spouses. As long as it remains unknown if and when the prisoner will be released, the marriage must continue for 5 years. During this time, neither spouse can remarry, and if they do, they would be deprived of the gifts they received during the wedding ceremony. After this time, the marriage can be dissolved.

If a man is in captivity, a woman must wait 10 years before requesting dissolution of the marriage, but only when it remains unknown whether the man is alive or when bail has been posted for him and he has not returned.

If the man has gone off to war and it remains unknown whether he is alive, the woman must wait 2 years (from his departure) until she applies for termination of the marriage. If the husband's commander provides information about his death, the woman must request confirmation. Only then can a mass for the deceased be arranged, and the woman is then given written permission (with signatures of witnesses present at the mass) to remarry, but the wedding ceremony must take place at earliest 1 year after the permission is issued. If the woman objects to this rule, then both she and her future husband will be punished as adulterers.

Witnesses who gave false testimony regarding the death of a woman's husband would be demoted and forced to pay a fine of ten pounds (about four kilograms) of gold. If, however, the allegedly deceased husband was alive, he could do as he saw fit—start a new life or take his spouse back (Tzadua and Strauss 1968, p. 151).

A marriage can be dissolved also when one spouse conspires against the other, or knows of such a conspiracy and does not inform the spouse. If the spouses are hostile to each other, and the instigator of the conflict is the woman, then the man "shall be patient with her and be merciful to her until she repents of her [evil ways] and returns to the good" (Tzadua and Strauss 1968, p. 152). If this does not happen, the man had to bring her before a priest, who was the negotiator between the parties. If this did not help, the couple had to go to the bishop for advice.

If the woman disobeyed the bishop and ran away from her husband, the bishop had to bring her back. If the woman continued to be disobedient and refused to return to her husband's home, the bishop would spill the dust from his shoes on the threshold of their home. This meant that the woman's husband could act according to his own conscience. He could stay with his quarrelsome wife or take a new one. However, if the husband was the cause of his wife's quarrelsomeness, he had to stay with her. If the husband refused to abide by this decision, he could not cross the threshold of the church or take communion (Tzadua and Strauss 1968, p. 153).

Most of the reasons described above relate to situations in which a woman breaks the rules. However, at the end of the subsection, there is a list included (without exhaustive explanation) of the reasons why a woman may leave her husband's home:

> If the husband schemes against the life of the wife in any manner; or if others so plot against her and he knows it and does not make her aware of it; or if he schemes against her purity and gives her to one who sins with her.[49] (Tzadua and Strauss 1968, p. 153)

[49] If there are witnesses confirming that the husband forced his wife to commit adultery, but did not achieve his goal, this is sufficient reason for the woman to leave the man's house, taking with her all the gifts and clothes she received before the marriage (Tzadua and Strauss 1968, p. 153).

## 5.11 Marriage Among the Clergy

The first part of the *Fəthạ Nägäśt*, dealing with the rights and duties of clergy and laity, does not cover marriage-related issues as a coherent topic; however, such information can be found in the various subsections of this part. In chapter five, which refers to bishops, it is stated that in order to become a priest, eighteen requirements must be met. In addition to personal qualities and health, a prospective clergyman must lead a virtuous life and be "the husband of one wife" (Tzadua and Strauss 1968, p. 24).[50] The chapter also notes that an acceptable wife is only one who has been married in a church (a *qal kidan bäqurban* marriage). The chapter goes on to say that a married cleric can only be elected bishop if there is no unmarried candidate, preferably a monk (Tzadua and Strauss 1968, p. 25). The section dealing with the duties of priests (chapter six), specifies that a priest was also allowed to marry and start a family, although their children should not "be accused of luxury" (Tzadua and Strauss 1968, p. 43). As mentioned above (Chapter 2), the wedding ceremony can only take place before ordination to the first degree (diaconate). As for lay people active in the church (e.g., the choirmaster, doorkeeper, lector, cantor), they too can marry and, unlike clergy members of the Ethiopian Orthodox Church, they can remarry after the death of their spouse (Tzadua and Strauss 1968, p. 53).

## 5.12 *Fəthạ Nägäśt* Rules Concerning Concubinage

A separate chapter of the code was devoted to concubinage. Its very title, ('Prohibition of concubines: concubine and women with marriage bond') indicates the position held on the topic by Ethiopian lawmakers. According to the *Fəthạ Nägäśt*, informal unions are forbidden because they contradict the institution of marriage. They are "continuous fornication" (Paulos Tzadua and Strauss 1968, p. 155; *Fəthạ Nägäśt* 1990 [1998], p. 242), so any such relationship should become a marriage as soon as possible, regardless of whether the concubine is a free woman or a slave.

The prohibition of concubinage also stands in stark contrast to custom in Ethiopia. It is known from historical sources that most of the rulers of the Ethiopian Empire also had multiple concubines, in addition to a wife married in a church ceremony (Molvaer 1995, p. 257). Moreover, the tradition of concubinage is still alive among Ethiopians. This can be observed, for example, in the research conducted in the 1990s by Reidulf K. Molvaer. When asked, Ethiopians themselves admitted that

---

[50] The quote comes from the Bible (1 Timothy 3) and indicates that a priest receiving ordination could be married only once in his lifetime.

having multiple extramarital relationships is a source of pride. However, social acceptance of extra-marital relationships does not apply to women, who have to hide their affairs for fear of their husband's wrath.

## 5.13 The *Fəṭḥa Nägäśt* and Common Law

There is no doubt that the law contained in the code operated in parallel to customary laws among the various ethnic groups of the Ethiopian Empire. This was mainly due to the fact that the higher oral and written forms of the Ge'ez language were known primarily to the clergy and aristocrats. The lower-born, who did not have the opportunity to attend a church school (and this was the only educational model that existed in Ethiopia until the twentieth century), did not have the opportunity gain a high working knowledge of the written word, which made the use of the code much more difficult. Walter Plowden (1868, p. 120), a British consul who stayed in Ethiopia from 1848 to 1860, noted that it was customary for lower court judges to open the book at "random" and deduce the appropriate sentence based on any quotation found on the page.

The *Fəṭḥa Nägäśt*, as a work created under social and cultural circumstances different from those of Ethiopia, did not fully reflect the cultural traditions of the Ethiopian Empire. As a result, the laws found in the code were not always applicable to the community. Thus, the principle was adopted that only offences aimed directly or indirectly at the emperor were subject to the imperial court, which passed its sentences based on the *Fəṭḥa Nägäśt*. In turn, other crimes were to be tried according to the prevailing common law (Seta 1999, p. 31). The accounts of (early) travellers to Ethiopia (e.g., Huyn and Kalmer 1935, pp. 246–249; Rey 1935, pp. 128–132; Walker 1933, pp. 137–152) provide many examples showing that customary laws and the regulations contained in the *Fəṭḥa Nägäśt* complemented each other, although at times they were mutually exclusive, as evidenced by the already mentioned George Krzeczunowicz (1970).

## 5.14 The Role of the *Fəṭḥa Nägäśt* in Ethiopian Society

Although the *Fəṭḥa Nägäśt* was difficult to read and understand due to the imperfect translation and the translator's lack of legal training, the book was held in high esteem by Ethiopians. This is evidenced by one of the funeral customs, according to which, after the death of an Ethiopian ruler, a copy of the code was placed in his coffin to symbolise that the emperor always followed the provisions of the book when passing judgments (Haile Selassie 1967, p. 417).

The strength of its influence is shown also by the fact that in 1890, in preparation for Italy's conquest of the Ethiopia, the army command commissioned Ignazio Guidi (1844–1935) to edit and translate the book into Italian, to function as the basis of colonial judicial administration. Despite the Italians' defeat at the Battle of Adua (1896), the *Fətḥa Nägäśt* was published with a commentary in 1899 (see Seta 1999, p. 24).

Moreover, the *Fətḥa Nägäśt* was the subject of in-depth study in the final, fourth year at traditional Ethiopian church schools. This stage of education was called *Mäṣähaf bet* ('House of the Book'), and only 10% of the students who passed the previous stages reached it.[51] During the course, a chapter of the book was read, and then translated by the teacher into Amharic and interpreted. The student would repeat both the translation and interpretation until he learned them by heart. Next, they would move on to learning the next chapter (Seta 1999, p. 72). The best students who grasped the contents of the book were given the title of *liq* ('scholar') and nominated as judges and legal advisors. They served not only in the imperial palace, but also imperial provincial courts (Bairu Tafla 1991, p. 102).

The *Fətḥa Nägäśt* was in use until the twentieth century, when Emperor Ḫaylä Śəllase I (1930–1974) decided to carry out a major codification and create legal codes following the European model. Inspiration was sought in various codes, including the Swedish, English and French ones, but traditional legislation was not fully discarded. When promulgating the first Ethiopian Penal Code in 1930, Emperor Ḫaylä Śəllase I made it clear that the new code was merely an adaptation of the laws contained in the *Fətḥa Nägäśt* to the social situation of the time. A confirmation of this assumption is found in the Penal Code itself, where there are references to the *Fətḥa Nägäśt* in as many as sixty articles. Moreover, in the introduction to the Civil Code, published in 1960, one can read that "the Codification Commission [...] has been inspired in its labours by the genius of Ethiopian legal traditions and institutions as revealed by the ancient and venerable Fitha Neguest" (quoted after Paulos Tzadua and Strauss 1968, p. xxviii).

## References

Andersen KT (2000) The queen of Habasha in Ethiopian history, tradition and chronology. Bull Sch Orient Afr Stud 63:31–63

Augustyniak Z (2009a) Małżeństwa polityczne w Etiopii na przełomie XIX i XX wieku. MA dissertation, Department of African Languages and Cultures, University of Warsaw

Augustyniak Z (2009b) Marriages in Ethiopia. Studies of the Department of Languages and Cultures 43:99–115

Bartnicki A, Mantel-Niećko J (1978) Geschichte Äthiopiens: von der Anfängen bis zur Gegenwart. Akademie-Verlag, Berlin

Bausi A (1992) Heritage and originality in the Ethiopic Sinodos. Journal of Ethiopian Studies 25:15–33

[51] The other stages bear the following names: *Nəbab bēt* ('House of Reading'), *Qädase bet* ('House of Liturgy'), *Zema Bet* ('House of Song') and *Qäne bet* ('House of Poetry'), see Seta (1999), p. 71 and Chernetsov (2005), pp. 228–230. For more on the subject of church-based education in Ethiopia, see Chaillot (2002), pp. 83–100.

# Chapter 6
# The Institution of Marriage in Ethiopian Legislation from Zärᵓa Yaᶜəqob's Death to the Reign of Mənilək II

## 6.1 The Reign of Bäᵓədä Maryam

After Zärᵓa Yaᶜəqob's death in 1468, he was succeeded by his son Bäᵓədä Maryam (1468–1474), who pursued a policy radically different than that of his predecessor. The emperor abandoned the idea of centralising the state in favour of increasing the autonomy of individual provinces. The new emperor's policy allowed local families to return to power in the provinces. There was also a change in the approach of the Empire to local customs, including law; Bäᵓədä Maryam gave precedence to the customary laws of individual districts over the provisions of the *Fətḥa Nägäśt*.

Historical sources show that the young emperor continued the policy of Zärᵓa Yaᶜəqob's in only two aspects – spreading the Christian faith and ensuring Ethiopia access to the sea (Bartnicki and Mantel-Niećko 1978, p. 77). The implementation of the former had a less bloody course than under his predecessor, perhaps also because Bäᵓədä Maryam himself was not very attached to the teachings of the Church, at least in terms of adherence to the principle of monogamy. It is known from many sources that the emperor had four wives at the same time (Kaplan 2003a, p. 432; Perruchon 1893, pp. 125, 155). This is yet another example of how Ethiopian rulers were not particularly zealous in following the *Fətḥa Nägäśt*'s provision concerning monogamy.

After a ten-year reign, Bäᵓədä Maryam died suddenly. Before his grandson ascended to the throne, Ethiopia was ruled by three more emperors who were more interested in staying in power than in introducing new laws. Only the accession to the throne of the eleven-year-old Ləbnä Dəngəl (1508–1540), son of Emperor Naᶜod and grandson of Bäᵓədä Maryam, stabilised the political situation in Ethiopia. On behalf of the underage ruler, it was his great-grandmother,[1] Empress Ǝleni, who exercised power, "[…] one of Ethiopia's most eminent political minds of the time

[1] Ǝleni (Admas Mogäsa) was one of Zärᵓa Yaᶜəqob's wives and the step-mother of Bäᵓədä Maryam.



Z. Augustyniak, *Marriage in the Ethiopian Empire*, Studies in the History of Law and Justice 33, https://doi.org/10.1007/978-3-032-26065-9_6

and one of the most famous female rulers in the country's history" (Bartnicki and Mantel-Niećko 1978, p. 85).

It is worth mentioning here that Empress Ǝleni, wife of Emperor Zärᵓa Yaᶜəqob, came from a Muslim dynasty ruling in the Hadija Sultanate (Perruchon 1893, p. 59). Undoubtedly, this was a political marriage through which the emperor was to influence the policies of the Muslim district administrators. The wedding took place around 1443 (Chernetsov 2005), and the ceremony was combined with Ǝleni's baptism. It can therefore be assumed that the wedding ceremony took place in a church and it was a *qal kidan bäqurban* type of marriage. Guided by similar considerations, Emperor Naᶜod married the daughter of the *gärad* of the Däwaro sultanate, giving her the Christian name Naᶜod Mogäsa (Derat 2010). Naᶜod's son, Ləbnä Dəngəl, was supposed to do the same, but he refused to marry a Muslim princess from Hadija because of a defect in her beauty. As the girl had already been baptised, "[...] she could not return to her father" (Beckingham and Huntingford 1961, p. 193), so the emperor decided to give her hand in marriage to one of the Christian noblemen.

These examples confirm that marriages between representatives of two religions could take place as long as the non-Christian party underwent conversion. Such a law is in accordance with the provisions of the *Fətḥa Nägäśt*, although the application of this code is not recorded in any of the chronicles of the above-mentioned rulers. It can therefore be assumed that such a law existed earlier.

## 6.2 Legislation in the Ethiopian Empire During the Reign of Ləbnä Dəngəl (1508–1540)

Ləbnä Dəngəl ascended the Ethiopian throne while he was still a child. Until 1515, the country was ruled on his behalf by a triumvirate consisting of *Ǝtäge* Ǝleni,[2] the ruler's mother Naᶜod Mogäsa, and *Ras* Wäsän Sägäd. This was a time when Ethiopian art (especially literature) flourished, and the country developed not only culturally but also economically.

The chronicler of a Portuguese mission that arrived in 1520,[3] Francisco Alvares, left also an account of the first Ethiopian legislation in the golden era of the Ethiopian Middle Ages. With regard to the rules related to marriage, Alvares writes that Ləbnä Dəngəl was the first ruler in the history of the Empire to decide to have only one wife, thus setting a model for subsequent rulers.[4] Perhaps the source of such

[2] According to James Bruce, an English traveller, Ǝleni "was skilled in the laws of the kingdom" (quoted after Beckingham and Huntingford 1961, p. 15).

[3] The Portuguese came to the Ethiopian Empire at the request of Empress Ǝleni, as she saw the rising threat from their Muslim neighbours and attempted to implement the idea of an Ethiopian-European anti-Muslim coalition. See Bartnicki and Mantel-Niećko (1978), pp. 85–96.

[4] The Jesuits, who came to Ethiopia in 1555, undermined Alvares' words, claiming that polygamy was common among the population of the Ethiopian Empire. Cf. Beckingham and Huntingford (1961), pp. 193, 240; also Cohen (2009), pp. 170–178.

provisions in the *Fətḥa Nägäśt* prohibiting bigamy is to be seen in this decision, although the ruler himself referred to St Matthew's Gospel when deciding to introduce monogamy. The Portuguese chronicle implies also that, as far as the institution of marriage was concerned, the emperor's subjects lived in a kind of legal dualism. On the one hand, they were bound by the precept of monogamy derived from ecclesiastical law, while—on the other—unions based on customary law were permitted, including temporary marriages of the *dämoz* type,[5] which in some cases enabled polygamy. According to the Portuguese priest, "men [...] keep two or three wives; and this is not forbidden to them by the King nor by their magistrates, only by the Church" (after Beckingham and Huntingford 1961, p. 105). As far as customs related to divorce are concerned, mainly common law provisions were in effect, according to which the separating spouses had to return gifts received before the marriage and divide the property accumulated during the marriage (Beckingham and Huntingford 1961, pp. 106–108).

Priests were the only social group that was exclusively governed by church law. A clergyman could only have one wife, with whom he could not divorce. After her death, he could also not remarry. The same rules applied to a clergyman's wife, who could remain widowed or join a religious order after his death (Beckingham and Huntingford 1961, p. 119; Pankhurst 1990, p. 36).

In describing his journey through the Ethiopian Empire, Alvares did not once mention any penal code operating in the country. If either the emperor or the judges passed judgment on a case, the justification for it was supported by relevant passages of Scripture or other religious texts. At first glance, this may support the conjecture presented in the previous chapter that the *Fətḥa Nägäśt* was not an official legal code. However, given the ubiquity of Biblical references in the code, Alvares may not even have been aware that the judges were quoting the *Fətḥa Nägäśt* rather than the Bible itself. What is puzzling, however, is the lack of information about the use of the code in the chronicle of Emperor Ləbnä Dəngəl.

## 6.3 The Judiciary System and Courts Under Emperor Śärṣä Dəngəl (1563–1597)

After Ləbnä Dəngəl's death, his son and successor Gälawdewos (1540–1559) managed, with the help of Portuguese troops, to end the thirty-year-long 'holy war' against the Muslims. After the victory, the ruler had to face a series of internal challenges, the most important among them being the restoration of imperial authority,

[5] Although Alvares does not specifically name the relationship, he writes that men who come to the town for the market take wives to help them sell their produce. Later, he describes a wedding ceremony he witnessed. Some of the rituals he describes take place during *sər'at* type ceremonies, but it is difficult to determine whether Alvares witnessed this particular ceremony (Beckingham and Huntingford 1961, pp. 104–106).

centralisation of power and reconstruction of the war-ravaged state. For the nearly twenty years of his reign, Gälawdewos fought constant battles with those of the peoples living in Ethiopia who refused to submit to imperial authority and against invading Muslim armies. During one such battle, the emperor was killed, leaving no male descendants.[6] Thus, it was the deceased emperor's younger brother, Minas (1559–1563), who became the ruler of the Ethiopian Empire.

The new emperor was not popular among either the aristocracy or the clergy, not only because of his unfortunate moves in domestic policy, but also due to his impulsive character (Bartnicki and Mantel-Niećko 1978, p. 142). After his death, a struggle began between groups of noblemen who supported different pretenders. The rivalry for the imperial throne was won in 1564 by the 13-year-old Śärṣä Dəngəl, the son of Emperor Minas from his union with *Ǝtäge* Admas Mogäsa. The young emperor decided to subjugate the peoples and districts that had been under imperial rule before the Muslim invasion. The ruler, however, did not limit himself to military conquests alone, but brought *č̣äwa* settlers[7] as well as monks and priests to the subjugated territories, while forcing district administrators to embrace Christianity. To bind local leaders even more firmly to the new ruler, Śärṣä Dəngəl arranged marriages between members of the imperial family and representatives of local families.

The unification of the Empire also had an economic purpose, as taxes from the subordinated districts and counties were to form an important share of the revenue supplying money to the imperial treasury. To obtain additional funds for his fight against Muslim invaders, Śärṣä Dəngəl introduced a law establishing a fixed level of taxes imposed on district administrators. Under the previous tax system, only a small portion of the income of each district had reached the imperial treasury. The imperial decree linked the amount of tax to the quantity of property owned by noblemen. This law was not welcomed by the district administrators, who up until then had held the exclusive right to determine the level of taxes. Encountering resistance from the noblemen, the emperor abandoned further legal reforms, including those concerning marriages.[8]

Following the example of his predecessors, Śärṣä Dəngəl had only one wife, Maryam Śəna. This would confirm that the law forbidding bigamy, decreed by Ləbnä Dəngəl, was respected by successive rulers of the country. However, Śärṣä Dəngəl adhered also to local customs, as in addition to his crowned wife, he had a mistress (from the Betä Ǝsraᵓel) named Ḥarägo, whose son Yaᶜəqob was to become the heir to the throne (Nosnitsin 2010, p. 547). It is far more probable, however, that the emperor chose to have only one wife, not so much abiding by the Ləbnä Dəngəl's decree but rather Ethiopian canon law, according to which one could be married in

---

[6] Sources only mention the ruler's long-time mistress, whom he took from her lawful husband, as a result of which he was reportedly tormented by remorse (Kleiner 2005, p. 657).

[7] The *čäwa* settlers played an important role in introducing the social structure characteristic of the Ethiopian Empire into conquered territories.

[8] *Abba* Baḥrəy's *Zenahu lägalla* ("The History of the Galla"), containing a critical assessment of Ethiopian society, shows the importance of the reforms related to social life. Cf. Nosnitsin (2010), p. 546; Getachew Haile (2014), pp. 180–181.

church only once in a lifetime. The fact that Empress Maryam Śəna bore the title of *ətäge* indicates that this was a *qal kidan bäqurban* marriage, as this title could be obtained by an imperial spouse only during an ecclesiastical wedding ceremony.

The reign of Śärṣä Dəngəl is also relevant to the present study because it was during his reign that the use of the *Fətḥa Nägäśt* in the judicial process was documented for the first time, i.e., in the Imperial Chronicle, in the chapter on the punishment of rebel leaders in one of the Ethiopian provinces (Paulos Tzadua and Strauss 1968, p. xxi). This passage confirms not only that Abū l-Faḍāᵓ'il bin al-ᵓAssāl aṣ-Ṣafī's *Nomokanōn* had already been translated into Ge'ez by that time, but also that Ethiopian judges used the book in passing sentences. It should be noted at this point that although the *Fətḥa Nägäśt* was the official legal code of the Ethiopian Empire, it was treated more as a book of legal advice on which judges could rely when conducting trials.[9]

A slightly different view on the use of the code at that time has been presented by Tsegaye Beru. According to him, the *Fətḥa Nägäśt* was not in common use, as few judges had mastered Ge'ez (Tsegaye Beru 2013, p. 347). This, however, cannot be completely true, as to become a magistrate, one had to complete the fourth level of education at a traditional church school, which entailed memorising the code. Even if a judge did not know Ge'ez (which seems unlikely), he was able at least to find the relevant passage and to read it in Amharic.[10] However, Tsegaye Bergu may be right when he writes that judges interpreted the same provisions of the book differently (which was also due to the way the book was taught in school) and, therefore, gave different judgements on similar cases. As an example, he cites the provision on inheritance. According to judges interpreting the provisions of the *Fətḥa Nägäśt* literally, a child from an extramarital union was not entitled to an inheritance unless the deceased parent had included such a provision in the will. In contrast, other judges, citing the same legislation, held that such a child would not inherit only if the deceased had acknowledged his offspring before death (thus giving them a right to the inheritance) but had not made a corresponding provision in his will (Tsegaye Beru 2013, p. 347).

As mentioned in the previous chapter, until the mid-twentieth century, the provisions of customary law and those of the *Fətha Nägäśt* were applied alternately. If, in a given case, the code provided otherwise than custom, the latter was disregarded. In contrast, in legal cases not covered by the code, the provisions of customary law were applied.

[9] This is confirmed by the Chronicle of Emperor Susənyos, which mentions that the book was used in the course of passing judgment by "[...] the learned men of the church who were versed in the Fetha Nagast". See Paulos Tzadua and Strauss (1968), p. xxi.

[10] According to Paulos Tzadua, the *Fətḥa Nägäśt* was available in manuscripts of two types soon after its appearance in Ethiopia. The more common one contained a Ge'ez text with glosses in Amharic and Ge'ez. The other, which served didactic purposes, had a literal Amharic translation with a commentary in Amharic below each legal provision in Ge'ez. Ethiopian judges most probably used the manuscripts of the second type. See Paulos Tzadua and Strauss (1968), p. xviii.

When discussing court hearings conducted in accordance with customary law, it is impossible not to mention the traditional Amharic way of resolving disputes called *(täṭäyyäq) mugt* or *mugt bätäṭätyäq sərat* (literally 'conducting a dispute through a hearing'). According to Tsegaye Beru, already quoted earlier, public dispute resolution was "[...] a national pastime where everyone in the neighborhood, including young children, would attend just about any court proceeding" (Tsegaye Beru 2013, p. 345). This is confirmed by Edward Ullendorff, who observed that "[...] most Ethiopians possess an astonishing knowledge of customary law, enhanced by clear thinking, memory and a wonderful facility of eloquent exposition" (Ullendorff 1962, p. 186). As Ethiopians highly valued rhetoric skills, they often spoke in their own cases. It was also not uncommon for a court dispute to be won not by the person who was in the right, but by the one who was a better speaker.[11] Most disputes of this type concerned defamation, appropriation of property or ownership of land, but there were also cases involving marriage, especially in conflicts over the division of property after divorce.

Traditional Ethiopian courts were also called street courts because anyone could be selected as a judge, e.g., a person passing by two people arguing (Abera Jambere 1988, p. 245; Mattausch 2007, p. 1040). According to some sources, refusing to attend a trial as a judge was considered an affront and rudeness. Once a suitable place for the trial had been found (e.g. the shade of a sprawling tree), both sides would present their arguments and the judge would deliver a verdict. If the complainant and the accused were satisfied with the verdict, the case was considered closed and the judge relieved of his duty. Most often, however (for reasons mentioned above), one of the parties felt aggrieved; thus, the village chief (*čəqa šum*) or the lowest-ranking judge (*aṭbiya daññа*, literally 'local or parish judge') was called in to settle the dispute, accompanied during the trial by two assessors (*täččiwočč*), who were either delegated by both parties to the dispute or chosen from among the trial observers.

The trial would begin with a representative of each of the sides presenting a *yäqəbqabä was* (or *yämäggža was*),[12] a kind of laudation, which was meant to convince the court and the audience about the virtuousness of the accused/accuser. The plaintiff would then present the allegations against the defendant (*kəss maqərräb*), which the defendant could accept or reject. If the defendant disagreed with the allegations, the plaintiff presented arguments against the defendant, to which the defendant responded with counter-arguments. To emphasise their truthfulness, both parties would start a bidding war (*wərərrəd mätkäl*). For example, the accused offered to give the judge a mule if his words proved to be untrue. The accuser, on the other hand, wishing to outbid his opponent, could

[11] A vivid description of an Ethiopian speaking before a customary court is found in the memoirs of the Swedish general Eric Virgin (1936, p. 90). See also Abera Jembere (1988), p. 245.

[12] *Was* – guarantee. For other forms of guarantees, see Abera Jembere (1988), p. 246.

promise the judge a horse.[13] If both parties were sure of their case, they outbid each other until they were on the verge of bankruptcy. Sometimes it happened that the defendant decided to plead guilty to an act committed in order not to lose all his property. In such a case, he only had to pay the court costs, the sum of which was fixed at one *bərr*.

If the accused pleaded not guilty, the trial entered the next stage, which was the examination of witnesses. Those called before the judge had to testify in favour of either party. Both the accused and the plaintiff were allowed to present three witnesses (*masräğğa*) each.[14] In addition, they were allowed to produce documentary evidence (e.g., a wedding contract or a list of pre-wedding gifts), if they had any. Witnesses did not have to take a *fəṭəm* oath, but they were obliged to tell the truth. If a witness's testimony pleased neither party, they could require the witness to swear on the Scripture that they were telling the truth.

The next stage involved direct confrontation between the claimant and the accused (*täṭäyyäq*). Each party answered a question posed by the adversary in an attempt to prove their case. Only one question could be asked during the session, and an answer that did not relate to the question was punishable by a fine. When the trial was nearing its end, each side would make a closing speech (*wərd mänzat*), in which they would try not only to convince the judge of their innocence, but also to ridicule the opposing side by proving that they had committed similar bad deeds before. Speeches were then made by the assessors. Finally, the judge would give a verdict with supporting arguments (*fərd*). The losing party had to pay not only the court costs, but also the amount of the bet.[15]

Both parties could appeal the verdict; however, subsequent hearings had to take place before the imperial courts. Until 1935, the following hierarchy of courts applied (compiled based on Abera Jembere 1988, p. 252; 1998, 214–219):

1. *Yäbota* or *Yakätäma Daññа* (Court of First Instance)
2. *Yäᵓakal Dañña* (District Court)
3. The *Šalläq* court (District Administrator's Court)
4. The court of the *Afä Nəgus* (The Supreme Court)
5. *Zufan Čəlot* (The Imperial Court).[16]

The traditional courts described above continued to function until 1942, when Emperor Ḫaylä Śəllase I carried out a reform that systematised the Ethiopian judiciary. Thus, people's courts disappeared not only from the streets of larger cities, but

[13] Often, the stake in the bet were not the goods themselves, but their financial equivalent.

[14] Relatives of the parties could not be witnesses, making it much more difficult to conclude the trial in a case involving divorce or marital violence.

[15] Immediately after the verdict, punishment followed. The most common included fines, confiscation of property, banishment from one's place of residence, whipping, mutilation and the death penalty. See Bairu Tafla (1991), p. 109. An exaggerated description of a street court can be found in Huyn and Kalmer (1935).

[16] An interesting comparison between the Ethiopian imperial court and the English royal court was presented by Sedler (1964, pp. 59–76).

also from the countryside. However, during the period discussed in this chapter, street courts were common. In addition, verdicts handed down in unusual cases often became precedent, which, over time, turned into a regulation of customary law.[17]

## 6.4 Emperor Susənyos' Reforms and the Jesuit Mission in Ethiopia

The Portuguese mission with Francisco Alvares left Ethiopia in 1526, three years before the beginning of the 30-year war against the Muslims, as a result of which the Ethiopian Empire faced annihilation. Ethiopian sources contain little information about this period of history. Also, any development of law can hardly be expected when the very existence of the state was threatened. Knowledge of Ethiopian legislation from that period is further obscured by the fact that the Muslim invaders plundered and burned all the Christian buildings they passed. Not only *gädams*, churches and monasteries were burnt down, but also the imperial residences at Gebergie and Baduki, where large numbers of manuscripts were kept, not only of a legal nature. In the absence of any information in Ethiopian sources concerning the development of the institution of marriage during this period, it is necessary to consult external ones—which are primarily the writings of Jesuit missionaries.

The Jesuits first arrived in Ethiopia in 1555, in the midst of the Ethiopian-Muslim war. The purpose of this first mission was to try to convert the ruler to Catholicism. The mission was partially successful. Although Emperor Gälawdewos refused the proposal from Bishop Andrés de Oviedo, who had arrived at the Ethiopian court in 1557, to convert himself, he did give his consent to a Jesuit evangelisation mission in Tigray. The missionaries travelled around Ethiopia until 1566, when they decided to establish a missionary centre at Firemona, located on the Adwa plateau. During this time, the missionaries' situation became much worse, as Emperor Gälawdewos died in a battle against Nūr ibn Muǧāhid,[18] and he was succeeded by Minas,[19] who was hostile to the Jesuit missionary activities. The emperor prevented the missionaries from having any contact with the local population.

[17] An example of such a precedence is provided by Huyn and Kalmer (1935, pp. 164–165).

[18] Nūr bin Muǧāhid was one of the most important generals of Imam Aḥmad bin Ibrāhīm al-Gāzī, who in 1529 invaded Ethiopia. Cf. Bartnicki and Mantel-Niećko (1978), p. 134; Muth (2007), pp. 1209–1210.

[19] Around 1550, Emperor Minas married the daughter of one of the influential Tigray rulers, Admas Mogäsa. This was a marriage of the *qal kidan bäqurban* type, which, as noted above (Chap. 2), was most common among members of the imperial family. See Kleiner (2010), p. 435.

In 1603, at the invitation of Emperor Zädəngəl (1603–1604), Father Pedro Páez came to Ethiopia.[20] With his arrival, a second period of intense Jesuit activity in Ethiopia began. This time, the reigning emperor was positively disposed towards the newcomers from Europe. Similar was the policy pursued towards the Jesuits by Emperor Susənyos (1607–1632), who allowed them to establish more than a dozen mission centres throughout the country (Cohen and Martínez 2007, p. 278). To overcome the separatist tendencies among some of the noblemen and the resistance of the clergy, the Emperor requested military assistance from the King of Spain and the Roman Pope. Most probably, the Europeans made the sending of troops to Ethiopia conditional on the Emperor's conversion to the Catholic faith. As a result, in 1624, Susənyos announced his conversion, along with that of several dignitaries. With this step, he contributed to the outbreak of a civil war that lasted four years. The Emperor, seeing his political and military defeat, publicly admitted that he had made a mistake in allowing the Jesuits to spread their faith and abdicated in favour of his son, Fasilädäs (1632–1637). Immediately upon assuming the throne, the new Emperor convened a council in Gonder, at which it was decided to banish the Jesuits to Firemona. From there, the missionaries fled to the *Bahər Nägaš* Yoḥannəs, who handed them over to the Turks (Bartnicki and Mantel-Niećko 1978, p. 169).

During their nearly 80-year sojourn in the Ethiopian Empire, Jesuits left accounts on the practical functioning of marriage law. Indeed, they set themselves the goal of Christianising the institution of marriage (Cohen and Martínez 2007).[21] According to their descriptions, Ethiopian marriages were far from the Christian ideal. Vows were usually made in the presence of a local magistrate or elders, and marriages were short-lived, (especially among the aristocracy), which actually contradicts the observations made by Francisco Alvares (Páez 2008, p. 378). Contrary to the words of the Bible, man and woman did not become one, and after marriage the wife did not take her husband's name (which particularly surprised the Jesuits) (Cohen 2009, p. 170). Manoel de Almeida argued that Ethiopian Christians treated marriage as a sacrament, which did not mean that they lived in monogamous relationships (Cohen 2009, p. 171). Witnessing the social acceptance of extramarital relationships and concubinage, European missionaries realised how the Christian ideal of the sacrament of marriage clashed with the practice of customary law in Ethiopia.

Pedro Páez noted that adultery was the main reason why men filed for divorce. Moreover, according to the Jesuit priest, men cheated on their wives with full deliberation solely so that they could have a relationship with another woman.

> [...] It is common for men to abandon their wives and for women to abandon their husbands. It is enough to go to a judge and declare that one no longer wants to live with her/him. This is a blatant violation of the evangelical rules of marriage. If both parties are in agreement, there is a division of property. If only one party wants a divorce, the abandoned

[20] Apparently, the Emperor wanted to get not only military support from the Spanish and Portuguese, but he was also interested in European legal systems. See Cohen (2014), p. 104.

[21] For the apologia for the Catholic doctrine of the indissolubility of marriage, see Páez (2008), p. 376.

> party gets everything. If the man is away from home for a few years, the wife may be allowed to marry someone else. In the case of the wife committing adultery, the husband does not even need the permission of the judge (Páez 2008, 375).[22]

Páez did attempt to explain to Ethiopians that a partner's infidelity was not sufficient grounds for divorce, and that only death could separate spouses. However, his opinions were not met with understanding, which only confirms how strong the attachment to customary law was among the Ethiopians (Cohen 2009, p. 171). From reports of the Jesuit missionaries, it is also known that among the Tigrayans there was a law requiring a widow to be married by her husband's brother, and that relationships between relatives were permissible (Páez 2008, p. 378). Almeida shows this on the example of Emperor Susənyos's daughter, Wängelawit, who married her deceased sister's husband. The Jesuits considered such a union unacceptable as there was too close a degree of affinity between the spouses.[23]

It was only after Emperor Susənyos converted to Catholicism that the marriage law changed. The Emperor decreed that henceforth a man could only marry one woman, and only in church, and disputes between spouses would be settled by church courts. Furthermore, in 1624, an imperial decree established that marriage was indissoluble, and that conduct contrary to the decree would be punished by death or confiscation of property (Cohen 2009, p. 174). The ruler's decisions did not meet with the approval of either the clergy or the local magistrates. The former were disgruntled because, since Susənyos' baptism, all weddings were to take place in the Catholic rite, while the magistrates feared their jurisdiction to be restricted and the benefits they derived from performing weddings and presiding over divorce cases to be reduced.[24]

Although the Jesuits were strongly opposed to marriages contracted under customary law, they resorted to the provisions of that law when the dissolution of the marriage caused one of the parties to change to the Catholic faith. The Jesuits, in particular, were keen to win the favour of Ethiopian noblewomen, and were therefore very willing to become involved in disputes between spouses who had entered into marriage under customary law. Father Thomas Barneto described the story of a young noblewoman, who against her will was given in marriage to the uncle of the

---

[22] The last regulation cited by Páez refers to the entry in the third part of the sixth section in Chapter 24 of the *Fəṯḥa Nägäśt*. Cf. Paulos Tzadua and Strauss (1968), p. 151; Páez (2008), p. 375.

[23] Almeida's writings show his dislike to Wängälawət, whom he considered promiscuous, because she had had seven husbands, while she became involved with her sister's husband even before separating from her own husband. This last accusation is confirmed by other sources; however, Almeida's aversion might rather have been caused by the fact that Wängälawət was a staunch opponent of the Catholics, while her husband *Däğğazmač* Zäkrəstos favoured the Jesuits. Cf. Cohen (2009), p. 173; Toubkis (2014), pp. 118–119.

[24] Emperor Susənyos is also credited with introducing changes to court procedures. According to the Emperor's decree, the imperial court was attended by four *azmačs* and four scholars familiar with the legal provisions of the *Fəṯḥa Nägäśt*. Representatives of the Ethiopian administration also sat in the imperial court, in order of their rank. The court session would begin with a prayer and then proceed to the consideration of the case. According to Aṣmä Giyorgis, this custom did not survive to Mənilək II's reign (1889–1913). See Bairu Tafla (1987), pp. 344–345.

administrator of one of the provinces. She promised to be baptised if Father Barneto would help her to get divorced. The missionary ensured the woman that he would allow her to leave her husband if she could prove before the judge of the customary law court that she had been married without giving her consent (e.g., by claiming that this was a marriage of the *ṭäläfa* type). In this case, the whole process was conducted without any difficulties and soon after the annulment of the marriage, she was baptised (Cohen 2009, p. 176).

As mentioned above, the Jesuits were expelled from Ethiopia in 1632 by Emperor Fasilädäs. Before this happened, the abdicating Emperor Susənyos promulgated a decree granting his subjects freedom of religion. In doing so, he revoked earlier decrees establishing marriage in the Catholic rite as the only valid model in Ethiopia. The Jesuit attempt to introduce Catholic morality in the Empire proved unsuccessful, and Fasilädäs' subjects returned to local customary laws.

## 6.5 Ethiopian Law and Inter-ethnic and Inter-religious Marriage

From the moment Fasilädäs ascended the throne, the number of Muslims in Ethiopia began to increase;[25] however, in multi-ethnic Gonder it was the Amhara who continued to gather most privileges (Quirin 1992, p. 110). Others were treated much worse: the Muslims, the Qemants, the Betä Ǝsraʾel, the Wäyṭo, and the 'šanqəlla'. Inter-ethnic and inter-religious unions were rare, perhaps because the groups were unwilling to renounce their faith and culture in favour of Christianity or the Amhara culture.[26] Inter-ethnic marriages were also opposed by some Ethiopian rulers. In 1668, Yoḥannəs I (1667–1682) issued a decree banning Muslims and Betä Ǝsraʾel from settling among Christians. Both Muslims and Ethiopian Jews were to live in separate neighbourhoods and were not allowed to marry Christians (Quirin 1992, p. 115). Iyasu I the Great (1682–1706), in turn, created an office whose sole task was to ensure that marriages arranged at the imperial court were homogeneous. Prospective spouses not only had to be from the same ethnic group, but also equal in rank and property (Quirin 1992, p. 116).[27]

Despite reluctance on both sides, marriages between people of different faiths and ethnicities did occur in the Ethiopian Empire. Such marriages were also arranged, especially if they served state interests. Arranging marriages as one of the

[25] There was even a rumour among the Emperor's subjects about the ruler's alleged conversion to Islam. This was not true, and the rumour was only intended to discourage the Jesuits from returning to Ethiopia. See van Donzel (2005), p. 502.

[26] However, on the other hand, according to Betä Ǝsraʾel oral tradition, "[…] about half of the Amhara [of Gonder] have Falasha ancestors" (quoted after Quirin 1992, p. 115).

[27] A similar prohibition was imposed by the Italians occupying the Ethiopian Empire between 1936 and 1941. Italian-Ethiopian marriages were strictly forbidden on pain of punishment, and children from such unions were taken away from their parents. See Perham (1969), p. 152.

ways of conducting domestic policy was known from the early days of Ethiopian statehood. The main purpose of political marriages was to strengthen or expand networks of influence by creating new alliances. At the same time, such a marriage could neutralise potential threats from other contenders for power. Another advantage of a political marriage was that by marrying the right person, one could be a frequent guest at court, which favoured the realisation of political aspirations. Another reason for marriages among the state elite was the desire to own more land and thus strengthen the control over strategic and economically important parts of the country. Such strategically important lands included the Debaroa area and other lands administered by the *bahər nägaš* as well as those through which trade routes ran, including but not limited to arms trade routes. Other important areas included Hadija and Ǝnnarya, where there were centres of slave and silver trade (Pankhurst 1997, p. 206).[28]

Political marriages also served to resolve conflicts and strengthen ties with noblemen of other faiths—the Muslims and Betä Ǝsraᵓel—and ethnicities, such as the Oromo. In the twentieth century, the topic of political marriages in Ethiopia and their impact on the state was addressed both by Ethiopian historians, such as Bairu Tafla (1972) and Beyene et al. (1990), as well as by Western scholars—Richard Pankhurst (1979, 1997, 1999) and Chris Prouty (1986). Their research shed light on the legal aspect of such relationships and on their impact on the political make-up of the state.

A good exemplification of legal issues related to inter-ethnic and inter-religious marriages can be found among members of the reigning dynasty during the Gonder period (1632–1784). The first of these was the union of Emperor Bäkaffa (1721–1730) with Bərhan Mogäsa (better known by the name Məntäwwab), originating from the Qwara district. Ethiopian tradition has it that the emperor, captivated by her beauty, married for love rather than for political reasons. In reality, however, Məntäwwab never became the emperor's crowned wife, as this title belonged to Awaldä Nəgəśt, whom the emperor married in 1723 and who died three years later.[29] Since there is not the slightest mention of Məntäwwab in the emperor's official chronicle, it seems that he married her according to local custom or it was a *sərat*-type marriage. One argument in favour of the latter is the fact that, according to the *Fəṭḥa Nägäśt*, the emperor could not have concubines, and a marriage according to local custom would be considered such a union. Due to his position, the emperor had to obey the law. The marriage was facilitated by the fact that Məntäwwab was a Christian.[30] However, a marriage of this type was in this case the most appropriate, because the emperor was already married in church.

[28] For more on political marriages in the Ethiopian Empire, see Augustyniak (2009) and Heran Sereke-Brhan (2002).

[29] The ceremony took place in church and was of the *qal kidan bäqurban* type (Crummey 2000, pp. 99–100).

[30] She was given the baptismal name of Wälättä Gyorgis and she belonged to the *qəbat* faction (Berry 2003, pp. 534–535).

Although Məntäwwab was not officially the emperor's wife, she crowned herself empress (*nəgəśtä nägäśtat*) after the emperor's death to rule on behalf of their son, Iyasu II (1730–1755).[31] One of the female regent's moves was to arrange the marriage of Emperor Iyasu II to Wəbit, daughter of Amiṭo, a Tulama-Oromo clan chief from Yäğğu.[32] It was a political marriage aimed at strengthening the Qwaranese position against the Amharic and Tigrayan dignitary families, who were reluctant to give up their dominant position at court. No sources provide information on the religion of the emperor's future wife, but certainly Wəbit was not a Christian, as it was only after her marriage that she was baptised and given the name Wälättä Bersabeḥ. As the sacrament of baptism took place after the wedding ceremony, it can be assumed that this was a *sərat* marriage. Wəbit was never given the title of *ətäge*, which also supports the idea that her marriage to the emperor was not a *qal kidan bäqurban*-type union.[33]

After Iyasu II's death, his seven-year-old son, Iyoᵓas I (1755–1769), ascended the throne. At this time, rivalry between Qwaran and Oromo factions at the imperial court intensified. The young emperor, although raised in his mother's culture and speaking primarily the Oromo language (Bruce 1790, p. 660), did not decide to abandon the Christian faith in favour of his mother's native beliefs. He was certainly aware of the great stir among the aristocracy caused by Emperor Susənyos' conversion to Catholicism and that his conversion would have been a pretext for overthrowing his rule. However, the emperor did not require other Oromo to convert, allowing them to retain their beliefs (Conte 1979, pp. 164–165). However, some of the Oromo groups, while residing among the Amhara, adopted their culture and the Christian faith, which encouraged intermarriage among representatives of the old Amharic and Tigrayan families, in turn strengthening the Oromo position at court. In contrast, some of the Oromo clans that settled on the eastern fringes of the Empire converted to Islam.

However, some of the Oromo groups, while residing among the Amharic, adopted their culture and the Christian faith, which encouraged intermarriage with representatives of the old Amharic and Tigrayan families, strengthening the Oromo position at court. In turn, some of the Oromo clans that settled on the eastern fringes of the Empire converted to Islam.

Since the beginning of their presence in the country, Muslims in Ethiopia have adhered to Sunni Islam, but not in a strictly orthodox version, as it incorporates elements of traditional beliefs. This is particularly evident during religious festivals, during which Muslims, also pilgrims, gather to pray, sing and dance together, and

[31] According to LaVerle B. Berry (2003, p. 534), after the death of Məntəwwab's husband, she did not declare herself *nəgəstä nägästat*, but her kinsmen at the court gave her the title of *ətäge*. Cf. Crummey (2003), p. 450.

[32] Earlier, the young Bäkaffa found refuge with the chief of the Tulama-Oromo. See Pankhurst (1997), p. 216.

[33] It is worth noting that, in addition to a marriage certificate, a marriage contract was also drawn up detailing all the goods the spouses brought into the union. For an example of such a contract from the time of the Gonder emperors, see Pankhurst (1979), pp. 457–466.

sometimes to perform rituals related to the Zar cult.[34] Although in Ethiopian Islam all Sunni schools of Islamic law are represented, the most important for Ethiopian Muslims are the Hanafi, Shafıʼi and Mālīki schools. Although it is not certain by which routes the schools of Islamic law arrived in Ethiopia, the Hanafi school is presumed to have come from Yemen, the Shafıʼi from Egypt, while the Mālīki probably came from eastern Sudan. It seems probable that the Hanafi school appeared in Etiopia earlier than the Shafi'i school, which in time became the dominant legal doctrine (Ahmed and Gori 2007, pp. 198–201).[35]

In the provinces of the Ethiopian Empire where Muslims were the majority, and in the former medieval Islamic sultanates, Sharia law was applied. Since Islam does not distinguish between the secular and religious sphere, all aspects of a Muslim's social and private life were subject to this law. Marriage and inheritance cases were also judged according to Sharia law, although in the Ethiopian Empire customary law was also taken into account.[36]

As far as the Islamic judiciary in Ethiopia was concerned, each of the legal schools elected judges in the areas that fell under the respective school. Despite differences between the schools, their approach to some legal issues was the same, determined by the stance of the Qur'an and Sunna. For example, the penalty for adultery was one hundred lashes in the case of unmarried persons or stoning if the case involved a married person. In addition, in order to pass a judgment in such a case, a *qadi* needed the testimony of four eyewitnesses, and giving false testimony was severely punished. Judges had the right to try only cases related to marriages contracted in accordance with Sharia law or if the spouses were Muslims (Zaki Mustafa 1973, pp. 138–139).

According to Islamic law, a male follower of Islam can marry a non-Muslim woman,[37] but a female Muslim cannot marry a non-Muslim man, unless he embraces Islam. Otherwise, the marriage will not be considered legal. However, numerous sources indicate that Ethiopian Muslims circumvented this provision by marrying according to local customary law, which did not require conversion.

According to Islamic law, marriage is the only legal way for a man and a woman to satisfy their sexual desires. As mentioned earlier, adultery is considered one of the most serious crimes within family law. Islam allows polygyny (although a man can have no more than four wives), but prohibits polyandry (Trimingham 1952,

---

[34] Zar—a cult of spiritual possession, present not only in Ethiopia, but also in the entire Horn of Africa, Egypt, Iran, Oman and Yemen. For more on Zar in Ethiopia, see Torrey (1970), pp. 51–59.

[35] Currently, the Hanafi school is present in historic Abyssinia and parts of modern Eritrea, the Mālīki school predominates in the Eritrean lowlands, and the Shafıʼi school is prevalent in Harer and among the Oromo and Somali. See Conte (1979), p. 179.

[36] For example, both Islamic customary law and normative Islam allow slaves to be their masters' concubines, and after being freed—their wives.

[37] A Muslim man can only marry "a woman of the book", i.e., a Jewish or Christian woman. However, a non-Muslim wife does not have the same full rights as a Muslim one. For example, a non-Muslim wife does not have the right to inherit after her husband; she can only receive 1/3 of his estate if he included her in the testament. See Sadowski (2014).

p. 190). In contrast to Christian doctrine, in Islam, marriage is not a sacrament, but a civil contract that is entered into by mutual consent, although the woman does not take active part in its formation.[38] It is sufficient that she gives consent (even tacitly) to the marriage being concluded. The marriage contract refers to the Qur'an and its provisions must comply with Sharia law. Breaking the contract is treated not only as a violation of the law, but also as a sin.

As in any contract, also a marriage contract has indispensable components, referred to by the Arabic term *rukn* ('pillar'). In addition to these, there are also *shart* ('preconditions'), which are necessary for the marriage contract to be valid and to have specific legal effects (Sadowski 2014). The pillars of the marriage contract include the matrimonial offer, its acceptance, and the parties to the contract, i.e., the future husband, the woman and her legal guardian (*wali*). The preconditions, in turn, include the presence of witnesses, the *mahr*,[39] and the content of the contract. In order to conclude a marriage according to Islamic law, in addition to the marriage contract and the consent of both parties, the presence is required of two witnesses (men) and of a *qadi* who publicly announces the marriage.

A woman marrying a Muslim man can include a number of conditions in the marriage contract, for example, that she will be allowed to continue her education or that she does not give consent to her husband's next marriage. However, a woman cannot stipulate that the children be brought up in their mother's religion if she is not a Muslim, as Sharia law demands that the children must follow their father's religion. All the terms of the contract have to be feasible and not incompatible with Islamic law.[40] The husband's failure to honour the terms of the agreement gives the wife the possibility to seek a divorce.

Despite such strict legal provisions regarding the institution of marriage, the practice of Ethiopian Muslims in this regard diverged greatly from the provisions in place. As for the rule concerning conversion before marriage, it was not even observed by Muslim noblemen who, when giving their daughters away to Christian members of the imperial family, not only did not demand that their future sons-in-law convert to Islam, but also allowed their daughters to be baptised. The princesses from the Sultanate of Hadija mentioned above are examples of such conversions. As in many other cases, for the Muslims (but also for followers of other religions), the benefits of the relationship far outweighed the importance of strict adherence to the rules of the book.

In addition to the Muslims, another religious group that entered into close relations with the imperial power through a series of marriages were the Ethiopian

---

[38] The Hanafi school recognises that a mature, sane woman can represent herself when negotiating a marriage contract. See Sadowski (2014).

[39] *Mahr*—a man's wedding gift to a woman. Half of the *mahr* is paid immediately after the wedding, the other half is paid to the woman in the case of divorce or the spouse's death.

[40] Terms of contract that are contrary to the law do not make the marriage invalid, but are still considered unlawful.

Jews.[41] Their exact origins are unknown. The Betä Ǝsraᵓel themselves believe that they arrived in Ethiopia with Mənilək I, the son of the Jewish King Solomon and the Queen of Sheba. In 1973, Israel's main Sephardic Rabbi, Ovadia Yosef, opined that the Betä Ǝsraᵓel are descendants of people from the tribe of Dan (Dana), one of the tribes of Israel that travelled south. In turn, researchers studying this ethnic group formulate three hypotheses regarding the origin of Ethiopian Jews. According to one, the Betä Ǝsraᵓel arrived in Ethiopia directly from Palestine in the thirteenth century BCE at the time of the Exodus (this theory is in line with Rabbi Yosef's opinion). The second theory is based on the assumption that Jewish emigrants arrived later than the thirteenth century and mixed with the Agew people, imposing their religion and customs on them. The last theory claims that the Jewish community in Ethiopia originated as a Christian sect that split from the Orthodox Ethiopian Church around the fifteenth century (Gawlik 1999, p. 43). None of the above-mentioned hypotheses is supported by sufficient evidence. It cannot be excluded that all three are partly true or complementary. There is also a hypothesis claiming the conversion of the local population to Judaism by Jewish immigrants (Gawlik 1999, p. 43).[42]

In European sources, the first reliable information on Jews living in Ethiopia dates back to 1438 (Hess 1970, p. 99). In Ethiopian sources, scant information on Betä Ǝsraᵓel can be found in the slightly earlier chronicle of ᶜAmdä Ṣəyon I, which records a campaign against rebellious Jews in the regions of Semien, Wegere, Selamynt and Segedie. The expedition initiated a conflict lasting more than three hundred years between the Betä Ǝsraᵓel and the Christian emperors of Ethiopia. Mutual resentment, however, did not prevent Ethiopian rulers from marrying Ethiopian Jews. For example, the above-mentioned Emperor Śärṣä Dəngəl, aside from his Christian wife also had a concubine from the Betä Ǝsraᵓel people named Ḥarägo (or Harägwé), sister of the ruler of Semien, Gedewon (Pankhurst 1997, p. 214). He had four sons from this union, two of whom he designated as his successors.[43] Although the title *əmabet* ('princess') appears before Ḥarägo's name in Ethiopian sources, it is not possible to state conclusively whether the emperor was married (through any type of marriage) to a woman of the Betä Ǝsraᵓel. Indeed, the law of this group forbade any contacts—including marriage—with followers of another religion (Kaplan 2003b, p. 553). It is possible that (as Jesuit sources would have it) the woman was baptised (Pankhurst 1999, p. 82), but no Ethiopian sources confirm either this information or that concerning a marriage ceremony involving her.

Another marriage between a member of the imperial family and a representative of the Betä Ǝsraᵓel took place a few years later, during the reign of Susənyos,

---

[41] By people from outside their ethnic group, the Ethiopian Jews were referred to using the term *Felasha*. They themselves prefer to use the term Betä Ǝsraᵓel (literally, 'the house of Israel').

[42] Earlier, imaginary theories about finding one of the lost tribes of Israel originated from the ninth century.

[43] The first, Zäkrästos, died a few days after his father summoned him to the imperial court. The other, Yaᶜəqob, was announced the ruler of Ethiopia a few days after the Emperor's death. See Nosnitsin (2010), p. 547.

Yaᶜəqob's successor. As mentioned earlier, the emperor converted to the Catholic faith, which provoked some Ethiopian noblemen to rise up against the ruler. One of the rebels was the emperor's brother, Yəmrəḥannä Krəstos, who wanted to marry off his daughter to Walay, son of Gedewon, to secure the support of the Betä Ǝsraᵓel (Pankhurst 1997, p. 215). The rebellion failed, and Yəmrəhanä Krəstos was exiled. One of the charges brought against the emperor's brother was that he had sought to consort with the Betä Ǝsraᵓel, for which he was punished with a lifetime prohibition on contact with Ethiopian Jews. Susənyos' victory ended the period of attempts at establishing friendly relations with the Betä Ǝsraᵓel and arranging marriages with members of this group.

The above examples of marital and non-marital unions between Christian members of the imperial family and representatives of other religions show that only those unions in which a non-Christian underwent conversion were permitted by law. This was in accordance with the provisions of the *Fətḥa Nägäśt*, which was the legal code in force at the time. While it is understandable that marriage to a Muslim was not welcome at the imperial court, the reluctance of representatives of the imperial family to marry the Betä Ǝsraᵓel is surprising. Ethiopian Jews had similar marriage customs to Christians. As with the Amhara, a Betä Ǝsraᵓel betrothal often took place when the prospective spouses were very young, and the marriage itself was a contract between two families rather than the completion of a union between a man and a woman (Shelemay 1989, pp. 43–44). The Betä Ǝsraᵓel also—like the Ethiopian Christians—were very cautious when it came to choosing a husband or wife and always checked that the two parties were not connected by blood ties, going as far back as seven generations. To be sure, an obstacle to unions between the Amhara and the Jews was the low social status of the Betä Ǝsraᵓel and the legal prohibition of such unions by the Jewish leadership in Ethiopia; thus, such marriages were practically impossible among Ethiopian noblemen. However, among lower classes, inter-religious marriages (including Christian–Muslim marriages) were not uncommon and were socially accepted as long as the wedding ceremony took place in accordance with local customary law.

## 6.6 Marriage in the Period of the Regress of Ethiopian Legislation

The death of Iyoᵓas I in 1769 marked the end of real imperial power in Ethiopia. The Empire broke up into districts, whose rulers sought independence from the Gonder governors exercising *de facto* power on behalf of puppet emperors. This fragmentation of the state, known in Ethiopian historiography as the *zämänä mäsafənt* ('the period of the princes'), was the result of historical processes that had already begun at the time of the Great War with the Muslims in the sixteenth century. The Ethiopian Empire, ruined by constant invasions, long could not recover from the economic crisis and, in such a situation, the emperors' efforts to centralise power were hampered. Even the periods of economic and cultural development under Bäkaffa and Iyoᵓas I did not change the internal politics of the state.

There was hardly any general development of Ethiopian legislation as such during that period, as each district had its own legal code—increasingly often written down—and its own judges. In each district, its ruler was considered the highest judge, although cases threatening the national interest were tried before the emperor (Abir 1968, pp. 169–170). As an example of the development of local legislation, the Shewa district can be cited, which was one of the most successful political centres during the *zämänä mäsafənt*. The district was the home of Śahlä Maryam, later Emperor Mənilək II, who attempted to implement the district's style of governance, learnt in his youth, throughout the Ethiopian Empire after assuming power in the state.

Although the applied legal code in Shewa was the *Fətḥa Nägäśt*, a great deal of discretion was given to local judges to pass sentences based on their own judgement and local customary law. During the reigns of Asfa Wossen (1755–1808) and Wossen Sägäda (1808–1812), the sentences handed down by the Shewan courts were very cruel. The most severe (but also the most common) punishments included the death penalty, forced amputations, branding with iron, and flogging.[44] The Shewan criminal law code (based on customary law) was only reformed during the reign of Śahlä Śəllase (1813–1847), grandfather of Mənilək II, since—as W.C. Harris wrote—"[...] blood flowing from the veins of a subject found no pleasure in the eyes of the ruler" (Abir 1968, 170). According to the decree issued by the king of Shewa,[45] capital punishment was inflicted only in cases of murder, sacrilege and high treason. Furthermore, any death sentence had to be approved by the ruler.[46] If possible, the death penalty was changed to life imprisonment and confiscation of property. In the case of proven murder, the *nəgus*—in accordance with customary law—had to hand the murderer over to the victim's family, although it often happened that the ruler tried to persuade the family to accept financial compensation instead of killing the murderer (Ege 1996, pp. 133–134). As for minor offences, such as theft or corruption, Śahlä Śəllase decreed imposing hard physical labour instead of branding. Another important change in the Shewan legislation were punishments for debtors and those who could not pay taxes. Instead of imprisonment as previously, debtors became slaves to the lender until the debt was considered repaid (Abir 1968, pp. 170–171). Unfortunately, the sources do not provide any information on the changes introduced by Śahlä Śəllase regarding the law related to the institution of marriage. It can only be surmised that in Shewa, inhabited mostly by

[44] A special whip called *ǧəraf*, made from hippopotamus skin, was used to carry out this punishment (Guébré Sellasié 1930, p. 112).

[45] In 1839, Śahlä Śəllase, as the first Shewan ruler, assumed the title of king (*nəgus*). See Bartnicki and Mantel-Niećko (1978), p. 237.

[46] The *nəgus* of Shewa was the supreme judge, who presided over cases of the highest state importance or where the matter was highly controversial. Since the times of Aksum, the role of the second-instance court was performed by a group of judges (there were 19 in Shewa) called *wämbäroč*. See Ege (1996), p. 133.

the Amhara, the customary law allowed *qal kidan bäqurban*, *sərat* and *dämoz* marriages.[47]

The first change in family law concerning marriage came after the period of the princes, when Kaśa Ḫaylu (of Qwara origin) proclaimed himself emperor, taking the name of Tewodros II (1855–1868). After subjugating the districts of Tigray and Shewa, whose rulers had also put forward claims to the imperial crown, the new emperor embarked on a series of internal reforms. This involved, above all, a reorganisation of the state administration and the tax system. Slavery was also formally abolished. However, the most relevant for the present study decree was the prohibition of polygamy. The emperor decided that each Christian could have only one wife (Bartnicki and Mantel-Niećko 1978, pp. 252–253; Pankhurst 1990, p. 139). This shows that, despite the declarations made by previous rulers of the Ethiopian Empire, polygamy was a common phenomenon, not only among the nobility but also among common subjects. With his decree, Tewodros intended to put an end to this practice, although the law he introduced did not apply to Muslims residing in Ethiopia, who were still allowed to have four wives under Sharia law.

Some sources add that the emperor, wanting to be a living example of Christian morality, married only one woman—Princess Täwabäč, daughter of Gonder governor *Ras* Ali Alula. The wedding ceremony took place in September 1854. It was a *qal kidan bäqurban* marriage, and, although the couple had no children, the emperor remained faithful to his wife until her death. According to the same sources, the widowed emperor had doubts about whether he should remarry. He believed that he was bound by the same laws as the Ethiopian clergy (Rubenson 1966, p. 56). After eighteen months of deliberation, the emperor was persuaded to remarry by a Briton, John Bell. Tewodros' choice was Təruneš (or Təruwärq), daughter of *Däǧǧazmač* Wəbe.[48]

After Tewodros' suicide, Täklä Giyorgis II (1869–1871) took over the imperial crown for three years, followed by Yoḥannəs IV (1872–1889). During the reigns of both emperors, little changed in terms of the development of Ethiopian legislation, as both rulers were more preoccupied with internal and external threats.

For the present study, the only interesting information comes from the reign of Emperor Yoḥannəs IV. According to sources, when Yoḥannəs was in his thirties, he married an Afar woman. As a Muslim, she had to be baptised before the wedding ceremony and took the name Ṭəbäba Śəllase (Bairu Tafla 2014, p. 74). This confirms the lack of change in Ethiopian family law, which allowed unions between Christians and followers of different religions only if the latter converted to Christianity. There was also an interesting rumour spread after the ruler's death

[47] For an in-depth description of the judiciary apparatus in Shewa during the reign of *Nəgus* Śahlä Śəllase, see Ege (1996), pp. 132–134.

[48] It should be mentioned that, having only one wife, the Emperor lived according to the law he himself established, but defied the law contained in the *Fətḥa Nägäśt*. Indeed, one chronicle states that Tevodros and Täwabäč had lived together for ten years before the church wedding. The outraged chronicler wrote that, in such a case, the *qal kidan bäqurban* marriage should be forbidden, for the code allows it only for virgins (Paulos Tzadua and Strauss 1968, p. XXVI).

(treated as fact by some historical studies) that Yoḥannəs IV had a son with his elder brother's widow whom he married. While the fact that there was an official heir to the throne came as a surprise to Ethiopians at the time, marrying one's brother's wife did not offend anyone. This proves that in certain districts of Ethiopia levirate was acceptable and in accordance with local customary law (Bairu Tafla 2014, p. 74).

## 6.7 The Institution of Marriage During Mənilək II's Reign (1889–1913)

In 1889, Emperor Yoḥannəs IV died at the Battle of Metemma, and was succeeded by Mənilək II. The Shewan Emperor devoted the first nine years of his reign to the conquest of the south-western Horn of Africa and the annexation of new territories, thus building an empire larger than contemporary Ethiopia. Mənilək II intensified also contacts with European powers, finding in them—as did rulers of Aksum in Byzantium—a model to be followed (Bartnicki and Mantel-Niećko 1978, pp. 349–352). Thus, the ruler's fascination with European states resulted in a number of reforms intended to modernise the state (see, e.g., Marcus 1995, Märsəᶜe Ḫazän Wäldä Qirqos 2004; Prouty 1986).

Concerning the law and the development of the judiciary system, one of the most important reforms was the formation of the cabinet in 1907 and the appointment of the first Minister of Justice (*yäfərd ministər*) in Ethiopian history, Näsibu Mäsqälo.[49] Until the nomination, Näsibu held the title *afä nəgus* and for sixteen years he was a judge of the Supreme Court in Shewa (Ege 1996, p. 356; Rubinkowska 2007, p. 1150). The severity of his sentences (e.g., it was him who introduced the practice of branding thieves with a T-shaped mark on the forehead) was so well known that an anecdote circulated about defendants seeking reconciliation with their victims by saying, "Please do not let me stand [accused] before Nesibu" (Märsəᶜe Ḫazän Wäldä Qirqos 2004, pp. 29–31). Also, there was a rumour that the judge accepted bribes. To corroborate this allegation, Märsəᶜe Ḫazän Wäldä Qirqos (2004, pp. 30–31) quotes a case which, however, seems to be rather an example of the judicial practice called *wərərrəd mätkäl*, discussed above (Maḫtämä Śəllase Wäldä Mäsqäl 1950 [1942], p. 29). When defining the duties of a Minister of Justice, the Emperor emphasised that *afä nəgus* should always refer to the provisions of the *Fətḥa Nägäśt* in his sentences (Maḫtämä Śəllase Wäldä Mäsqäl 1950 [1942], p. 71; Paulos Tzadua and Strauss 1968, p. XXVII). As the Prime Minister and Minister of Justice, Näsibu Mäsqälo oversaw the twelve judges appointed to their positions by the Emperor

[49] Mənilək II's reform was met with disdain by representatives of Western powers in the Ethiopian Empire. In contrast, the Emperor's official chronicler, Gäbrä Śəllase, describes this reform as one of the most important for the modernisation of the state. Cf. Ege (1988), p. 351 and Guébré Sellasié (1930), pp. 527–528.

himself.[50] Mənilək divided the country into six judicial districts, to which he assigned two judges each. The appointed arbitrators bore the tile *aläqa* ('scholar'), but also *mälakä bərhan* ("guarding the light [the law]"), which was given to "[...] the most distinguished doctors of [legal] sciences, who knew and applied the *Fətḥa Nägäśt*" (Guébré Sellasié 1930, p. 153). In addition, there were three legal clerks in each sector, whose task was to keep the trial books.[51] This was another reform in imperial administration as, until Mənilək's reign, both the proceedings of the trial and the verdict were transmitted orally by imperial messengers. By writing down the names of the parties to the trial and the indictments, it was easier to conduct appeals (Märsəᶜe Ḫazän Wäldä Qirqos 2004, p. 43; Marcus 1995, p. 226).

The first panel of judges was appointed on 25 March 1908. In his memoirs, Märsəᶜe Ḫazän Wäldä Qirqos mentions the names and titles of only the five judges "on the right bench" pointing out that the same number of judges sat to the left in the Palace of Justice, with *Afä Nəgus* Näsibu Mäsqälo supposedly also a member of this group (Märsəᶜe Ḫazän Wäldä Qirqos 2004, pp. 42–43). The author also writes that, according to ancient custom, the office of the *afä nəgus* was located next to the entrance to the main hall of the Imperial Palace, and anyone passing these buildings had to dismount from his horse to show respect for the ruler and his justice (Märsəᶜe Ḫazän Wäldä Qirqos 2004, pp. 42–43; Perham 1969, p. 145). The offices of the other judges were built of corrugated sheet metal and were located in various places within the palace complex.[52]

In addition to the twelve appointed judges and *Afä Nəgus* Näsibu, the other imperial ministers also had the right to pass judgement. The Minister of War, *Fitawrari* Habtä Giyorgis, in particular, was famous for the justice of his sentences. Two court cases related to the institution of marriage in which the *Fitawrari* had passed judgment will be presented below.

> A man took a prostitute to his home for the night agreeing to pay her two Birr. As they liked each other after that first night, they cohabitated without contracting a marriage. She moved in, and fortune smiled on them and he became wealthy. After they had lived together for about five years, he wanted to marry another woman and asked her to move out. She agreed to leave on condition that she get[s] her share of wealth they built up together. He countered that she lived on her own free will, that they had not contracted marriage, and that he, therefore, was not going to share his wealth with her.
>
> Their case finally came to the court of *Fitawrari* Habte Giyorgis. After they each presented their case, judgment was pronounced. All the others judges passed verdict against her saying that they could not see how she could claim a share of the property, as she had no marriage contract. *Fitawrari* Habte Giyorgis, on the other hand, asked the man how many years they had lived together. The man replied that they had lived together for five years. He fur-

[50] According to Bairu Tafla (1991, pp. 91–111), the nomination of such a number of judges was supposed to be a return to Aksum tradition, in which the emperor had twelve advisors. In turn, Maḫtämä Śəllase Wäldä Mäsqäl (1950 [1942], p. 70) claims that there were sixteen judges.

[51] The superior of all the clerks was Ḫaylä Šumye (Märsəᶜe Ḫazän Wäldä Qirqos 2004, p. 43).

[52] Märsəᶜe Ḫazän Wäldä Qirqos' memoirs (2004, pp. 42–43) contradict the information provided in Emperor Mənilək II's official chronicle. Indeed, Gäbrä Śəllase (1930, p. 153) writes that ten magistrates resided in Adwa, one in Gonder and one in Addis Ababa.

> ther asked him how much he had agreed to pay her on the first night he took her home. The man replied that he agreed to give her two Birr and that he did give her that amount. [...] At that rate, his liability reached Birr 3,650 and was more than his property was worth. The man found himself in dilemma. Therefore, he pleaded with the woman to reconcile with him, gave her a marriage contract, and they started living as husband and wife (Märsəᶜe Ḫazän Wäldä Qirqos 2004, pp. 44–45).
>
> A gentlemen related that he spent the night with another man's wife in his dream. The husband heard the story and charged the gentleman to pay him *yinafa*[53] compensation. The case reached the court of *Fitawrari* Habte Giyorgis where he heard the litigants present their cases.
>
> On hearing the case, *Fitawrari* Habte Giyorgis, asked the accused if he had a mule. He replied that he had one. *Fitawrari* Habte Giyorgis then ordered him to bring his mule with all its accessories (saddle, bridle, strap...etc.). When he brought the mule, *Fitawrari* told him to give it to the plaintiff. Then *Fitawrari* turned to the plaintiff and said [sarcastically], "You have surely been victimized and wronged. The mule is your compensation; mount it here immediately and ride it home". The plaintiff was happy, mounted the mule and galloped it. He had gone only a short distance when *Fitawrari* sent a messanger to call him back. When the man returned, the *Fitawrari* ordered him to give back the mule to the owner. The man protested. [...] The *Fitawrari* then said: „What a strange thing, indeed! The accused slept with your wife only in a dream. Therefore it was not real. But you wanted *yinafa* compensation for a crime that was not actually committed". [...] The litigants each went their way, and the accused returned to his home with his mule (Märsəᶜe Ḫazän Wäldä Qirqos 2004, p. 45).

From the above it can be concluded that, officially, Ethiopian legislation at the turn of the twentieth century did not recognise the institution of concubinage, according to the rules of the *Fəṭḥa Nägäśt*. A woman who was not in a legalised relationship with a man was entitled neither to a share of the property after divorce nor to a retainer in the event of her partner's death. Furthermore, during the reign of Emperor Mənilək II, officials passing judgements did not have to adhere strictly to the provisions of the *Fəṭḥa Nägäśt*, but could refer also to the customary law, but above all to their own judicial assessment and to the principle of equality before the law.[54] Therefore, the *Fitawrari* had the right to order compensation for the woman. Moreover, the second quote implies that in nineteenth-century Ethiopia, according to customary law, a compensation was due to the betrayed husband. The aforementioned anecdote does not state whether or what punishment was applied to the woman the man dreamt of, although customary law also punished the woman for adultery, and the *Fəṭḥa Nägäśt* provides a more severe punishment against a woman than that applied to a man (Paulos Tzadua and Strauss 1968, p. 153).

Although the judicial apparatus in the Empire had undergone a major expansion by the end of the nineteenth century, Emperor Mənilək continued to act as supreme

[53] According to Märsəᶜe Ḫazän Wäldä Qirqos, *yinafa* is the compensation paid by an adulterer to the husband of the woman with whom he had an affair.

[54] For more on the principle of equality in Ethiopian legislation, see Abera Jembere (1998), pp. 93–95.

judge and he settled judicial disputes twice a week, for 5–6 h a day.[55] On Wednesdays, the Emperor issued judgements in civil cases, while on Fridays he dealt with criminal cases. The Emperor strictly adhered to the rule that court cases should not be dealt with on Saturdays and Sundays (Marcus 1995, p. 218). Unlike his grandfather, Mənilək was a strict judge and "[…] as cruel towards criminals as Pontius Pilate" (Marcus 1995, p. 197). The severity of his judgements increased further after the Battle of Adwa (1896); although, in the opinion of his contemporaries, the Emperor's sentences served more political needs than justice (Marcus 1995, p. 197). When issuing sentences, the Emperor usually relied on the legal provisions contained in the *Fətḥa Nägäśt*, although the imperial chronicler also described one case in which the death penalty was passed "[…] in accordance with customary law and the *Fətḥa Nägäśt*" (Gäbrä Śəllase 1967/1959, pp. 147, 178–179, 242–243, 286–287, 301, 314–315, 327 & 331).[56] As already mentioned, the Emperor only dealt with cases that threatened the existence of the state or in those involving murder, while family law cases were judged on a lower level. The official imperial chronicle records only one Mənilək's verdict in a case relaetd to a conflict between two dignitaries concerning marriage.

> A nobleman named Wäldä Ammanu'el married his sister to a man named Täsfa Mika'el. Some time later, Wäldä Ammanu'el demanded that his brother-in-law divorce his sister because he wanted to marry her off to another man.[57] Täsfa Mika'el loved his wife and did not want to part with her, so his brother-in-law took her from him by force and remarried her. The embittered Täsfa Mika'el forged a letter in which Wäldä Ammanu'el swore allegiance to Tewodros II and dropped it off at the latter's house. He then reported his find to Mənilək at his brother-in-law's house. However, the forgery soon came to light and Täsfa Mika'el was sentenced to death. (Gäbrä Śəllase 1967/1959, pp. 60–62).

A year after the cabinet was formed by imperial decree, Mənilək II issued a law against polygamy.[58] The punishment for it was confiscation of property and 2 years of imprisonment (Maḫtämä Śəllase Wäldä Mäsqäl 1950 [1942], p. 603).[59] As Bairu Tafla writes, the reasons why the Emperor decided to issue the decree are unclear (Bairu Tafla 1972, p. 13), especially if Mənilək II himself did not follow the laws

---

[55] Mənilək's extraordinary activeness as a supreme judge was also highlighted by Gäbrä Śəllase (1967/1959, pp. 60–66; Guébré Sellasié 1930, pp. 107–161), the emperor's official chronicler, who devoted as many as three chapters of the imperial chronicle to his judicial activities. Cf. Ege (1988), p. 353.

[56] In turn, Harold G. Marcus (1995, pp. 197, 219) claims that Mənilək often applied strict common law rules, of which he was accused by foreigners residing in the Empire (including by his advisor, Alfred Ilg). Cf. Gäbrä Śəllase (1967/1959), p. 198.

[57] The imperial chronicler does not explain what type of marriage was entered into between Täsfa Mika'el and Wäldä Ammanu'el's sister, but it was almost certainly not a marriage of the *qal kidan bäqurban* type, as – in this case – according to the law, divorce would not have been possible.

[58] Maḫtämä Śəllase Wäldä Mäsqäl (1982, p. 586) claimed also that Emperor Mənilək promulgated a decree under which no marriage could take place unless the bride and groom had previously met each other. However, such information does not appear in any of the other sources relating to the period.

[59] Bairu Tafla (1972, pp. 13–14) claims that the imperial decree only referred to church marriages.

related to marriage found in the *Fətḥa Nägäśt*. For example, a devout Ethiopian Christian should not marry more than twice in a lifetime (according to the rules in Part Eleven, Section Two of Chapter 24) (Paulos Tzadua and Strauss 1968, p. 137). Meanwhile, Mənilək married as many as three women,[60] though only one of them (Ṭaytu Bəṭul) was married in a church and crowned the Emperor's wife (*ətäge*). In the chapter on weddings, the code states that the wedding ceremony should take place in a church and the young couple should receive communion together (Paulos Tzadua and Strauss 1968, p. 142). In all probability, the Emperor believed that the provisions of the *Fətḥa Nägäśt* only applied to marriages contracted before the *abunä* and his other unions did not bear the features of a marriage, although the code does not define that a union contracted under customary law is not treated as a marriage.

Another legal provision that was frequently violated by the Emperor was the prohibition of concubinage expressed twice in the *Fətḥa Nägäśt* (Chapter 25 and Chapter 24, Part Five Section Five) (Paulos Tzadua and Strauss 1968, p. 144; 155). According to an Italian traveller, Orazio Antinori, who met Mənilək II in 1876, the King of Shewa not only bore a physical resemblance to his grandfather, but also inherited from him a predilection for women (Prouty 1986, p. 46). The constant affairs of the Shewan ruler irritated his wives to such an extent that one of them decided to take up arms against their unfaithful husband (Bafäna),[61] while another attempted to poison her rivals to get a place in the imperial bed (Ṭaytu).[62] However, it should be mentioned that none of the ruler's wives was opposed to his extramarital relationships, as long as they served their purposes. For example, according to some sources (Bairu Tafla 2014, p. 74) it was Ṭaytu who brought Šäwaräga (the offspring of the Emperor's affair with a servant) to the imperial court in order to marry her off to her nephew, *Ras* Mikael. Ṭaytu was also actively involved in the upbringing of Zäwditu, who was Mənilək's illegitimate daughter. Both of these moves (as well as other marriages arranged by the Empress) were aimed at increasing the *Ətäge*'s influence in the imperial court and on the choice of the heir to the throne.

Yet another legal provision violated during the reign of Mənilək II was related to marriages between relatives and affinities. According to the *Fətḥa Nägäśt* (Chapter

[60] The Emperor's wives were as follows: Alṭaš (the daughter of Emperor Tewodros II), Bafäna and Ṭaytu Bətul. For more information on Emperor Mənilək II's relationships, see Augustyniak (2009), pp. 25–43.

[61] In 1877, taking advantage of the absence of her husband, who was at war, Bafäna declared herself ruler of Shewa. The Queen herself claimed that she was pushed into this transgression and her scheming with Emperor Yoḥannəs IV by her jealousy of her husband. Cf. Zewde (1975), p. 89; Augustyniak (2009), p. 35.

[62] Ṭaytu was jealous not only of Mənilək's contacts with his previous wife, Bafäna, but also of the Emperor's relationship with his first wife, Alṭaš. Ṭaytu is said to have been involved in Alṭaš' mysterious and sudden death, which occurred shortly after her reunion with Mənilək in 1892 in Yäǧǧu (the meeting was said to have resulted in the princess' pregnancy). Cf. Prouty (1986), pp. 40–41; Bairu Tafla (2003), p. 211.

24, Part 2), marriage between a man and a woman who are separated by less than nine degrees of consanguinity is forbidden. Yet, in the imperial court under Mənilək, such unions occurred frequently, an example being the marriage between Šäwaräga and *Ras* Mikael, whom Mənilək regarded as his adopted son (Prouty 1986, p. 103). When courtiers (including Ṭaytu) were admonished for disobeying the law when arranging marriages between close relatives, they said that such unions were "[...] like mixing of milk and water, whereby the latter increased and whitened the former" (Bairu Tafla 1972, p. 21).[63] Perhaps Emperor Mənilək II's 1908 decree was intended to curb precisely these practices.

Whatever purpose the Emperor's decree may have served, it was a dead regulation. As Aṣmä Giyorgis wrote, "In Ethiopia a law is legislated but not put into practice" (Bairu Tafla 1987, p. 119). Paradoxically, the law introduced by Mənilək II was later used to overturn his crucial decision. The accusation of polygamy was one of the reasons (along with conversion to Islam) for the 1916 *coup d'état*, which resulted in the overthrow of *Ləǧ* Iyasu, the heir to the throne anointed by Mənilək II himself. However, his influence on the development of Ethiopian legislation should not be judged solely in the context of the aforementioned decree. He modernised the whole judicial apparatus, using Western models but preserving local traditions. All these measures provided the basis for the great codification of the law, which was undertaken by Ḫaylä Śəllase I.

## References


Abebe Z (2010) Wäyṭo. In: Uhlig S (ed) Encyclopaedia Aethiopica, vol 4. Harrassowitz, Wiesbaden, pp 1162–1164

Abir M (1968) Ethiopia: the era of the princes. The challenge of Islam and the re-unification of Christian empire, 1769–1855. Longmans, London

Ahmed H, Gori A (2007) Islam. In: Uhlig S (ed) Encyclopaedia Aethiopica, vol 3. Harrassowitz, Wiesbaden, pp 198–202

Augustyniak Z (2009) Małżeństwa polityczne w Etiopii na przełomie XIX i XX wieku. MA dissertation, Department of African Languages and Cultures, University of Warsaw

Bartnicki A, Mantel-Niećko J (1978) Geschichte Äthiopiens: von der Anfängen bis zur Gegenwart. Akademie-Verlag, Berlin

Beckingham CF, Huntingford GW (eds) (1961) The Prester John of the Indies. A true relation of the lands of the Prester John being the narrative of the Portuguese Embassy to Ethiopia in 1520, written by Father Francisco Alvares, vol 1. University Press, Cambridge

Berry LVB (2003) Bərhan Mogäsa. In: Uhlig S (ed) Encyclopaedia Aethiopica, vol 1. Harrassowitz, Wiesbaden, pp 534–535

Beru T (2013) Brief history of the Ethiopian legal systems – past and present. Int J Leg Inf 41(3):335–388

Beyene T, Pankhurst R, Shiferaw B (eds) (1990) Kasa and Kasa. Papers on the lives, times and images of Téwodros II and Yohannes IV (1855-1889). Institute of Ethiopian Studies, Addis Ababa University, Addis Ababa

Bruce J (1790) Travels to discover the source of the Nile, II. J. Ruthven, Edinburgh


[63] For more on political marriages in nineteenth-century Ethiopia, see Heran Sereke-Brhan (2002).

Chernetsov S (2005) Education. In: S. Uhlig (ed) Encyclopaedia Aethiopica vol 2, Wiesbaden, Harrassowitz, pp 228–230
Cohen A, Martínez A (2007) Jesuits. In: Uhlig S (ed) Encyclopaedia Aethiopica, vol 3. Harrassowitz, Wiesbaden, pp 277–281
Cohen L (2009) The missionary strategies of the Jesuits in Ethiopia (1555-1632). Harrassowitz, Wiesbaden
Cohen L (2014) Zädəngəl. In: Uhlig S (ed) Encyclopaedia Aethiopica, vol 5. Harrassowitz, Wiesbaden, pp 103–104
Conte C (1979) Ethiopia. An introduction to the ethnology of law. Giuffrè Editore, Varese
Crummey D (2000) Land and society in the Christian Kingdom of Ethiopia. From the thirteenth to the twentieth century. University of Illinois Press, Urbana and Chicago
Crummey D (2003) Bäkaffa. In: Uhlig S (ed) Encyclopaedia Aethiopica, vol 1. Harrassowitz, Wiesbaden, pp 449–450
Derat M-L (2010) The Zāgwē dynasty (11–13th centuries) and King Yemreḥanna Krestos. Annales d'Éthiopie 25(2010):159–195
Ege S (1988) The first Ethiopian cabinet: background and significance of the 1907 reform. In: Beyene T (ed) Proceedings of the Eight International Conference of Ethiopian Studies, vol I. Institute of Ethiopian Studies, Addis Ababa; Frobenius Institut, Johann Wolfgang Goëthe Universität, Frankfurt am Main, pp 351–360
Ege S (1996) Class, state, and power in Africa. A case study of the Kingdom of Shäwa (Ethiopia) about 1840. Harrassowitz, Wiesbaden
Gawlik K (1999) Exodus? Powrót? Niezwykła historia niezwykłego ludu w Rogu Afryki. In: Mantel-Niećko J (ed) Afrykański wygnaniec. Tożsamość a prawa człowieka Dialog, Warszawa
Haile G (2014) Zenahu lägalla. In: Uhlig S (ed) Encyclopaedia Aethiopica, vol 5. Harrassowitz, Wiesbaden, pp 180–181
Heran Sereke-Brhan (2002) Building Bridges, Drying Bad Blood: Elite Marriages, Politics and Ethnicity in 19th and 20th Century Imperial Ethiopia (PhD dissertation written at the Faculty of History at Michigan State University, 2002)
Hess RL (1970) An outline of Falasha history. In: Pankhurst R, Chojnacki S (eds) Proceedings of the Third International Conference of Ethiopian Studies, III. Institute of Ethiopian Studies, Haile Sellassie I University, Addis Ababa
Huyn L, Kalmer J (1935) Abessinien – Afrikas Unruhe-Herd. Das Bergland-Buch, Salzburg
Jembere A (1988) Tatayyaq Muget: the traditional Ethiopian mode of litigation. In: Beyene T (ed) Proceedings of the Eight International Conference of Ethiopian Studies, vol 1. Institute of Ethiopian Studies, Addis Ababa; Frobenius Institut, Johann Wolfgang Goëthe Universität, Frankfurt am Main, pp 245–262
Jembere A (1998) Legal history of Ethiopia, 1434-1974. Erasmus Universiteit, Leiden; Afrika-Studiecentrum, Rotterdam
Kaplan S (2003a) Bäədä Maryam I. In: Uhlig S (ed) Encyclopaedia Aethiopica, vol 1. Harrassowitz, Wiesbaden, p 432
Kaplan S (2003b) Betä Əsraᵓel. In: Uhlig S (ed) Encyclopaedia Aethiopica, vol 1. Harrassowitz, Wiesbaden, pp 552–559
Kleiner M (2005) Gälawdewos. In: Uhlig S (ed) Encyclopaedia Aethiopica, vol 2. Harrassowitz, Wiesbaden, pp 656–657
Kleiner M (2010) Säblä Wängel. In: Uhlig S (ed) Encyclopaedia Aethiopica, vol 4. Harrassowitz, Wiesbaden, pp 434–436
Marcus HG (1995) The life and times of Menelik II. Ethiopia 1844-1913. The Red Sea Press, Lawrenceville
Mattausch B (2007) Muggət. In: Uhlig S (ed) Encyclopaedia Aethiopica, vol 3. Harrassowitz, Wiesbaden, pp 1040–1041
Mustafa Z (1973) The substantive law applied by Muslim courts in Ethiopia. Possible justifications for the continued application of the Sharia. J Ethiop Law 9(1):138–148

Muth F-C (2007) Nūr b. Muǧāhid. In: Uhlig S (ed) Encyclopaedia Aethiopica, vol 3. Harrassowitz, Wiesbaden, pp 1209–1210
Nosnitsin D (2010) Śärṣä Dəngəl. In: Uhlig S (ed) Encyclopaedia Aethiopica, vol 4. Harrassowitz, Wiesbaden, pp 544–547
Páez P (2008) História da Etiópia. Assirio & Alvim, Lisboa
Pankhurst R (1979) An eighteenth-century Ethiopian dynastic marriage contract between Empress Mentewwab of Gondar and Ras Mika'el Sehul of Tigre. Bull School Orient Afr Stud 42(3):457–466
Pankhurst R (1990) A social history of Ethiopia. Addis Ababa University, Addis Ababa
Pankhurst R (1997) Dynastic inter-marriage in medieval and post-medieval Ethiopia. In: Fukui K, Eisei K, Shigeta M (eds) Ethiopia in broader perspective. Papers of the XIIIth International Conference of Ethiopian Studies, vol I. Shokado Book Sellers, Kyoto, pp 206–220
Pankhurst R (1999) Ethiopian dynastic marriage and the Beta Israel. In: Parfitt T, Semi ET (eds) The Beta Israel in Ethiopia and Israel. Studies on Ethiopian Jews. Curzon, Richmond, pp 206–220
Perham M (1969) The Government of Ethiopia. Faber and Faber, London
Perruchon J (ed) (1893) Les chroniques de Zar'a Yâeqôb et de Ba'eda Mâryâm rois d'Éthiopie de 1434 a 1478. Émile Bouillon, Paris
Prouty C (1986) Empress Taytu and Menelik II. Ethiopia 1883-1910. The Red Sea Press, Trenton
Quirin J (1992) The evolution of Ethiopian Jews. A history of the Beta Israel (Falasha) to 1920. University of Pennsylvania Press, Philadelphia
Rubenson S (1966) King of Kings Tewodros of Ethiopia. Haile Sellassie I University, Addis Abeba; Oxford University Press, Nairobi
Rubinkowska H (2007) Näsibu Mäsqälo. In: S. Uhlig (ed) Encyclopaedia Aethiopica, vol 3, Wiesbaden, Harrassowitz, pp 1150.
Sadowski M (2014) Małżeństwo z muzułmaninem – aspekty prawne. http://www.temidium.pl/artykul/malzenstwo_z_muzulmaninem_aspekty_prawne-1018.html
Sedler RA (1964) The Chilot jurisdiction of the Emperor of Ethiopia: a legal analysis in historical and comparative perspective. J Afr Law 8(2):59–76
Śəllase G (1967/1959) Tarikä zämän zä-dagmawi Mənilək Nəgusä nägäśt zä-Ityopya. Artistik, Addis Abeba
Sellasié G (1930) Chronique du règne de Ménélik II, roi de rois d'Éthiopie. Libraire Orientale et Américaine, Paris
Shelemay KK (1989) Music, ritual, and Falasha history. Michigan State University Press, East Lansing
Tafla B (1972) Marriage as a political device: an appraisal of socio-political aspect of the Menelik period 1889-1916. J Ethiop Stud 1(10):13–23
Tafla B (ed) (1987) Aṣma Giyorgis and his work. History of the Gāllā and the kingdom of Šawā. Franz Steiner, Stuttgart
Tafla B (1991) The dispensation of justice in traditional Ethiopia. An appraisal of legal historiography. In: Philipps L, Ádám A, Wittman R (eds) Rechtsentstehung und Rechtskultur. Heinrich Scholler zum 60. Geburtstag. Decker & Müller, Heidelberg, pp 91–111
Tafla B (2003) Alṭaš Tewodros. In: Uhlig S (ed) Encyclopaedia Aethiopica, vol 1. Harrassowitz, Wiesbaden, p 211
Tafla B (2014) Yoḥannəs IV. In: Uhlig S (ed) Encyclopaedia Aethiopica, vol 5. Harrassowitz, Wiesbaden, pp 73–80
Torrey E.F. (1970) The Zar Cult of Ethiopia. In: Pankhurst R, Chojnacki S (eds) Proceedings of the Third International Conference of Ethiopian Studies, III. Institute of Ethiopian Studies, Haile Sellassie I University, Addis Ababa, pp 51–59
Toubkis D (2014) Zäkrəstos. In: Uhlig S (ed) Encyclopaedia Aethiopica, vol 5. Harrassowitz, Wiesbaden, pp 118–119
Trimingham JS (1952) Islam in Ethiopia. Oxford University Press, London
Tzadua P, Strauss PL (1968) The Fetha Nagast. The law of the Kings. Faculty of Law, Haile Sellassie I University, Addis Ababa

Ullendorff E (1962) The Ethiopians: an introduction to country and people. Oxford University Press, London
van Donzel E (2005) Fasilädäs. In: Uhlig S (ed) Encyclopaedia Aethiopica, vol 2. Harrassowitz, Wiesbaden, pp 499–502
Virgin E (1936) The Abyssinia I knew. Macmillan, London
Wäldä Qirqos MH (2004) Of what I saw and heard. The last years of emperor Menelik II and the brief rule of Iyassu. Centre Français des Études Éthiopiennes & Zamra Publishers, Addis Ababa
Zewde G-S (1975) Yohannes IV of Ethiopia: a political biography. Clarendon Press, Oxford

# Chapter 7
# The Great Codification

## 7.1 The Legal Reforms of Iyasu V: Changes in Civil Law

In 1909, Emperor Mənilək II, weakened by an illness that he had been suffering from for a number of years, announced *Ləǧ* Iyasu (1910–1916) his successor to the Ethiopian throne.[1] Until recently, the opinions on the latter's reign was unequivocally negative. This was due not only to the mistakes he made during his reign, but also to the *Ras* Täfäri Mäkʷännən's (later Emperor Ḫaylä Śəllase I) propaganda, which led to the heir to the throne being seen as a playboy and apostate, with no respect for tradition. Due to the efforts of the last Ethiopian Emperor, any reliable research on Iyasu's reign was for a long time impossible. The *Ləǧ*'s descendants had felt so threatened that they did not reveal their origins, or left Ethiopia forever. It was believed that even mentioning the name of the heir to the throne, let alone keeping mementos of him, could cause severe problems. Little is therefore known about the political thought of Mənilək II's successor, although recent research confirms that *Abeto* Iyasu wanted to continue the processes of modernisation of Ethiopia begun by his predecessor, both in terms of foreign policy and the country's domestic affairs (Ahmed Hassen Omar 2014; Rubinkowska-Anioł 2000/2001). However, the reluctance of the Shewan noblemen to change and the resentments of the Western European colonial powers, combined with the ruler's impulsive character and political immaturity, meant that Iyasu was unable to implement these plans.

During his short reign, *Ləǧ* Iyasu only managed to carry out limited number of reforms.[2] Two concerned the prohibition of certain customary law practices. The most important of these involved the prohibition of *qʷäräñña* (literally 'bound').

[1] *Ləǧ* Iyasu was the son of the Emperor's daughter—Šäwaräga and *Ras* Mikael, governor of the district of Uello.

[2] According to Iyasu's chronicler (Gäbrä Əgziʾabəḥer Elyas and Molvaer 1994, pp. 37, 328), most of the reforms were introduced in 1912. This is also confirmed by Märsəʿe Ḫazän Wäldä Qirqos (2004, p. 115).



Z. Augustyniak, *Marriage in the Ethiopian Empire*, Studies in the History of Law and Justice 33, https://doi.org/10.1007/978-3-032-26065-9_7

This was the practice of chaining the right hand of the transgressor with the left hand of the accuser or his relative. The two people had to walk around chained until the judge decided that the punishment had been served. According to Richard Pankhurst (2010, p. 316), punishment of this type could be ordered regardless of the crime committed, and its main purpose was to induce remorse in the offender. *Abeto* Iyasu banned this type of practice, but only when it involved a murder case. The ruler considered this type of punishment to be a double persecution of the victim's family (Märsəᶜe Ḫazän Wäldä Qirqos 2004, p. 113; Gäbrä Ǝgziᵓabəḥer Elyas and Molvaer 1994, pp. 37, 328–329). Also, the ruler ordered that only prison guards should be responsible for guarding a prisoner.

Another customary law practice banned by Iyasu was *leba šay* ('thief seeker'), a traditional method applied in cases theft. Although banned in Tigray by Emperor Yoḥannəs IV, it was still practised in Shewa and neighbouring districts. After a crime had been reported, a man and a young boy, just before puberty, would be summoned to the scene of a theft. A strong drug was administered to the boy who, in a trance induced by the psychoactive substance, recreated the act of stealing. The boy would then walk around the village visiting various farmyards. The person deemed guilty of the theft was the one in whose house the intoxicated boy would pass out. The alleged thief had to not only give back the stolen goods, but also cover the costs incurred in the search for the perpetrator.[3] Often there was abuse during the performance of the *leba šay* ritual, as it would happen that the owner of the house where the intoxicated boy fell asleep would pay the 'seeker' to give the boy even more of the drug to stimulate the sleeper to continue his search. This could be repeated many times, leading the boy to overdose and die. In addition, the growing dissatisfaction of people who had to pay for crimes they had not committed led Ethiopians to offer hospitality to strangers less and less, fearing that it was a case of *leba šay*.[4] *Ləǧ* Iyasu, seeing the fraud both in the practice itself and in the use of it by thief seekers to enrich themselves (Märsəᶜe Ḫazän Wäldä Qirqos 2004, pp. 113–114; Gäbrä Ǝgziᵓabəḥer Elyas and Molvaer 1994, pp. 37, 329–330), decreed that the search for the thief was to be carried out by the victim himself, and that if he decided that he wanted the assistance of a *leba šay*, he had to pay for his services. In addition, the ruler enacted a law according to which a person in whose house a drugged boy would pass out did not have to cover the costs of the search and pay compensation to the victim, as long as the stolen object was not found in his farmyard. Although the law enacted by *Ləǧ* Iyasu came into force, *leba šay* continued to be used in the detection of crimes. It was not until Empress Zäwditu that the practice was finally forbidden (Gäbrä Ǝgziᵓabəḥer Elyas and Molvaer 1994, pp. 166, 462–463; Ficquet and Smidt 2014, p. 192).

In addition to outlawing the above-mentioned practices, Iyasu took steps to amend the law relating to the confiscation of a nobleman's property in the event of

---

[3] An exceptionally colourful description of the *leba šay* ritual was presented by J. I. Eadie (1924, pp. 79–83).

[4] Refusing to give hospitality to a stranger who knocked on one's door was one of the more serious transgressions against good custom.

his misuse of power. Before Iyasu took over, any state official caught embezzling money or committing any other crime was deprived not only of his office, but also of all the property he owned. However, the punishment was not severe enough to prevent the noblemen from swindling. It happened that officials hid precious objects and gave their cattle to their families, thus avoiding confiscation. Iyasu abolished the confiscation order, replacing it with an obligation to make reparations. If the fine (corresponding to the seriousness of the crime) was not paid within the indicated period, the culprit faced imprisonment (Gäbrä Ǝgziᵓabəḥer Elyas and Molvaer 1994, pp. 37–38, 330; Märsəᶜe Ḫazän Wäldä Qirqos 2004, p. 114). To more effectively counter financial embezzlement at his court, Iyasu conducted frequent audits of ministries and offices (Gäbrä Ǝgziᵓabəḥer Elyas and Molvaer 1994, pp. 48, 342–343; Bahru Zewde 2007, p. 254).

The above decree did not meet with the approval of some of the Ethiopian noblemen. In addition, it is also certain that they were also dissatisfied with another law introduced by the ruler. Iyasu had decided to simplify the method of transferring tithes to the palace. Until the reform was introduced, teams of four officials inspected districts shortly before the harvest season, assessing the abundance of the year's grain harvest. On this basis, they determined the amount of tithes to be paid to the imperial treasury. As the assessments were inaccurate, fraud and misappropriation of grain by local administrators was common. Moreover, no farmer (on threat of punishment) was allowed to start harvesting until the imperial officials had visited him, even if this risked damaging the crops (e.g., due to heavy rain). In addition, each of the visited peasants had to host a feast in honour of the visitors. All this meant that the Ethiopian farmers delivered increasingly smaller tithes to the imperial palace, and suffered hunger. *Ləǧ* Iyasu decided that each farmer would himself declare the amount of grain he owned and on this basis the tithe amount would be calculated (Gäbrä Ǝgziᵓabəḥer Elyas and Molvaer 1994, pp. 38–39, 330–331; Märsəᶜe Ḫazän Wäldä Qirqos 2004, pp. 114–115).

Iyasu also introduced minor changes in civil law. He decreed that upon the death of a childless person, their estate would not pass to the state, as was the case until then, but would be inherited by a relative of the deceased, who should pay for the funeral mass with the inherited money.[5]

However, Iyasu did not change the law prohibiting polygamy. Numerous sources (Bahru Zewde 2007, 255; Augustyniak 2014b, pp. 39–47; Gäbrä Ǝgziᵓabəḥer Elyas and Molvaer 1994, pp. 64, 358–359; Gobäze Ṭafäṭä 1996, p. 130; Bahru Zewde 1991; Prouty 1986) indicate that he himself married at least ten women, half of them Muslim.[6] Being involved in these relationships, the *abeto* was breaking *Fətḥa Nägäśt* law, according to which a man can only marry three times and all wives should embrace the Christian faith (Paulos Tzadua and Strauss 1968, pp. 136–137,

[5]Until Iyasu's reign, no mass was celebrated after a childless person died (Gäbrä Ǝgziᵓabəḥer Elyas and Molvaer 1994, pp. 38, 331; Mers'é Hazen Wolde Qirqos 2004, p. 115).

[6]The ruler's promiscuity and his alleged conversion to Islam were the official reasons for the *coup d'état* in 1916. For more on the reasons behind the ruler's downfall, see Rubinkowska-Anioł 2000/2001, pp. 25–38.

144). Also, his first marriage to Aster Mängäša, the granddaughter of Yoḥannəs IV, described as the only legitimate union (Gäbrä Ǝgziᵓabəḥer Elyas and Molvaer 1994, p. 358), was in fact an illegitimate one, as it was concluded in violation of the *Fətḥa Nägäśt*. Indeed, on the day of the marriage, *Ləǧ* Iyasu was a 12-year-old boy, while Yoḥannəs IV's granddaughter was only 6 years old. According to the code, the appropriate age for marriage is 20–25 for a man and 12–15 for a girl (Paulos Tzadua and Strauss 1968, p. 140). Despite the obvious breach of the rules, the marriage was never dissolved, perhaps because it was a political union and the marriage was never consummated. As the *Fətḥa Nägäśt* emphasises the importance of procreation, and it can be assumed that *Ləǧ* Iyasu's marriage to Aster Mängäša was not consummated, thus according to the law it did not exist. However, the Shewan noblemen plotting against Iyasu considered this marriage to be valid, and his subsequent unions to be a breach of the law.[7] However, the most important reason why the Ethiopian aristocracy decided to break the oath given to the dying Mənilək and go against their ruler was Iyasu's alleged conversion to Islam. Indeed, in chapter 44 of the *Fətḥa Nägäśt*, the first section states: "And if the king becomes a heretic, from that moment he is no longer a king, but a rebel" (Paulos Tzadua and Strauss 1968, p. 271).[8]

## 7.2 Marriage During Täfäri Mäkʷännən's Regency (1916–1930)

After a successful *coup d'état* in 1916, Zäwditu, the eldest daughter of Emperor Mənilək, ascended the imperial throne. As the Empress had no political experience, Täfäri Mäkʷännən (appointed as regent) and *Fitawrari* Habtä Giyorgis, minister of war in Mənilək II's government, were to rule alongside her.[9] Although formally Zäwditu decided, Habtä Giyorgis, who had provided distinguished service to the country over many years, unquestionably held a high position. The *Abune* Matewos was an equally important advisor to the Empress, as Zäwditu was very religious and more focused on the affairs of the church than on the *raison d'état*.[10] Despite the

[7] The fact that the ruler's other marriages were also political unions aimed at expanding his influence and ensuring the loyalty of the rulers of the Muslim provinces did not matter to Iyasu's opponents. For more on Iyasu marriages and their significance for the internal politics of Ethiopia, see Augustyniak (2011), pp. 45–54.

[8] For more reasons for breaking the oath given to Mənilək, see Gäbrä Ǝgziᵓabəḥer Elyas and Molvaer (1994), pp. 63–65, 357–360.

[9] Rubinkowska-Anioł (2010, pp. 17–46) discusses the difficulties of accessing Ethiopian sources from this period.

[10] Despite her fervent faith, the Empress failed to observe (as did her father and nephew) the marriage regulations of *Fətḥa Nägäśt*. She was first married off to Arᵓaya Yoḥannəs, the son of Yoḥannəs IV. Because she was seven years old, and her husband only eight years older, arranging such a union, as in the case of Iyasu, was unlawful. Nevertheless, the wedding took place with

apparent chaos, there was a strict division of responsibilities between the members of the triumvirate. The Empress was responsible for maintaining good relations with the Ethiopian Orthodox Church, *Fitawrari* Habtä Giyorgis was given authority over the army, while the management of state administration and diplomatic relations were appointed to Täfäri Mäkʷännən (Rubinkowska-Anioł 2010, p. 147).

In view of the above, changes in Ethiopian legislation have to be attributed to Täfäri Mäkʷännən, although officially the law was made by the Empress. However, Zäwditu did so in consultation with or at the instigation of the regent, as she seems to have supported Täfäri's ideas on modernising the country despite her conservatism. For example, in 1918, she issued an edict upholding her father's decision to ban slavery (Perham 1969, p. 225). Such a prohibition was one of the requirements that Ethiopia had to fulfil when joining the League of Nations, and membership in the organisation was of particular interest to the regent. Zäwditu was not happy with this regulation, as she herself owned many slaves (Rubinkowska 2014, p. 158), so Täfäri Mäkʷännən proposed a law banning the slave trade but allowing slave ownership. In doing so, he argued that total abolition would have unbalanced the Ethiopian economy.[11]

Täfäri Mäkʷännən also took on the responsibility of presiding over the imperial courts (*zufan čəlot*), although traditionally this role was held by the ruler (Bairu Tafla 1991, p. 97). According to the chronicle written by Gäbrä Ǝgziᵓabəḥer Elyas, Täfäri Mäkʷännən dealt with court cases three times a week. On Wednesdays, he handled appeals, on Fridays he tried murderers in accordance with the *Fətḥa Nägäśt*, while Saturdays were devoted to Special Court cases (Gäbrä Ǝgziᵓabəḥer Elyas and Molvaer 1994, pp. 208, 500; Haile Sellassie I 1976, p. 65).[12] The assumption of judicial duties by the regent was not welcomed by the Shewan nobility, for whom this was a clear signal that *Ras* Täfäri was set on reaching for the imperial crown. According to Gäbrä Ǝgziᵓabəḥer Elyas, in 1924, Zäwditu was approached by noblemen demanding that she start presiding over the court every Wednesday and Friday. The Empress, recognising her duty, agreed, but she held only one session, finding it extremely distressing to hand out the final verdicts (Gäbrä Ǝgziᵓabəḥer Elyas and Molvaer 1994, pp. 160, 455–456).

As for laws relating to the institution of marriage, during the period of the triumvirate, both the Empress and the Regent took certain legal steps to limit the number of divorces and to favour church marriages. During her reign, Zäwditu enacted a law according to which any of her subjects who chose a *qal kidan bäqurban* marriage, or who declared their intention to join a monastery after the death of a spouse thus

great pomp and in accordance with the provisions of the code. Six years after the ceremony, Zäwditu Mənilək was widowed—her husband died of smallpox and she married three more times. All of her marriages were legal and performed according to a secular rite. See Augustyniak (2009), pp. 64–74.

[11] M. Perham (1969, pp. 225–226) included the content of the decree in her book. Ethiopia was admitted to the League of Nations in 1923, but had to fulfil its obligations *post factum*.

[12] The Special Court, which was established after Habtä Giyorgis' death, dealt with the resolution of conflicts between Ethiopians and foreigners residing in Ethiopia.

married, would receive the entire wedding trousseau from the imperial palace (Gäbrä Ǝgziᵓabəḥer Elyas and Molvaer 1994, pp. 160, 455–456). As mentioned earlier, the Empress was a very religious person and perhaps in this way she wanted to encourage her subjects to dispense with civil ceremonies or to marry according to customary law.

In 1918, Täfäri Mäkʷännən, during a flu epidemic, which led to the death of many Ethiopians, sent an official letter to *Abune* Matewos with a request for him to intervene and to "bring moral reform" (Bairu Tafla 1972, p. 21), paying particular attention to issues relating to the institution of marriage. In his letter, the Regent proposed to issue a special statement on the matter, stamped at the top with the seals of the Empress and *Abune*, and at the bottom with the seal of Täfäri Mäkʷännən. The letter received no clear response from the Church and the subject of frequent divorce among Ethiopian Christians was dropped.

Both *Abune* Matewos and *Fitawrari* Habtä Giyorgis died in 1926.[13] The latter's death ended the rule of the triumvirate, while contributing to the growing animosity between the Empress and Täfäri Mäkʷännən. Up to this point, as both Ethiopian sources and Western studies emphasise, cooperation between the ruling trio had been excellent (Gäbrä Ǝgziᵓabəḥer Elyas and Molvaer 1994, pp. 125, 424; Ḫaylä Śəllase I 1937, p. 44; Haile Sellassie I 1976, p. 64; Rubinkowska-Anioł 2010, pp. 182–186). In the chronicle of Zäwditu's rule, its author, Gäbrä Ǝgziᵓabəḥer Elyas, lists the legal and administrative initiatives undertaken by the Empress and regent "[...] to remove the speck of ignorance from the eyes of Ethiopia [...]" (Gäbrä Ǝgziᵓabəḥer Elyas and Molvaer 1994, pp. 163, 458):

1. Establishment of the Criminal Court
2. Creation of the lower and upper houses of the parliament[14]
3. Establishment of a Ministry of Foreign Affairs
4. Establishment of a prison with wards for those on death row[15]
5. Division of the Ethiopian Empire into twelve districts and nomination of one judge per district

[13] In a passage in the chronicle dedicated to the *Abune* Matewos' successor, Gäbrä Ǝgziᵓabəḥer Elyas mentions that according to the *Fətḥa Nägäśt*, the archbishop of Ethiopia had to originate from Alexandria, because "one Egyptian wrote [out] of his own head ("thought") in the [book] Justice of Kings (*Fitha Negest*) in the name of the 300 [i.e. 318 clergymen said to have gathered at the Council of Nicaea in A.D. 325]." (Gäbrä Ǝgziᵓabəḥer Elyas and Molvaer 1994, pp. 137, 526). This quote confirms that in the first half of the twentieth century, it was still commonly thought that the code was created during the Council of Nicaea.

[14] Gäbrä Ǝgziᵓabəḥer Elyas is mistaken in this statement, as the parliament was established by the Constitution promulgated in July 1931 (Gäbrä Ǝgziᵓabəḥer Elyas and Molvaer 1994, pp. 163, 458; Augustyniak 2014a, pp. 25–38).

[15] According to the Regent's order, the death penalty could only be prescribed in cases listed in the *Fətḥa Nägäśt* (Maḫtämä Śəllase Wäldä Mäsqäl 1950 [1942], p. 91; Paulos Tzadua and Strauss 1968, p. xxvii).

6. Printing and publishing an abridged version of the *Fətḥa Nägäśt*
7. Publishing the constitution[16]
8. Banning the practice of *wərərrəd mätkäl*
9. Setting working hours for judges[17]
10. Introduction of a system to help maintain the order of filing with the imperial court[18]
11. Establishment of the Special Court of Ethiopia.

The establishment of the last institution was the first step towards regulating the legal relations between Ethiopia and foreigners residing therein. Most of the cases dealt with commercial or civil law. Occasionally, there were cases bordering on criminal law. All case files were bilingual, i.e. in Amharic and in a relevant European language, making these minutes another important source for the development of legislation in Ethiopia, especially as regards case law. In addition, Ethiopian legislation had to be applied to an Ethiopian standing before the Special Court, and the documents were sent to the embassies. As a result much information on Ethiopian customary law can be found in the archives of the foreign ministries of the European powers.

The records of the Special Court were analysed by Heinrich Scholler (1985) and Jacques Vanderlinden (1966). However, among the cases they quote, there is none related to the institution of marriage. There may be two reasons for this: either such cases were dealt by Ethiopian courts (if the marriages were contracted in Ethiopia), or in the 15 years of the court's operation there was not a single divorce case that required judicial intervention. The first is much more likely, especially given the many types of marriages in Ethiopia.

## 7.3 The First Constitution of Ethiopia: The Issue of Inter-ethnic Marriages

Empress Zäwditu died on 2 April 1930. Many historians suppose she was poisoned by order of the Regent (cp. Greenfield 1967, p. 163; Seunarine 1999, p. 69; Marcus 1987, p. 96; Rubinkowska-Anioł 2010, p. 240) and, even though there is no

[16] The chronicler is once again mistaken as the Ethiopian constitution was announced in 1931, after Empress Zäwditu's death. Cf. Gäbrä Ǝgziᵓabəḥer Elyas and Molvaer (1994), pp. 163, 458; Augustyniak (2014a), p. 25.

[17] The judges were to rule on criminal and civil cases until one o'clock in the afternoon. After a two-hour break, they were to focus exclusively on studying new laws and decisions adjudicated by higher courts.

[18] Until the system was introduced, those who paid more to the palace servants would be admitted to the imperial judges. According to the law introduced by Zäwditu and Täfäri, the petitioner first had to pay a fixed fee, and then the imperial secretaries would record the type of case and set a date for a hearing.

evidence for his involvement, Täfäri Mäkʷännən doubtless benefitted from the Empress' death, as there were no obstacles for him to reach for full power. Exactly seven months after Zäwditu's death, the coronation of the Emperor, who took the name Ḫaylä Śəllase I, took place.[19] One of his first decisions was to promulgate the first constitution in the history of Ethiopia.

While he was still the regent, Täfäri Mäkwännən commissioned *Abba* Jérôme Gäbrä Mädḫən Gäbrä Muse[20] to translate a few European codes into Amharic and write a draft version of the constitution based on them. Nonetheless, according to Ḫaylä Śəllase himself, the project was blocked by "some nobles", who were afraid "it would diminish the dignity and authority" of the Empress (cf. Haile Selassie I 1976, p. 178), leading to the abandonment of the project. After the Empress died, *Abba* Jérôme's work was completed by *Bäğrond* Täklä Ḥawaryat Täklä Maryam. While writing the Ethiopian Constitution, he drew on the laws of European countries, including England and Italy, as well as on the Japanese constitution.

The promulgation of the constitution took place on 16 July 1931, less than a year after the Emperor's coronation. After the ceremonial signing of the document by Ḫaylä Śəllase, representatives of all social groups paid homage to the new Emperor. The ruler then gave a fiery speech, comparing Ethiopia to a great family in which all are subject to the same law and rule is exercised by one emperor (cf. Haile Selassie I 1967, p. 389; Perham 1969, pp. 423–432). The monarch also stressed that all provisions in the constitution were in line with Ethiopian customs, and that representatives of the noblemen, government officials and "other Ethiopian subjects" had been involved in drafting the text of the document (Marcus 1987, p. 117).[21]

Although the new ruler claimed that having a constitution was the next step towards modernising the state,[22] its overriding aim was to legitimise the right of Ḫaylä Śəllase and his descendants to the throne and to introduce absolute monarchy (for more, see Augustyniak 2014a, pp. 25–38). This is clearly stated in the three articles of the first chapter of the constitution, which read:

> […] Art. 3. The law determines that the imperial dignity shall remain perpetually attached to the line of His Majesty Haile Selassie I, descendant of King Sahle Selassie, whose line

[19] The Regent was announced as the country's new ruler on the second day after the Empress died, but the official ceremony was postponed for six months to allow for the attendance of representatives of countries with which Ethiopia had established diplomatic relations during Täfäri Mäkʷännən's regency.

[20] Jérôme Gäbrä Mädḫən Gäbrä Muse was a Catholic priest educated by the French Lazarists and Capuchins and a close associate of Ḫaylä Śəllase. In 1918, he left the priesthood for civil service. Able to speak many languages (including Tigrinya, Amharic, Ge'ez, Latin, Italian and French), he also assisted various European researchers of Ethiopia (Rouaud 2007, pp. 272–273).

[21] The English translation of the Emperor's speech on the announcement of the constitution is included in Haile Selassie I's autobiography (1967, pp. 388–391).

[22] The Emperor's modernisation initiatives during the first period of his reign are discussed by R. Pankhurst (2006, pp. 181–201). The Emperor himself explains the reasons why he decided to create the constitution in his autobiography (Haile Sellassie I 1976, pp. 178–201).

descends without interruption from the dynasty of Menelik I, son of King Solomon of Jerusalem and the Queen of Ethiopia, known as the Queen of Sheba.

Art. 4. The throne and the crown of the empire shall be transmitted to the descendants of the Emperor pursuant to the law of the imperial house.

Art. 5. By virtue of his imperial blood, as well as by the anointing which he has received, the person of the Emperor is sacred, his dignity is inviolable and his power indisputable. He is consequently entitled to all the honors due to him in accordance with tradition and the present Constitution. The law decrees that anyone so bold as to seek to injure His Majesty the Emperor will be punished (*Ethiopian Constitution of 1931*).

The circumstances of the drafting, publication and reception of the constitution are outside the scope of the present study, but it is worth noting that its promulgation on 16 July 1931 marked the beginning of a period of change in Ethiopian legislation that culminated in the 1960s. It was in this document that the term "nation" first appeared (Articles 1, 2, 32, 35) and institutions were established that had a tremendous impact on the development of legislation in the Ethiopian Empire. In this respect, the most important points in the constitution are articles 7, 9, 10 of Chapter 2, which define the law-making bodies:

[...] Art. 7. The Emperor of Ethiopia will institute the Chamber of the Senate (Yeheggue Mewossegna Meker Beth) and the Chamber of Deputies (Yeheggue Memriya Meker Beth). The laws prepared by those chambers become executory by imperial promulgation.

[...] Art. 9. When the chambers are not sitting, the Emperor has the right in case of necessity to promulgate decrees taking the place of laws, so as to maintain order and avert public dangers. The law determines that these decrees shall in due course be presented to the chambers at their first subsequent meeting, and that they shall be abrogated for the future if the chambers do not approve of them.

Art. 10. The Emperor shall give the necessary orders to ensure the execution of the laws in force, according to the letter and the spirit thereof, for the maintenance of public order and for the development of the prosperity of the nation. (*Ethiopian Constitution of 1931*)

Members of the upper house of parliament were elected by the Emperor from among representatives of the nobility who had already served at the imperial court as ministers, judges, army commanders or members of the imperial council. Members of the lower house of parliament were elected by senators and district administrators (*šumoch'*). This was a temporary solution to be replaced by a general election. Parliament was to meet once a year and last about 6 months. During this time, both chambers were busy drafting and passing laws. Every law had to be accepted by both houses of parliament, but only after it had been approved by the Emperor. Moreover, the Emperor himself could issue decrees which immediately became law. Although they required parliamentary approval and the lack of it was supposed to lead to the suspension of this law, in practice it never happened that the parliamentarians, as subjects of the ruler, opposed the Emperor's will. The more so that the upper house was headed by the Emperor's trusted officials: *Bitwäddäd* Wäldä-Ṣadəq Gošu (Chair of the Senate) and *Blatten Getta* Śahlä Ṣädalu (Vice-Chair). As a result, despite the legislature being established, the enactment of laws was within the competence of the Emperor.

A separate chapter of the constitution was devoted to judicial power, quoted in full below.

**Chapter VI Jurisdiction**

Art. 50. Judges, sitting regularly, shall administer justice in accordance with the laws in the name of His Majesty the Emperor. The organization of the courts shall be regulated by law.

Art. 51. Judges will be chosen from men who have experience in legal matters.

Art. 52. Judges will sit in public. In cases which might affect public order or endanger public morals, they may sit, according to the law, in camera.

Art. 53. The jurisdiction of each court shall be fixed by law.

Art. 54. Special courts shall judge all matters relating to administrative affairs, which are withdrawn from the jurisdiction of other courts (*Ethiopian Constitution of 1931*).

The chapter on the organisation of the judiciary is much shorter than the one on the organisation of parliament, but it leaves no doubt that judicial power was largely independent of imperial will, although Ḫaylä Śəllase I still remained the supreme judge, with the power to overrule and amend sentences of lower courts (in accordance with Article 16). While not mentioned in the Constitution, since the promulgation of the Penal Code in 1930, Ethiopian judges no longer invoked the *Fətḥa Nägäśt* when passing sentences in criminal cases, although lower courts continued to justify verdicts with common law provisions.

According to the aforementioned penal code, corporal punishment such as flogging or forced amputations was prohibited. It also sought to unify and systematise the methods of punishment and countermeasures. Before, judges had issued sentences based on their own judgement, which sometimes led to abuse and bribery. The new code precisely defined punishments for particular offences, simultaneously attempting to find a compromise between the rules of customary law and the requirements of modern Western legislation. For example, the amounts set for fines were correlated with the level of the court. A court of first instance could fine up to 50 *bərr* or three months' imprisonment, while a district court (*awraya*) could impose up to 500 *bərr* or 1 year's imprisonment. A separate imperial decree in 1942 ('Administration of Justice Proclamation') replaced the traditional courts described in the previous chapter with modern court procedures.[23]

A Swiss citizen, Jacques Auberson, was put in charge of the Ministry of Justice. He was one of Ḫaylä Śəllase I's closest collaborators in 1934-35, and his main task was to modernise his subordinate ministry and to reform the legal system of the Empire (Marcus 1987, pp. 138–140). Moreover, in 1962, the Emperor officially opened the Faculty of Law at Ḫaylä Śəllase University (now Addis Ababa University), to which he appointed an American, James C.N. Paul, as dean.

Despite the intense efforts of its authors, most of the provisions contained in the 1930 draft of the Penal Code (Abera Jembere 1998, p. 191), which was written

[23] This decree established a four-tier judicial system (Regional Court, Provincial Court, Higher Court, Imperial Supreme Court). See Mattausch (2007), p. 1041; Aberra Jembere (2007), pp. 509–511. For more on the Civil Procedure Code, see Scholler (2003), pp. 751–752.

before the promulgation of the Constitution, referred to the social, political and economic situation of Ethiopia at the time of Mənilək II. Therefore, it did not correspond to rapidly changing Ethiopian reality, thus the Emperor decided to create a new criminal law code, which was legislated in 1957 and published four years later (Penal Code 1961). Its publication was the result of a major legal reform initiated in the 1950s by Ḫaylä Śəllase I.[24]

With regard to the law concerning the institution of marriage, there was no major change in legislation during the first years of Ḫaylä Śəllase I's reign. During this period, the main objective of the Emperor's domestic policy was the unification of the Ethiopian nation, in which Amharic culture would play a dominant role. For this reason, for example, the decision was taken to open schools throughout the country where the Amharic language was taught. Due to the lack of qualified teaching staff, Western missionaries were hired to teach exclusively in this language. With the universal education programme and indoctrination into Amharic culture and language, the issue of inter-ethnic marriages arose.

In 1933, in the government newspaper *Bərhanənna Sälam* ('Light and Peace'), an article appeared criticising Western missionaries teaching in local languages, because "[...] it creates obstacles to unity. [Government policy aimed] to have all the people in the country to speak Amharic. With language unity there is also unity of ideas [...] thus the border peoples and the central inhabitants [will] become related" (quoted after Marcus 1987, p. 137). This was a significant change in the approach of the imperial authority to such unions, compared to the edicts of previous rulers prohibiting marriages between representatives of different ethnic and religious groups. The new emperor favoured such unions, as long as they served the unity of the Empire.

## 7.4 The Great Codification of Law

One of the stages in the modernisation of the state that the Emperor had in mind was the creation of legal codes based on the European models. However, in order to avoid problems with the incompatibility of the provisions contained in the codes with Ethiopian reality (as was the case with the *Fətḥa Nägäśt*), in 1950, the Emperor decided to create a compendium of knowledge on customary law in Ethiopia. This was an extremely difficult task, as most of the legal traditions of the Ethiopian peoples had never been written down. Thus, the decision was made to collect court judgments with brief justifications. The collection was to be a resource for the Codification Commission, which was tasked with creating modern Ethiopian legal codes. Over a period of 2 years, 7290 case files were collected, then divided thematically and translated into English. This twelve-volume unpublished work,

[24] Both in the 1930 code and in the 1957 one, the codifiers referred to the same injunction found in the preface of the *Fətḥa Nägäśt* to carry out changes in the law in accordance with changing social conditions (Paulos Tzadua and Strauss 1968, pp. xxvii–xxviii).

entitled *Digest of Ethiopian Case Law*, is now housed in the library of the Faculty of Law at Addis Ababa University.

The next step in the legal reform of the Ethiopian Empire was the establishment of the aforementioned Codification Commission. As already stated, Ḫaylä Śəllase I was keen that the resulting codes should be created according to the Western models, but reflect Ethiopian reality. Therefore, not only Ethiopian judges and lawyers, but also comparative law experts from European countries were invited to work on the codification of the law.[25] The composition of the Codification Commission was ultimately settled in 1952, headed by *Säḥafe Təʾəzaz* Wäldä Giyorgis Wäldä-Yoḥannəs, Minister of Justice at the time.[26] The other members were:

1. *Blatta* Märsəʿe Ḫazän Wäldä Qirqos, Vice-Chair of the Commission and Vice-Minister of Justice
2. Tamrat Yəgäzu, the second Vice-Minister of Justice
3. *Däǧǧazmač* Käbbädä Täsämma, Chair of the Supreme Court
4. *Däǧǧazmač* Mäsfən Gämäč, retired Chair of the Supreme Court
5. *Blatta* Kätaw Yətatäku, Vice-Chair (and later Chair) of the Supreme Court
6. *Blatta* Wäldä Qirqos Gäbrä Mäsqäl, retired judge of the Court of Second Instance
7. Minas Lämma, Vice-Minister of Finances
8. Mammo Täddäsä, Minister of Commerce and Industry
9. *Däǧǧazmač* Zäwde Gäbrä-Śəllase, Minister of Public Affairs, Transport and Civil Aviation
10. *Liqä Mäṭṭañ* Wärädä-Kal Wändəm, judge of the Court of Second Instance
11. *Liqä* Kaṣäla Wäldä-Mädhən, retired Vice-Chair of the Supreme Court
12. *Nəburä'əd* Mäkʷariya Abiʿyähoy, judge of the Court of Second Instance
13. *Fitawrari* Dässaleän Čäränät, judge of the Court of Second Instance
14. *Balambaras* Ašäbbär Gäbrä-Ḥəywät from the Ministry of Justice
15. Səyum Akale-Wäld, Director General of the Ministry of Public Affairs
16. *Däǧǧazmač* Lämläm Wäldä-Sänbet, judge of the Court of Second Instance
17. *Aläqa* Jérôme Gäbrä Mädḫən Gäbrä Muse, judge of the Court of Second Instance
18. Näraᵒio Ǝsayas, Chair of the committee preparing the Civil Procedure Code
19. Judge Roberts, Chair of the Court of Second Instance (not listed by name in the composition of the Codification Commission)
20. Witold Grabowski, judge at the Criminal Division of the Court of Second Instance

---

[25] The text of the imperial speech given on the occasion of the appointment of the Codification Commission is available in the collection of the Emperor's speeches (Haile Selassie I 1967, pp. 393–396 & 408).

[26] The Emperor removed him from this position in 1955 and appointed *Blatta* Ayele Gebre as chair of the commission. Emperor Haile Sillasē remained the honorary chair of the Codification Commission.

21. Prof. Jean Graven, Dean of the Faculty of Law of the University of Geneva, Chair of the committee preparing the Criminal Code
22. Prof. René David from the Department of Comparative Law at the University of Paris, chair of the committee preparing the Criminal Code
23. Prof. Jean Escarra, expert in comparative law, Chair of the committee preparing the Commercial Law Code
24. Prof. Alfred Jauffrett, a jurist, Chair of the committee preparing the Commercial Law Code after J. Escarra's death
25. Paul Varghese, legal advisor to Ḫaylä Śəllase (not listed by name in the composition of the Codification Commission)
26. Olin. B. Scott, legal advisor in the Ethiopian Ministry of Commerce and Industry
27. Mr Kvostff, lawyer (not listed by name in the composition of the Codification Commission)
28. Mr Babian, Chair of the Chamber of Commerce (not listed by name in the composition of the Codification Commission)
29. Mr Perdikis, lawyer (not listed by name in the composition of the Codification Commission)
30. I. Menezes, manager of the Central Bank of Ethiopia (not listed by name in the composition of the Codification Commission)
31. Nathan Marein, Advocate-General
32. Charles Mathew, legal advisor to the Emperor, Chair of the committee preparing the Criminal Law Code.

Once the composition of the Codification Commission was determined, its members were divided into expert teams. Each group was tasked with preparing a draft of the various parts of the code. The draft version of the code (created in French) was then translated into Amharic and presented to the other members of the commission, with the head of each team clarifying any ambiguities. Once the amendments proposed by the members of the Codification Committee had been incorporated, the drafts were read once more and sent to the government. During the meeting of the Council of Ministers, the draft code was presented by the vice-chair of the commission who also answered questions from the ministers.[27]

As Abera Jembere writes (1998, p. 196), the representatives of the Council of Ministers did not study the Code article by article, contenting themselves only with the speech of the Vice-Chair of the Codification Commission. Much more attention was paid to the draft codes by members of both houses of parliament, with one day out of the General Assembly devoted to the reading of the code. The parliamentary session following the reading of the code was focused on questions and proposed amendments. Once these were taken into account, the draft was presented to Ḫaylä Śəllase, who approved the final version of the code by imperial decree.

[27] The only exception was the draft Code of Civil Procedure presented by representatives of the Ministry of Justice, see Abera Jembere (1998), p. 196.

In the course of the Great Codification, the greatest difficulty for legislators was the drafting of the Civil Code. The sections of the Code presented at the commission meetings were the subject of long and passionate discussions. This was caused by the fact that it was problematic to take into account all the differences arising from the diversity of customary laws of the various ethnic groups. Equally heated discussions took place during the work on the Criminal Code. By contrast, the maritime and commercial law drafts were the least controversial, primarily because these types of laws were alien to Ethiopians. Therefore, the basis for these codes was the 'Proclamation on Maritime Law' (Maritime Proclamation 1953) and the imperial decrees on trade from before the Italian occupation.

Although the reform of the entire Ethiopian legislation was an extremely ambitious task, the efficient work of the Codification Commission resulted in the promulgation of as many as six codes in less than a decade. In order, these were as follows: Penal Code (1957), Civil Code (1960), Maritime Law Code (1960), Commercial Law Code (1960), Criminal Procedure Code (1961) and Civil Procedure Code (1965).[28]

Moreover, in 1955, on the twenty-fourth anniversary of Ḫaylä Śəllase's ascension to the imperial throne, a new constitution was promulgated. Compared to its predecessor, the mid-twentieth century constitution had more than twice as many articles, and each chapter was also significantly expanded, although there were few changes in the content of the constitution itself. In the first article, it was once again reiterated that all of the emperor's subjects "[...] whether living within or without the Empire" form the Ethiopian nation (Perham 1969, p. 435). In turn, Article 5 of the constitution stated that the imperial throne could be inherited only by a male descendant of the ruler "[...] born in lawful wedlock" (Perham 1969, p. 435). This provision was in conflict with Ethiopian customary laws, according to which children both from marriages and illegitimate inherited (not only property) from the deceased. Certainly, by introducing these restrictions, the Emperor wished to avoid the situation that had arisen with the election of Zäwditu (the illegitimate daughter of Mənilək II) as Empress of Ethiopia.

## 7.5 The Ethiopian Civil Code of 1960

On 11 September 1960, the Civil Code came into force.[29] Earlier, on 5 May, the Code was published in a special edition of *Nägarit Gazeṭa*[30] as Proclamation no. 165/1960. In the preface, Prime Minister *Säḥafe Təᵓəzaz* Aklilu Habtäwäld stated

[28] It is interesting to note that the creation of the Criminal and Civil Procedure Codes was based on the Anglo-Saxon system of case law, while the creation of the other codes was modelled on continental law.

[29] In Article 3347 of the Code, there was information that from the moment the books were published " all rules whether written or customary previously in force concerning matters provided for in this Code" cease to be in force ('Civil Code' 1960, p. 561).

[30] *Nägarit Gazeṭa* was a government magazine between 1942 and 1974, in which acts passed by parliament, imperial decrees and ordinances were published (in Amharic and English). No law

that the code was created under the direct supervision of Emperor Ḫaylä Śəllase I[31] and was approved by both houses of parliament, in accordance with Articles 34 and 88 of the Constitution of the Ethiopian Empire. Moreover, in the preface the Emperor himself declared that the purpose of creating the code was to modernise the state along Western lines, but with the preservation of Ethiopian values, especially "[...] the genius of Ethiopian legal traditions and institutions, embodied in the ancient and venerable Fetha Neguest" (Civil Code 1960, VII).

The Civil Code consists of 3367 articles in five books concerning various aspects of private law. Each book is divided into sections, devoted to particular aspects of the law. The provisions concerning the institution of marriage are found in Book Two, which consists of two parts further divided into chapters and sections.

As already mentioned, the group preparing the civil law code was headed by René David of the Department of Comparative Law at the University of Paris. Unable to rely entirely on the customary law of one of the ethnic groups living in Ethiopia, the codifiers decided to use the comparative law method. In the course of its work, the Codification Commission drew not only on the post-1950 compendium of Ethiopian case law, but also on the codes of Western countries, most notably the Napoleonic Code and the civil codes of Switzerland, Germany, Greece, Italy, Portugal, Egypt, Iran, Lebanon, Israel, Turkey, Quebec and the Philippines. The commercial law of the United Kingdom, the United States and India were also consulted. Furthermore, the chapter on managing large estates used the Code of Agricultural Law, which originated in the Soviet Union (Scholler 2006, p. 144; David 1967, pp. 347–348). It should also be mentioned that some parts of the code were based neither on the laws of Western countries nor on Ethiopian customary law. Paragraphs on access to water sources, determination of citizenship status and (to a lesser extent) articles on the appointment of legal guardians, wills and registration of property were created completely anew.

As mentioned earlier, the Civil Code was intended not only to incorporate modern solutions known from Western codes, but also to take into account the legal heritage of the Ethiopian Empire. In deciding to use common law provisions, the codifiers relied on four considerations:

1. The provision had to appear in most known common law codes so that it could find the widest possible application.
2. The provision is not in conflict with the rights contained in the *Fətḥa Nägäśt* and 'natural justice' (*fətha fəṭärätawi*).
3. The provision does not hamper economic development.
4. The provision is sufficiently clear and meets the definition of a legal provision.

could enter into force until it had been promulgated in *Nägarit Gazeṭa*, which, however, was not always respected. For more, see Krzeczunowicz (1972), pp. 15–17.

[31] Statements of this type can often be found in the prefaces to various codes and resolutions. Their purpose was to reinforce the belief that the Emperor personally supervised all aspects of state governance. It was also an element of propaganda favouring the Emperor (Rubinkowska-Anioł 2010, pp. 17–46).

Analysing the individual books of the Code, it can be observed that in the first three books ('Persons', 'Family and Successions', 'Goods') the codifiers relied on common law provisions and those derived from the *Fətḥa Nägäśt*, while in the next two books ('Obligations', 'Special Contracts') the Codification Commission was assisted by the civil law codes of Western countries (David 1967, pp. 345–346).

As discussed above, a team of experts drafted successive chapters and presented the results at meetings of the lower house of parliament, together with a commentary on the sources used. As a result of these comments, the origin of a particular paragraphs and the changes made to them could easily be traced. Unfortunately, these commentaries were never published and, as the committee's work progressed, the number of commentaries diminished, as parliamentarians were more interested in the content of individual articles than in their origin.

The members of the Codification Commission encountered various obstacles in the course of their work. Although the constitution made all the emperor's subjects equal citizens before the law, discrepancies or even contradictions between the rights of the different ethnic groups emerged. One problem the codifiers had to deal with when writing Section Two of the Civil Code involved the differences between the biblically derived law prohibiting bigamy and Sharia law allowing a Muslim to have as many as four wives.[32] An explicit prohibition of polygamy could have outraged the Muslim community, which is why the decision was made to introduce Article 577, which reads: "(§2) Marriages contracted according to the religion of the parties or to local custom shall also be valid under this Code" (Civil Code 1960, 97).

The problem of the incompatibility of Sharia law with that established by the Emperor and the Ethiopian government had already arisen earlier; thus, on 29 May 1944, Ḫaylä Śəllase I promulgated Proclamation no. 62, which established three-tier courts to exercise jurisdiction over the Muslims living in the Empire.[33] A council of Islamic judges (*qadi*) constituted the court of the first instance, while that of the second instance consisted of a *Nāʾib* Council (Miran and van Donzel 2007), and the highest court was the Sharia Court, at least three judges of which were elected by the Minister of Justice from among the members of the *Qadi* Council. Muslim judges had the right to rule on civil matters, such as marriage, divorce, inheritance and the appointment of a legal guardian. Their decisions were final and not subject to the rest of the judicial apparatus, except the Supreme Court, of which the Sharia Court was a branch (Constitution 1931).

---

[32] The prohibition of bigamy is expressed explicitly in Article 585 of the Civil Code and Article 618 of the Criminal Code.

[33] Upon announcing the proclamation, the Emperor stated "[...] when We established Kadis' Courts by law We did it in order to achieve national unity" (Perham 1969, p. 156).

## 7.6 Provisions Regarding Marriage in the Civil Code

The provisions concerning the institution of marriage are to be found in Book Two of the Code, although articles relating to this issue can also be found in Book One (Articles 17 and 117). Title V of Book Two contains the provisions setting out the rules of inheritance, while Title IV, entitled 'Bonds of Relationship by Consanguinity and by Affinity', consists of the provisions relating to matrimonial relationships. Title IV is divided into twelve chapters:

Chapter 1 Relationship by consanguinity and affinity in general.
Chapter 2 Betrothal.
Chapter 3 Conclusion of marriage.
Chapter 4 Sanction of the conditions of marriage.
Chapter 5 Effects of marriage.
Chapter 6 Dissolution of marriage.
Chapter 7 Proof of marriage.
Chapter 8 Irregular unions.
Chapter 9 Conflicts in cases relating to marriages, divorces and irregular unions.
Chapter 10 Filiation.
Chapter 11 Adoption.
Chapter 12 Obligation to supply maintenance (Civil Code 1960, 569–570).

Analysing the structure of Title IV, it can be noted that it is similar to that of chapter 24 of the *Fətḥa Nägäśt*. In addition, in the Civil Code, the chapter on informal relationships ("irregular unions") constitutes part of Title IV, while concubinage is discussed in a separate chapter in the *Fətḥa Nägäśt*.[34] Moreover, the marriage section of the Civil Code was supplemented with chapters relating to the determination of parentage and adoption. The intention to maintain similarity in this respect between the *Fətḥa Nägäśt* and the Civil Code was confirmed by René David himself, who claimed that the aim of the Codification Commission was to systematise and formalise the law on marriage, rather than to reform it completely (Allehone Mulugeta 2000, p. 1344).

The first chapter of Book Two refers to the determination of the degree of kinship, both among relatives and affinities. Article 551 upheld the *Fətḥa Nägäśt* provision defining the degree of close kinship to seven generations. Demonstrating the absence of a common ancestor up to seven generations back was required during premarital negotiations. As far as affinities were concerned, the absence of a common ancestor up to three generations back had to be demonstrated (Art. 553). It should also to remembered that ties of affinity are not severed even after the cessation of the marriage (Art. 555).

The chapter 'Betrothal' consists of 16 articles. The first states that a betrothal is a "contract" between representatives of the two families to which the prospective

[34] It is worth noting that in the English translation of the *Fətḥa Nägäśt*, the term "concubinage" is directly used, while we can read about "irregular unions" in the Civil Code.

bride and groom belong. A betrothal was not considered legal unless both parties agreed to it (Art. 560). A "simple promise of marriage' was also not considered a betrothal, as indicated in the next article (Art. 561). This provision can be interpreted as a rejection of marriages that were not arranged and where the role of matchmakers was limited. Moreover, the absence of matchmakers may have made it more difficult to conduct any divorce negotiations later. The next two articles listed the persons who could act as matchmakers; additionally, the presence of two witnesses for each party was required for the betrothal ceremony to be considered legal (Art. 568). As in the provisions of the *Fətḥa Nägäśt*, the right to consent to the marriage was primarily held by the father of the groom or bride, but unlike the *Fətḥa Nägäśt*, the Civil Code allowed that—in the absence of the father—the mother could also negotiate the marriage. In her absence, the family was represented by grandparents or great-grandparents (both men and women). If they also were absent, an older brother or uncle from the mother's or father's side could act as the matchmaker (Art. 562 and 563). If the fiancé was over thirty and the bride over twenty-five, they did not need matchmakers. However, regardless of the age of the prospective bride and groom, the consent of each of them to the marriage was required (Art. 565).

Article 567 of the Code is very significant, as it states that the form of betrothal is subject to "[...] the usage of the place where it is celebrated". In this way, the legislators allowed the betrothal ceremony to be conducted in accordance with local customary law, which can be seen as a tribute to the well-established traditions of the ethnic groups living in the Empire.

If the betrothal was broken, the one who contributed to the breaking of it had to reimburse all costs incurred by the other party and return all gifts received on the occasion of the betrothal (Art. 572). In determining the amount of costs incurred by the abandoned party, the court took into account local custom, although the compensation could not be more than the sum of 1000 *bərr*. The court determined the amount of compensation only if the parties had not included a clause regarding such a situation in the betrothal contract. The sum of damages could be reduced in two cases: if its amount was overstated during negotiations or when the betrothal was broken due to exceptional circumstances (Art. 574). Any disputes relating to the breaking of the engagement had to be resolved within 1 year of the event, and were to be dealt with by family arbitration courts (Art. 723).

The most important change in the perception of the institution of marriage is recorded in the next chapter of the book ('Conclusion of marriage'), for, unlike the *Fətḥa Nägäśt*, the Civil Code recognised as legal both religious marriages and those contracted under customary law or before a public official (Art. 577). This was another provision of the Code that took into account the existence of customary laws (including legitimising marriage by abduction), which was confirmed by Articles 580 and 606 stating that a customary marriage was considered legal as long as all the rituals necessary for the conclusion of the marriage took place during the wedding ceremony. The only exception were temporary marriages (*dämoz*), which did not belong to any of the listed categories. Thus, based on Art. 3347, which abolished all laws prior to those contained in the code, such marriages became prohibited.[35] The Code also mandated the registration of marriages, regardless of how they were concluded. The written marriage record, in addition to the date of the ceremony, should contain the names of the spouses and their dates of birth. The same data should be included regarding the witnesses to the marriage ceremony (Art. 117 and 118). The marriage certificate may be drawn up at the request of the spouses or by order of a government official. In the latter case, the signatures of both the newlyweds and the witnesses are required (Art. 119 and 120).

Despite such revolutionary changes in the perception of the institution of marriage, the Code partly maintained and partly lowered the age for marriage. According to Article 581, a woman could marry at the age of fifteen, while a man had to be at least eighteen. In exceptional situations, the emperor could agree to lower the age limit, but by no more than 2 years. This provision also aimed to meet the expectations of various ethnic groups among which early marriage of girls was practised. Later in the Code, however, the codifiers sought to limit the application of customary law. Article 607 mentions the penalties under the Penal Code for marrying minors (without an imperial dispensation) or the lack of consent from the bride or groom's relatives to the ceremony.

Both in the case of the marriage of minors and in a marriage ceremony between those meeting the requirements of Article 581, the bride and groom had to express their wish to marry. In addition, in the case of the nuptials of minors, consent had to be given by the parents or legal guardians listed in Article 562 of the Code. The absence of such consent or consent given under duress made such a marriage illegal. Consent to marriage could also be withdrawn in the following cases:

1. If one of the spouses had been misled about the other person's identity.
2. If one of the spouses belonged to another faith than the other person.
3. If one of the spouses had been misled concerning the physical or psychological condition of the other person.[36]

Section two of Chapter 3 deals with civil marriages, which should be performed before a public official. The wedding ceremony should take place in the place of residence of one of the spouses, their parents or ancestors, where they have lived for at least six months. As with church weddings, four witnesses should be present at the signing of the marriage certificate, two for each party.

The subsequent section is entitled "Other marriages" and it describes unions concluded before a member of the clergy or in accordance with local customary law. In both cases, the wedding ceremony should take place in accordance with the principles of church law or local custom (Art. 605–606). It is noteworthy that the *Fətḥa Nägäśt* dealt exclusively with religious marriage, without taking into account other types of marriages. Meanwhile, the 1960 Civil Code, includes prominently civil

[35] John Markakis (1975, p. 297) maintained that the Civil Code valued church marriages higher than civil or customary marriages. However, none of the articles of the code supports his opinion.

[36] This last point was in particular referring to people suffering from leprosy and those who do not "[...] have the requisite organs for the consummation of the marriage" (Art. 591).

marriages (devoting a separate section to this issue), while religious and customary marriages are considered in another jointly.

Chapter 4 describes the sanctions that could befall both newlyweds and the official who grants them a wedding violating the code. Punishable under the Penal Code was to grant a wedding to a bigamist,[37] to widowers before the end of the period of mourning, to a minor (without parental consent and the dispensation of the emperor) and to a person suffering from mental illness. In the last case, the application for annulment of the marriage should be made no later than six months after the cessation of the illness. Persons who had been subjected to violence (both physical and psychological) in order to force them to consent to a marriage could request an annulment up to six months after the cessation of the violence and up to 2 years after the wedding ceremony (Art. 617).

Section 3 of this chapter describes situations in which the marriage could not be annulled by a decision of a state court, even when the conclusion of a religious or customary marriage did not fulfil the requirements of customary law and religion. In such a case, the aggrieved person could apply to the court for a compensation of damages or a determination of the amount of the fine. The court could also reduce the amount of such a fine if it considered it to be excessive.

In Chapter 5 ('Effects of marriage'), it was once again reiterated that each of the three types of marriage mentioned earlier (religious, civil, customary) was legal. Article 627 also allowed marriage contracts in which both parties defined rights and obligations, both in terms of personal and material-financial relationships. Four witnesses should be present at the signing of the contract, two for each party, and a copy of the contract could either be given to a notary or filed in the archives of the Registry Office. According to Article 632, during the marriage, both the spouses and the family arbitrators (acting for and on behalf of the spouses) could amend the contract. Any contracts signed by the spouses, but without a judicial seal, were not considered legal.

The above-mentioned articles seem to be strongly modelled both on customary law, which strictly distinguishes between the property of each spouse and their joint property, and on Islamic law, whereby a contract is written before the wedding ceremony, which contains declarations by both parties as to the nature of their relationship. In addition, the code's allowance for amendments to the marriage contract by the spouses or their family members allows for the insertion of common law provisions that may be in conflict with those of the Civil Code.

Section two of this chapter was devoted to the relationship between spouses. The first article established the husband as the head of the family, to whom the wife "[...] owes (...) obedience in all lawful things which he orders" (Art. 635). The spouses should take care of the spiritual and material welfare of the home together, albeit under the leadership of the husband. They should also raise their children together (Art. 637), while children from previous relationships should be raised by

[37] In accordance with Art. 613, a bigamist did not face imprisonment if, shortly after the second marriage, the first spouse died.

each parent separately (Art. 639). The husband also had the sole right to decide on the place of residence. Furthermore, the section emphasises that the spouses owed each other respect, support and marital fidelity. No marriage contract could challenge this right. The articles cited above are almost a copy of the provisions found in the *Fətḥa Nägäśt* (cf. Paulos Tzadua and Strauss 1968, pp. 141–142). They may derive also from customary laws, most of which apply to patriarchal societies. The only difference between the relevant provisions of the two codes is that according to the Civil Code, unless the husband is able to provide servants for his wife, he should assume some of the responsibilities of running the household (Art. 646).

Chapter 6 contains provisions relating to the dissolution of marriage, which apply to all types of marriage.[38] In this part, one can clearly see the guiding thought of the legislators, whose intention was not merely to codify customary laws, but to modify them in such a way as to make these laws as close as possible to moral law (*həg ləbuna*). They considered a marriage terminated in three cases:

1. The death of one of the spouses
2. Non-legality of the marriage
3. Divorce.

The first two grounds for the termination of a marriage have already been discussed earlier, while the grounds for divorce are elaborated in the next two sections of the chapter. Interestingly, according to Article 665, no divorce procedure could be carried out in the Ethiopian Empire without an adjudication of guilt. Moreover, in cases of uncomplicated divorce, the entire procedure was carried out by family arbitrators, who had three months to do so from the moment either party filed for divorce. The code also divides the grounds for filing for divorce into serious and less serious ones.[39] Four serious reasons are listed:

1. Adultery
2. When one of the spouses has deserted the conjugal residence for at least 2 years without letting the other spouse know
3. Mental illness lasting more than 2 years
4. When the absence of one of the spouses has been judicially declared (e.g. in the case of a final prison sentence).

The above reasons for the dissolution of marriage are fewer than those contained in the *Fətḥa Nägäśt*. For example, neither the desire by one of the spouses to join the clerical state, nor a provision that "life [will become] less burdensome and more agreeable" is included (Paulos Tzadua and Strauss 1968, p. 149). The legislators also failed to take into account another provision of the *Fətḥa Nägäśt*, in which the grounds for divorce were that the wife was possessed by the devil or that she was plotting against her husband. Another change from the provisions of the *Fətḥa Nägäśt* was the addition of an article about the legal dissolution of a religious

[38] The right to marry and the right to seek divorce is guaranteed by Article 17 of the Civil Code.

[39] In the code, the "less serious" reasons are not listed (Art. 667–673).

marriage if the decision to terminate the union is first issued by the institution that granted the marriage (Art. 671).

Before filing for divorce, family arbitrators started a negotiation procedure to reconcile the spouses. If the attempts failed, they proceeded to negotiations aimed at the division of joint property. Above all, custody of the children was granted to one of the parties. In contrast to the *Fətḥa Nägäśt*, children—regardless of their gender—remained under the care of the mother until the age of five, although the father had to contribute to their upkeeping. According to Article 689, the common property was divided equally between both spouses, while the received marriage gifts should be divided according to the arbitrators' decisions or those contained in the marriage contract. The family arbitrators also had the right to transfer all of the common property and no more than 1/3 of the other party's property to the injured party. The arbitrators had 1 year from the date the divorce was filed to carry out the entire procedure. In special cases, this period could be extended to 5 years. In addition, within six months of the pronouncement of the award, either party could request an additional judicial divorce procedure. Importantly, the arbitrators' decisions, including their award of divorce, were treated as decisions with the force of law and a state court opinion was not necessary unless requested by either party.

Another major change from the *Fətḥa Nägäśt* is the inclusion of a chapter on irregular unions in the book on marriage. In the first article, the code gives a definition of an informal relationship: "An irregular union is the state of fact which is created when a man and a woman live together as husband and wife without having contracted marriage" (Art. 708). Contrary to the provisions of the *Fətḥa Nägäśt*, this type of relationship was legal as long as the persons involved behaved as spouses (§1 Art. 709) but needed not to represent themselves in this way to third parties (§2 Art. 709). A relationship based solely on sexual relations was not treated as an irregular union (§3 Art. 709). According to some commentators (Buhagiar 1964, p. 96; Krzeczunowicz 1963, p. 63), the last paragraph of this article refers to *dämoz*-type relationships; this is not convincing, however, as such a relationship was not based solely on sexual relations, but rather was a type of marriage contract in which the woman was a rightful wife for a specific period of time.

According to the code, in irregular unions—as in *dämoz* marriages—no kinship relations are formed between the woman and the man's families. According to the law, there is no common property in such a relationship and the partners have no obligation to support each other. As in the *Fətḥa Nägäśt*, in the case of an informal relationship, the woman did not inherit from the man, although the children from the relationship were entitled to a share of the property after the father's death. Both parties could end the relationship at any time, but if the man ended it, he was obliged to support the woman for the following 6 months.

The next two chapters deal with the determination of parentage, of children both conceived during marriage and adopted. In the case of children born out of wedlock, the man who was married to the woman more than one hundred and eighty days before the child was born was considered to be the father. The same applied to children born within three hundred days of the dissolution of a marriage (Art. 743). In the case of informal/irregular unions, the man who was the woman's partner more than one hundred and eighty days before the birth of the child was considered to be its father.

In the case of adopted children, bonds of kinship and affinity arise at the moment of adoption, which was allowed only to spouses, unless the one adopted was the child of one of the adoptive parents. If the adopted child was more than 15 years old, then a contract was drawn up between them and the adopting person or persons. Such a contract had no legal force unless it was accepted by the court, which first interviewed the adopted child (if they were over 10 years old) and then the prospective adoptive parents to ascertain their intentions (Art. 796–806).

The last chapter of Book Two deals with the obligation of the spouses to provide for each other. According to this chapter, spouses should provide each other with housing, clothing and food. They should also take care of their partner, in health and in sickness, as required by society and local customs. Similar obligations applied to relatives and affinities. All the provisions in this chapter are in the Christian spirit of the *Fətḥa Nägäśt* and the provisions of customary law, which refer to the responsibility of the whole community for individuals.

## 7.7 The Civil Code and Customary Law

As Margery Perham writes, the introduction of the new legal codes went smoothly in Addis Ababa and other major cities of the Ethiopian Empire. In the provinces, however, customary law was still in force, and the use of the new codes depended mainly on how well the lawyers knew their contents (Perham 1969, p. 415). An additional problem was the vagueness of the code on some issues. As far as the institution of marriage was concerned, these included mainly provisions on irregular/informal unions and bigamy.

An open question is whether a *dämoz*-type marriage can be considered as an irregular union. As defined in Chapter 8 of Book Two, an irregular union is one between a man and a woman who act as husband and wife although formally they are not. As in a marriage, children born during the union are recognised as legitimate heirs to the property of both the mother and the father (Art. 715 & Art. 745), and the woman's partner is liable for her debts if their incurring was necessary to ensure the family's livelihood (Art. 714 & Art. 660). Therefore, a *dämoz* marriage fulfils the characteristics of an extramarital relationship, but has been prohibited under Article 3347 of the Code. Since the legislators did not provide precise definitions of the types of relationships covered by Article 708, this part of the Code is open for interpretation by judges, who in such cases preferred to use the customary law, which they knew better.

Another issue with the imprecision of the law concerning the institution of marriage involved the problem of the prohibition of bigamy expressed in both Article 585 of the Civil Code and Article 616 of the Criminal Code. At the same time, in other articles of both codes, one can read that the prohibition of bigamy "shall not apply in cases where polygamy is recognised under civil law in conformity with tradition or moral usage" (Art. 617 of the Criminal Code) and that "marriages contracted according to [...] local custom shall also be valid under this Code" (Art. 577). According to René David's notes, the article on the prohibition of bigamy was to include a waiver on the prohibition of bigamy in the case of marriages in which one of the parties is a follower of Islam. The provision on the dissolution of such a relationship was to read: "[...]Where the husband is of the Muslim religion the dissolution of marriage may be pronounced only at the request of the public prosecutor" (O'Donovan 1972, p. 446). However, the fast pace of the work done by the Codification Commission meant that parliamentary translators could not keep up with the translations and this version of the article was not presented to parliamentarians, with the result that Article 585 of the Civil Code remained in force and Ethiopian civil law only recognised monogamous marriages. The existing contradictory provisions of the two codes therefore meant that a potential bigamist could not apply for the dissolution of one of the marriages without risking a criminal trial. Moreover, as long as the first wife was alive, the second marriage of a bigamist did not exist legally, and therefore neither the husband nor the second wife could apply for its dissolution. A second marriage became legal if the first wife died, but the code does not mention whether a second marriage becomes legal if the first one is terminated due to divorce. Most likely, the legality of such a marriage was established on the grounds that there were no obstacles to the union.

Another issue is the status of a woman in a relationship with a bigamist. If a man's second wife leaves him and remarries, will her second marriage also be bigamous? As the woman's first marriage was illegal under civil law, her second marriage may be legal.

Although the 1960 Civil Code was vague on many issues, it lived up to the hopes placed in it for the codification of the law and the modernisation of the state. Although, in Margery Perham's words, the code was only used in proceedings before higher magistrates or in the larger cities of the Ethiopian Empire, the provisions it contained were responsive to societal needs. This state of affairs continued until the collapse of the Ethiopian Empire in 1974, when the provisions of the code were replaced in many legal situations by laws that had been introduced during the Ethiopian revolution and under the Därg government. Changes in civil law did not occur until after the regime change in 1991. Some of the provisions on private law were included in the articles of the 1995 Constitution of the Federal Democratic Republic of Ethiopia, including provisions on family law, the establishment of customary and religious courts and the equal status of men and women (Articles 34–35 of the Constitution). Further changes to Ethiopian legislation regarding the institution of marriage did not occur until 2000, when Ethiopian legislators promulgated the Revised Family Code (2000). Currently, the newly established Institute for Law Reform in Addis Ababa is working on the reform and consolidation of civil law.

# References


Augustyniak Z (2009) Małżeństwa polityczne w Etiopii na przełomie XIX i XX wieku. MA dissertation, Department of African Languages and Cultures, University of Warsaw

Augustyniak Z (2011) Małżeństwa polityczne jako sposób umacniania pozycji władcy w Cesarstwie Etiopskim za panowania lydża Ijasu. Afryka 33:45–54

Augustyniak Z (2014a) Konstytucja Cesarstwa Etiopskiego z 1930 roku – pierwszy krok ku modernizacji państwa czy próba wprowadzenia monarchii absolutnej. In: Kraska-Szlenk I, Wójtowicz B (eds) Current research in African studies. Papers in honour of Mwalimu Dr. Eugeniusz Rzewuski. Elipsa, Warszawa, pp 25–38

Augustyniak Z (2014b) Lïj Iyasu's marriages as a reflection of his domestic policy. In: Ficquet É, Smidt WGC (eds) The life and times of Lïj Iyasu of Ethiopia. New Insights. LIT, Zürich, pp 39–47

Buhagiar W (1964) Marriage under the civil code of Ethiopia. J Ethiop Law 1:73–99

Civil Code (1960) Civil Code of the Empire of Ethiopia. Negarit Gazeta, Addis Ababa, 5 May 1960

Civil Procedure Code (1965) Civil Procedure Code of Ethiopia. Negarit Gazeta. Extraordinary Issue 1

Commercial Law Code (1960) Commercial Code of the Empire of Ethiopia of 1960. Addis Ababa

Constitution (1931) Ethiopian Constitution of 1931. In: Perham M (1969) The government of Ethiopia. Faber and Faber, London, pp 407–416

Criminal Procedure Code (1961) Criminal Procedure Code of the Empire of Ethiopia. Negarit Gazeta 1

David R (1967) Sources of Ethiopian Civil Code. J Ethiop Law 4(2):341–349

Eadie JI (1924) An Amharic reader. Cambridge University Press, Cambridge

Elyas GƎ, Molvaer RK (1994) Prowess, piety and politics. The chronicle of Abeto Iyasu and empress Zewditu of Ethiopia (1909-1930). Rüdiger Köppe, Köln

Ficquet É, Smidt WGC (eds) (2014) The life and times of Lïj Iyasu of Ethiopia. New insights. LIT, Zürich

Greenfield R (1967) Ethiopia: a new political history. Pall Mall, London

Haile Selassie I (1967) Selected speeches of his imperial majesty Haile Selassie First, 1918-1967. The Imperial Ethiopian Ministry of Information. Publication and Foreign Languages Press Dept, Addis Ababa

Haile Sellassie I (1976) The autobiography of emperor Haile Sellassie I: my life and Ethiopia's progress. Oxford University Press, London

Ḫaylä Śəllase I (1937) Həywätenna yä-Ityopya ərməǧa. Bərhanənna Sälam, Baz

Jembere A (1998) Legal history of Ethiopia, 1434–1974. Erasmus Universiteit, Leiden; Afrika-Studiecentrum, Rotterdam

Jembere A (2007) Law and judiciary. B: judicial system. In: Uhlig S (ed) Encyclopaedia Aethiopica, vol 3. Harrassowitz, Wiesbaden, pp 509–511

Krzeczunowicz G (1963) A new legislative approach to customary law: the 'repeals' provision of the Ethiopian Civil Code of 1960. J Ethiop Stud 1(1):57–67

Krzeczunowicz G (1972) An introductory theory of laws in the context of the Ethiopian legal system. J Ethiop Law Occasional Pap 3:1–34

Marcus HG (1987) Haile Sellassie I. The formative years, 1892-1936. University of California Press, Berkeley

Maritime Proclamation (1953) Maritime Proclamation No. 137 of 1953. Addis Ababa

Markakis J (1975) Ethiopia. Anatomy of a traditional polity. Oxford University Press, Addis Ababa

Mattausch B (2007) Muggət. In: Uhlig S (ed) Encyclopaedia Aethiopica, vol 3. Harrassowitz, Wiesbaden, pp 1040–1041

Miran J, van Donzel E (2007) Nā'ib. In: Uhlig S (ed) Encyclopaedia Aethiopica, vol 3. Harrassowitz, Wiesbaden, pp 1116–1118

Mulugeta A (2000) Women, state and the family; issues of legal pluralism and challenges to family law. In: Yimam B (ed) Proceedings of the XIVth International Conference of Ethiopian Studies. Institute of Ethiopian Studies, Addis Ababa University, Addis Ababa, pp 1334–1358

O'Donovan K (1972) Void and voidable marriages in Ethiopian law. J Ethiop Law 3(2):439–451
Omar AH (2014) Lïj Iyasu: a reformist prince? In: Ficquet É, Smidt WGC (eds) The life and times of Lïj Iyasu of Ethiopia. New insights. LIT, Zürich, pp 81–89
Pankhurst R (2006) The quest for "civilization": the pre-World War II modernizing policies of Ras Täfäri Mäkonnen (later Emperor Haylä Sellasé) as expounded in his autobiography, and in the chronicle of Empress Zäwditu. In: Witakowski W, Łykowska L (eds) Wälättä Yohanna – Ethiopian Studies in Honour of Joanna Mantel-Niećko on the Occasion of the 50th Year of Her Work at the Institute of Oriental Studies. Warsaw University, Elipsa, Warszawa, pp 181–201
Pankhurst R (2010) Qwəraññа. In: Uhlig S (ed) Encyclopaedia Aethiopica, vol 4. Harrassowitz, Wiesbaden, p 316
Penal Code (1961) Penal Code of the Empire of Ethiopia of 1957. Addis Ababa
Perham M (1969) The Government of Ethiopia. Faber and Faber, London
Prouty C (1986) Empress Taytu and Menelik II. Ethiopia 1883-1910. The Red Sea Press, Trenton
Rouaud A (2007) Jérôme. In: Uhlig S (ed) Encyclopaedia Aethiopica, vol 3. Harrassowitz, Wiesbaden, pp 272–273
Rubinkowska H (2014) Zäwditu. In: Uhlig S (ed) Encyclopaedia Aethiopica, vol 5. Harrassowitz, Wiesbaden, pp 157–159
Rubinkowska-Anioł H (2000/2001) Wybrane aspekty polityki lydża Ijasu, władcy Etiopii (1909-1916). Afryka 12:25–38
Rubinkowska-Anioł H (2010) Ethiopia on the verge of modernity: The transfer of power during Zewditu's Reign, 1916–1930. Agade, Warsaw
Scholler H (1985) The special court of Ethiopia, 1920–1935. Franz Steiner, Stuttgart
Scholler H (2003) Civil procedure code. In: Uhlig S (ed) Encyclopaedia Aethiopica, vol 1. Harrassowitz, Wiesbaden, pp 751–752
Scholler H (2006) Ethiopian constitutional and legal development. Volume II: Essays on Ethiopian Legal Development. Rüdiger Köppe, Köln
Seunarine L (1999) Ethiopian women of power: From Denkenesh to empress Menen. Trican Book, New York
Ṭafäṭä G (1996) Abba Tena Iyasu. Maison des Études Éthiopiennes, Addis Abeba and Paris
Tafla B (1972) Marriage as a political device: an appraisal of socio-political aspect of the Menelik period 1889-1916. J Ethiop Stud 1(10):13–23
Tafla B (1991) The dispensation of justice in traditional Ethiopia. An appraisal of legal historiography. In: Philipps L, Ádám A, Wittman R (eds) Rechtsentstehung und Rechtskultur. Heinrich Scholler zum 60. Geburtstag. Decker & Müller, Heidelberg, pp 91–111
The Revised Family Code (2000) The Revised Family Code. Proclamation no. 213/2000. Negarit Gazeta. Extra Ordinary Issue, 4 July 2000
Tzadua P, Strauss PL (1968) The Fetha Nagast. The law of the Kings. Faculty of Law, Haile Sellassie I University, Addis Ababa
Vanderlinden J (1966) An introduction to the sources of Ethiopian law from the 13th to the 20th century. J Ethiop Law 3(1):227–639
Wäldä Mäsqäl MŚ (1950) Zəkrä Nägär. Näsanät, Addis Abäba
Wäldä Qirqos MH (2004) Of what I saw and heard. The last years of emperor Menelik II and the brief rule of Iyassu. Centre Français des Études Éthiopiennes & Zamra Publishers, Addis Ababa
Zewde B (1991) A history of modern Ethiopia, 1855–1974. James Currey, London
Zewde B (2007) Iyasu. In: Uhlig S (ed) Encyclopaedia Aethiopica, vol 3. Harrassowitz, Wiesbaden, pp 253–256

# Chapter 8
# Conclusions

Tracing the development of the institution of marriage in the times of the Ethiopian Empire has proved to be an extremely difficult task, mainly because of the small number of internal sources. Crucial for the present study were the *Fətḥa Nägäśt* and the Civil Code; both are available not only in Amharic but also in translations which—although for different resaons—helped significantly in analysing their contents. In the case of the *Fətḥa Nägäśt*, the linguistic and historical comments were valuable in understanding the vagueness of some parts of the text. The Civil Code was written not only by Ethiopians but also by invited European experts and it was published simultaneously in two language versions which gives a clearer indication of the authors' intentions.

In addition to codes, imperial decrees also had the force of law. There were far fewer relevant sources of this type than it initially appeared, perhaps for the reasons mentioned in the introduction. For the imperial chroniclers, the military conquests of the rulers and their contribution to the overall development of the state were more important than decrees concerning everyday matters such as marriages. Some information on imperial decisions concerning marriages are found in the memoirs of imperial dignitaries, but these sources referred only to the Ethiopian nobility, while remaining silent on their application among the emperor's subjects.

Despite the scant amounts of sources, the comparative material was sufficient to analyse the evolution of the institution of marriage in light of the legal codes and decrees of the Ethiopian rulers. Above all, the amount and nature of similarities between the two codes was surprising. Both were based on much earlier texts (the *Fətḥa Nägäśt* on the *Nomokanōn* and the Civil Code on the *Fətḥa Nägäśt*) adapted to different circumstances. It is worth noting that the *Nomokanōn* had to be adjusted to divergent social conditions, political systems and local customs. However, the Civil Code is much more inclusive than the *Fətḥa Nägäśt*, which leaves a significant part of the society outside its scope.

First and foremost, both codes are based on Christian doctrine, which can be seen above all in the provisions prohibiting adultery and bigamy. Although the Civil Code in no way favoured monogamous marriages contracted in accordance with the



Z. Augustyniak, *Marriage in the Ethiopian Empire*, Studies in the History of Law and Justice 33, https://doi.org/10.1007/978-3-032-26065-9_8

Christian religion—and only such did the *Fətḥa Nägäśt* consider legal—when reading the individual articles one can sense the intention of the codifiers, who sought to convince all ethnic groups to adopt the principle of monogamy. Hence, the code included vague provisions on informal unions and bigamy to discourage Ethiopians from entering into such relationships.

With regard to individual provisions in the two codes, it was surprising to discover that the Civil Code not only did not increase the age at which one could legally marry, but lowered it for men by 2 years. According to the *Fətḥa Nägäśt* regulations, a man could marry at the age of twenty, while a woman could marry at the age of fifteen. Moreover, persons who had not reached the appropriate age could also marry, as long as the emperor gave his permission. Such a low (especially for women) age for marriage was explained in the *Fətḥa Nägäśt* by a clause found in *Śenä Feṭrät*, according to which God had created Eve as a girl of fifteen and Adam as a man of thirty (Haile and Amare 1991, pp. 13, 48, 63).[1] In the Civil Code, the codifiers did not state the reason why they decided to keep the age so low, nor are there any legal commentaries surviving from the discussion of this section of the code in the parliamentary forum.

Another provision found in both the sixteenth-century and the 1960 code states that there is no distinction between legitimate and illegitimate children. According to both codes, children, regardless of the relationship from which they come, have the right to inherit from their deceased parents. The Civil Code also leaves no room for interpretation of the provisions on the establishment of paternity. Interestingly, in the case of these provisions, the source was not the Christian dogma, but the rules of customary law stemming from the belief present in many African cultures that children belong to the community as a whole and it is the community's duty to care for their welfare and upbringing (see, e.g., Mbiti 1970, pp. 143, 152).

Another similarity is the husband's dominant position in the family, which is emphasised in both codes. In the Civil Code, he is explicitly referred to as the head of the family, while the *Fətḥa Nägäśt* states that the wife owes her husband obedience in everything he does. The 1960 Code amends this provision slightly by adding that the wife is to obey unless the husband's actions are unlawful. The presence of a provision indicating the husband's authority over his wife in both codes confirms the patriarchal nature of most societies living in the Ethiopian Empire, both in the sixteenth century and four centuries later.

Although both codes share a number of provisions, they also differ on many issues. This is, obviously because every society is transformed as the surrounding reality develops. This was no different in the case of Ethiopian society, where change was stimulated not only by the development of Ethiopian statehood, but also by external influences, such as the presence of representatives of European countries at the imperial court. While the institution of marriage itself does not seem to

[1] I would like to express my gratitude to Sophie Dege-Müller for providing me the reference to the apocryph.

have changed over the years, the perception of it by Ethiopian legislation has evolved.

Above all, attitudes towards the institution of marriage have changed. In the *Fəth̨a Nägäśt*, the only legal union was a marriage contracted in a church, during a ceremony of receiving communion together. Meanwhile, the Civil Code recognised all marriages as legal unions: religious, civil and customary. This meant that most types of marriages, including *qal kidan bäqurban*, *sər'at* and *ṭäläfa* marriages, were legal, although the last of these in some cases could be declared invalid if the kidnapped person proved that the marriage has been concluded without her consent. A marriage of the *dämoz* type was excluded from the legality clause for all types of marriage as not fulfilling the characteristics of a marriage (no wedding ceremony).

Moreover, there is no provision in the 1960 Code limiting the number of marriages that can be performed in a lifetime. In the first part of the chapter on marriages, the *Fəth̨a Nägäśt* condemns those who marry for the third and fourth time, while the Code allows multiple marriages as long as the next union does not begin before the previous one ends. The codes also differ on the time to elapse between the termination of one marriage and the conclusion of another. According to the *Fəth̨a Nägäśt*, both the man and the woman should wait 9 months after the end of the relationship, whereas according to the Civil Code, only 6 months were sufficient. This change may have been due to the more precise provisions for establishing paternity, which were included in the Civil Code. The sixteenth-century text lacked such provisions, so it was assumed that a child born within 9 months after the cessation of marriage was the child of the woman's former husband. In addition, according to the new regulations, before entering into a new marriage, the degree of consanguinity had to be checked up to seven generations back and the degree of affinity up to three generations. This was a slight simplification from the provisions in the *Fəth̨a Nägäśt*, which mandated that the absence of a common ancestor be established up to the seventh or ninth generation. It is clear that both provisions were intended to prevent incestuous relationships, which included also those involving god-children.

Considering the wedding ceremony itself, there are also differences in the legislation. According to the *Fəth̨a Nägäśt*, the nuptials should take place within 2 years after the engagement, otherwise the engagement may be broken off. The Civil Code reduces this period to 6 months, unless the parties agree otherwise. It is not known what guided the legislators to set a shorter time between the betrothal and the wedding ceremony. One can only assume that this was due to changes that occurred in social life (simplification of the rituals associated with the wedding ceremony, fewer arranged relationships requiring lengthy matchmaking). Moreover, in the Civil Code, an entire chapter was devoted to the legal sanctions for performing an illegitimate wedding, whereas the *Fəth̨a Nägäśt* only described the types of penance for the illegitimately married and for the one performing such a wedding.

Another significant change from the *Fəth̨a Nägäśt* was the Civil Code's recognition of informal unions, referred to as concubinage in the previous code. In sixteenth-century Ethiopia, such unions were formally prohibited, whereas in the 1960 Code, the chapter on informal unions is included in the section dealing with marriage. The very existence of this section once again demonstrates the codifiers' sensitivity to the needs of Ethiopian society in the twentieth century. Both then and now, informal unions are much more common in Ethiopia than formal ones, especially church marriages. Although on the aforementioned issue of inheritance, the laws did not distinguish between children from formal and informal unions. However, women in informal unions were deprived of the right to inherit from their husbands. The Civil Code changed this provision, making married and cohabiting partners equal in rights and obligations.

The last important difference between the codes was the reduced number of reasons for the termination of marriage. The *Fətḥa Nägäśt* listed eight reasons why a marriage terminates. Among them were the desire of one of the spouses to join a monastery, possession by the devil or the belief that living alone would be more pleasant for both spouses. The Civil Code lists only three reasons for the cessation of a marriage (death of one of the spouses, illegitimacy of the union, divorce), while it divides the reasons for divorce into serious and less serious ones. The two codes differ also with regard to the division of property after divorce. Surprisingly, the provisions in the Civil Code are less precise than those contained in the *Fətḥa Nägäśt*. This is probably due to the fact that the twentieth century code gives more discretion to family arbitration and common law provisions.

An in-depth analysis of the chapters on the institution of marriage found in the two codes under discussion shows how much change has taken place in terms of the legal perception of what marriage is. The individual articles of the Civil Code leave no doubt that it was created for the whole society and not just for its part adhering to Christianity, as was the case with the *Fətḥa Nägäśt*. Consequently, the Civil Code was much longer and more precise than the code of the sixteenth century, as it took into account the existence of other forms of marriage and also the presence of religious and ethnic groups other than Christians. Although both codes were mainly written by non-Ethiopians, the 1960 code was more reflective of the social situation in the Ethiopian Empire. Even though the provisions of the code were vague in some parts, the code fulfilled its role in modernising the legislative apparatus as planned by the last emperor.

An analysis of the development of the institution of marriage in Ethiopia until the fall of the Empire in 1974 would be incomplete without a comprehensive account of the sources of law in Ethiopia and the legal and judicial reforms carried out by successive rulers. For the most part, these reforms did not directly affect family law, but were influential in changing it. Thanks to the historical, religious and social context, it was possible to present a kind of parallelism in the Ethiopian legal system, which was expressed in the coexistence of customary law and written codes. The position of the latter was linked to the consolidation of Ethiopian statehood (following the centralisation of power) and the influence of European models.

Nonetheless, even the Great Codification did not displace customary law from public space. This was not solely due to the ignorance of the content of the codes by judges in the Ethiopian provinces. The phenomenon of the persistence of customary law can also be seen in terms of the wider changes taking place in Ethiopian society.

Although these were not as rapid and profound in the Ethiopian Empire as they were in European societies, there was still a social demand for customary law norms.

The coexistence of customary laws (not always of Christian origin) with codes of statute law (the origins of which can be traced to Christianity) has been—and still is to some extent—possible in the case of Ethiopia, since a common feature of customary law is its focus on forgiveness and on bringing about reconciliation between the two parties to a conflict rather than punishing the offender. This approach coincides with the teachings of Christianity, which also preaches the need for forgiveness. As far as the institution of marriage is concerned, the minor similarities between the customary laws in Ethiopia and the state codes are far more numerous than it may initially appear, which is why (even today) in Ethiopia any formalisation of a relationship between a man and a woman, accompanied by a ceremony or ritual, is considered a legal marriage.

## References

Haile G, Amare M (1991) Śenä Feṭrät [Beauty of the creation]. Journal of Semitic Studies Monograph 16. University of Manchester, Manchester

Mbiti J (1970) African religions and philosophy. Anchor Books, New York

MIX
Papier aus verantwortungsvollen Quellen
Paper from responsible sources
FSC® C105338

If you have any concerns about our products,
you can contact us on
**ProductSafety@springernature.com**

In case Publisher is established outside the EU,
the EU authorized representative is:
**Springer Nature Customer Service Center GmbH**
**Europaplatz 3, 69115 Heidelberg, Germany**

Printed by Libri Plureos GmbH
in Hamburg, Germany